THE FULL ENGLISH

STUART MACONIE
THE FULL ENGLISH

A JOURNEY IN SEARCH OF A COUNTRY AND ITS PEOPLE

Harper
North

HarperNorth
Windmill Green
24 Mount Street
Manchester M2 3NX

A division of
HarperCollins*Publishers*
1 London Bridge Street
London SE1 9GF

www.harpercollins.co.uk

HarperCollins*Publishers*
Macken House, 39/40 Mayor Street Upper
Dublin 1, D01 C9W8

First published in hardback by HarperNorth in 2023
This revised and updated paperback edition published 2024

1 3 5 7 9 10 8 6 4 2

A catalogue record for this book
is available from the British Library

HB ISBN: 978-0-00-849826-9
PB ISBN: 978-0-00-849829-0

Printed and bound in Great Britain by
CPI Group (UK) Ltd, Croydon

MIX
Paper | Supporting
responsible forestry
FSC
www.fsc.org
FSC™ C007454

This book contains FSC™ certified paper and other controlled
sources to ensure responsible forest management.

For more information visit: www.harpercollins.co.uk/green

For 'Baz' Cryer and Graeme Garden,
who introduced me to JBP.

'I wished I had been born early enough to have been called a little Englander ... That *little* sounds the right note of affection. It is little England I love. And I considered how much I disliked Big Englanders ... red-faced, staring, loud-voiced fellows, wanting to go and boss everybody about all over the world, and being surprised and pained and saying "Bad show!" if some blighters refused to fag for them.'

'Let us be too proud ... to refuse shelter to exiled foreigners, too proud to do dirty little tricks because other people can stoop to them, too proud ... to tolerate social injustice here, too proud to suffer anywhere in this country an ugly mean way of living.'

J B Priestley, at the conclusion of *English Journey*

N
NORTH SEA
Whitley Bay
Tynemouth
Newcastle
North Shields
Seaham
Shotton Colliery
Ilkley
Bradford
Manchester
DEEP LANCASHIRE
Hull
Liverpool
Lincoln
Nottingham
Boston
The POTTERIES
The BLACK COUNTRY
Leicester
Norwic
Coventry
Birmingham
The COTSWOLDS
Swindon
Bristol
Gower
Southampton
FULL ENGLISH CHANNEL

CONTENTS

A NOTE ON THE
PAPERBACK EDITION

The speed and turbulence of change in England since I journeyed it in 2021/2022 has been such that here and there I've tweaked and updated, or added a new perspective on events. But largely the text is unaltered so that, just as with Priestley's original, it stands as a snapshot of fascinating, exasperating, pivotal time in our nation's history.

1

TO SOUTHAMPTON

In which I enjoy the sybaritic luxury of the
Megabus, raise the *Titanic* and learn of old football
curses, Queen Victoria's 'big shop' and
Jane Austen's 21st bash

'This isn't a very good start, is it?'

The driver of the Megabus, Karl, is a heavy set, gently melancholic
man in his late forties perhaps. As he speaks, he 'vapes' thoughtfully,
shrouding his head in a swirling grey mist like a Victorian illusionist.
We left Birmingham bound for Southampton, jewel of the
Hampshire coast. But twenty minutes in we have reached only
Coventry before meeting with that curse of the English traveller, the
'unforeseen circumstance'.

'Does this happen a lot?' he asks me plaintively.

'I don't know,' I reply truthfully. 'I've never been on a Megabus
before.'

This is meant to be merely informative, but it comes out freighted
with implication. It implies, haughtily, that I am the kind of sophis-

ticated, affluent man of the world who would never normally travel in this way, but for the fact that the Rolls-Royce Phantom Drophead Coupé is in for its MOT and there is no scheduled Learjet service between Birmingham New Street and Southampton. It insinuates that I have opted only reluctantly for this frankly proletarian budget charabanc, now making an unscheduled stop on a Coventry bus station forecourt on a drab, rainy Sunday afternoon. This is where we should be met by a new relief driver: energetic, purposeful, rested in line with the soon-to-be-abandoned European working time directive. But he or she is nowhere to be seen, AWOL. 'I can go no further,' says current driver Karl, though whether he means for legal or existential reasons is not clear.

Our lugubrious chat occurs against the enormous, cheery, pink-faced logo gracing the side of the bus. You will have seen this portly, liveried figure on your motorway journeys. The effect intended by his plumply benign presence is cheap but cheerful efficiency, fun even, but his look of bland amiability grows ironic, sinister even, in the gathering dusk. Brakes exhale, reversing alarms beep, fat dark raindrops begin to stain the grimy concourse. 'Stay Safe, Stay Apart' says a sign on the waiting room door. They still linger, these injunctions and slogans that once were the stuff of Hollywood disaster movies and dystopian novels, which became the humdrum furniture of everyday life.

Mindful of the long journey, now even longer, to come, I ask if the Megabus has a toilet.

'I don't know,' he says, making a comedic embarrassed face. 'I've never driven one of these before. I'm a minibus guy normally. But there's one on the concourse there …' He catches a flicker of anxiety on my face. 'Don't worry. I won't let him go without you.' Karl has a tired, slightly defeated face but a kindly one, so I believe him. We have forged a kind of bond, he and I, here on the concrete walkway of this unprepossessing West Midlands transport concourse. Eighteen minutes later, with me 'refreshed' and Barry, a new, understandably flustered driver arrived from Barnstaple and installed in the hot-ish seat, I wave to his friendly predecessor through the smudgy darkened windows of the Megabus as we pull away, headed south through rain and dusk at the start of my English journey.

2

There are fashions in books just as in trousers, tattoos and TV shows. In the 50s and 60s, it was all angry young men and kitchen sink realism. In the 90s and 00s, strappy sandals and fizzing prosecco bottles on the cover of what was patronisingly dubbed 'chicklit'. England in the 30s saw a boom in domestic travel writing. At one end of the spectrum were sentimental and nostalgic reveries of rural life such as H V Morton's *In Search Of England* and C Henry Warren's *England Is A Village*, all cycling spinsters and dovecotes and Herefordshire churches. At the other were grittier expeditions such as the two commissioned by the left-leaning publisher Victor Gollancz. In 1936, George Orwell visited industrial Lancashire, surveyed the brutal and dehumanizing conditions there and produced a slim but powerful piece of reportage called *The Road To Wigan Pier*, which continues to haunt the imaginations of documentary makers and the occasional politician. But three years before the old Etonian and former colonial policeman Orwell made his expedition north, a former Bradford wool clerk called John Boynton Priestley cast his net wider in a book subtitled 'a Rambling but Truthful Account of What One Man Saw and Heard and Felt and Thought During a Journey Through England During the Autumn of the Year 1933.' That book was *English Journey*, an instant bestseller that today is rightly regarded as a classic, if frequently misunderstood.

English Journey is a record of the author's gruffly amiable travels through the country, by train, coach and sometimes chauffeured

Daimler, taking in largely urban and industrial England (with one rural detour to the Cotswolds). On publication in 1934, it was enormously successful, displacing P G Wodehouse's collection of sustained silly-arsery 'What Ho! Jeeves' at the top of the bestsellers chart.* That seems very telling to me. Long before Bob Dylan, J B Priestley knew that the times in England were a-changing.

English Journey has become a key text in understanding England, never out of print, often re-issued, much loved. Vincent Brome, one of Priestley's many biographers, says that *English Journey* saw him add 'yet another string to his creative bow; that of "popular sociologist."' Yet, as John Baxendale has pointed out, in 2014's *Priestley's England*, 'this esteem … does not mean that there is any universal agreement as to how the book should be read. Contemporary reviews quoted on the dust-jacket hailed it variously as a searing indictment of Britain on the dole, a collection of racy anecdotes about unforgettable characters, and an evocation of cosy Englishness.' Whatever, *English Journey* proved highly influential, not just on Orwell but on a burgeoning trend for realist sociological travelogue and commentary such as the films of Humphrey Jennings and John Grierson and the Mass Observation movement. Some, and I am one, feel it contributed to a national appetite for change that persisted through the war and can be credited with winning the 1945 election for the Labour party.

Knowing of my admiration for Priestley, and enthusiasm for working-class history, popular culture, British travel, humour and the like, people had been suggesting that I 'retread' this English journey for a number of years. But it felt now that the time had come.

So. Why Priestley? Why *English Journey*? Why now?

For me, Priestley exemplifies a kind of figure who seems to have disappeared from our national life; the genuinely popular, engaged

---

* That must have pleased him. In his memoir *Margin Released* he witheringly describes Wodehouse as 'writing as if he never left school.'

and respected public intellectual. In England in the first half of the twenty-first century, we are 'blessed' with any number of voluble and high-profile culture warriors, contrarians and opinionators whose 'hot takes' on everything from pronouns to footballers wages we have had to become accustomed to. None have the same talent, reputation, body of work or reach of Priestley, who I'd call the last great man of English letters.

Priestley is that cliché beloved of profile writers, the 'bundle of contradictions': misrepresented, caricatured and gloriously uncategorisable. Those who think of him at all in modern intellectual circles tend to have him down as a bluff and sentimental little Englander, a phlegmatic everyman. In fact, he was a radical and experimental innovator, a progressive patriot, an internationalist with socialist beliefs. He turned down a knighthood and a life peerage, though he did accept an Order of Merit since that was personally awarded by the late Queen Elizabeth II, who he admired. His bulk and pipe and sheer Yorkshireness suggest conservatism, stolidity, fogeyism even. But he helped found the National Council for Civil Liberties, CND, and the Albany Trust gay rights lobbying group. He loved the music hall but he was also a huge fan of Monty Python and asked John Cleese and Graham Chapman to lunch. He was both enormously popular and daringly experimental. He wrote about vaudeville and time travel both with the same verve and elan.

Perhaps more importantly, in plays like *An Inspector Calls* and the wartime *Postscripts* broadcasts for the BBC, he genuinely changed the mood and tenor and governance of England by holding up a mirror to his country, and never more so than in *English Journey*. It both captured and catalysed the public mood and its huge popularity was part of a sea change in the national mood that found its fullest expression in the post-war settlement and the coming of the welfare state and Atlee's civic socialism. According to Tony Benn, 'J B Priestley shaped the political thinking of a whole generation.'

During the war some 15 million Britons crowded to their wire-lesses every Sunday night to hear his trenchant, patriotic but honest musings on the conflict and its impact on everyday life. He'd been a critic of the establishment's preferred broadcasting style and argued that, in the face of Nazi propagandists like Lord Haw-Haw, what was needed was 'a little less Lincoln's Inn Fields and a little more Gracie Fields.' Brilliant and popular though they were, his *Postscripts* were loathed by Churchill and mistrusted by a fearful BBC for their candour and perceived left-wing slant. Priestley knew that propaganda and flag-waving were less effective than the cold and galvanising truth. He recognised both that this would be a long, hard war but one that Britain must win, and if necessary alone, for the sake of humanity. 'Let the Nazis in and you will find that the laziest loudmouth in the workshop has been given power to kick you up and down the street … If the kindness of England, of Britain … is overshadowed by that vast dark face … it will not be a world worth living in … We will break their black hearts.'

Because he filled so many different roles so well – novelist, dramatist, social historian, short story writer, political observer, broadcaster – and was brilliant and popular in them all, he was sneered at by influential critics like F R Leavis and dismissed by peers such as T S Eliot and Virginia Woolf who described him and Arnold Bennett as 'the tradesmen of letters.' 'If I had written *Anna Karenina*' he said, 'it would have been assumed among the elite, that I was still turning out twaddle for the mob.' The novelist Christopher Fowler called him 'an author bullied out of print by the arrogance of the intelligentsia.' Boyd Tonkin has said that he sought to unite the string quartet, the variety act and the football crowd into a single democratic culture.

Why *English Journey*?

Because it is a work ripe for a proper revisit. While train carriages full of eager, earnest writers have revisited Orwell's *Road To Wigan Pier*, Cobbett's *Rural Rides*, Johnson and Boswell's tour of the Isles,

Kemp's Jig, the Canterbury pilgrimage and even the Jarrow March (I can recommend that particular one highly) no one has given *English Journey* a similar treatment. Beryl Bainbridge produced a curious but diverting 80s BBC TV series about it – you can find desultory chunks of it on YouTube – but the book that accompanied it is out of print and an odd, slight and unsatisfying thing it is too.

So I thought JBP and *English Journey* could stand another shot, sticking closely to the original itinerary and staying true to Priestley's intentions and enthusiasms. He recalled 'Hitherto I have always written what I wanted to like. But when it was suggested to me that the time is ripe for a book which shall deal faithfully with the English industrial life of today, and that I was the man to write such a book, it seemed my duty to undertake it.'

Why now?

Taking a break from the punishing research schedule of this book (eating oatcakes in Stoke-on-Trent, curries in Bradford, cocktails in Leicester etc), I went to a music festival in Oslo: my first foreign trip in a year and a half. As I left, Britain had no HGV drivers thanks to Brexit, empty shelves and a collapsing gas industry thanks to rampant idiotic privatisation.* There was no petrol in the pumps, no pasta or loo rolls on the shelves and rumour had it the army was about to be deployed on the streets. While in Norway I caught their most popular TV satire comedy show, their equivalent of *Have I Got News For You*. In it there was a long riff about Britain's malaises greeted with hearty gales of Nordic laughter. It concluded with one contributor saying, effectively, 'well, England's had a good run. But it's over for them now.' It was hard to disagree. The England I was exploring was, viewed from a grown-up nation like Norway, a dog's breakfast.

---

* De Gaulle said of France that no one could really govern a country that had 257 different types of cheese, the same I think goes for a small island that at one point had fifty-seven different energy providers.

It's a mild but delusional egocentricity to believe that one's own time is somehow different from every other; more complex, more dangerous, more culturally vibrant. Every age thinks this. But today's England had plenty of new, weird quirks and failures. There were times in the writing when England seemed to be revelling in a kind of crazed downward spiral, or, if you prefer, an exciting period of 'creative chaos' and disruption after the twin ruptures of Brexit and Covid; the brief, suicidal madness of Truss and Kwarteng; and the ongoing, befuddled dog-whistling of the Sunak government.

The England of Priestley's journey was just as turbulent and complex as ours. It was frothing with political and economic churn against a backdrop of global recession and menacing political demagoguery on the rise across Europe. The monarchy was in crisis, industry was failing, unemployment was rising remorselessly, but alongside all this the country was heading into uncharted territory. A modern mass media was exploding across several new technologies. People were obsessed with sport, music, movies and the stars thereof. Those who could afford it were listening to dance bands, going on holiday or to the 'pictures', hiking, swimming, eating out. Those who couldn't were demonstrating, striking, marching …

The England I found bubbled with new concepts and ideas that Priestley would have found fascinating, energising, maybe exasperating: MeToo, Black Lives Matter, 'Wokeness', social media, the 'Culture Wars'. Other themes would have seemed more familiar to him: globalisation, Americanisation, celebrity culture, populism. Would Priestley have been on Twitter? I think he wouldn't have been able to resist. TikTok and Insta? Not so much.

My research fell into two sections. A spring and summer of watching and reading everything I could find by the man. And I mean everything. I realised how 'deep' my 'dive' was getting when at 9pm on a glorious July evening I was indoors watching a Spanish amateur dramatic version of his play *Time and The Conways* (El Tiempo Y Los Conway) on YouTube. Then came an autumn, winter and spring of travel. I stuck pretty firmly to Priestley's itinerary and his format. So that's why I ended up visiting Shotton and Seaham Harbour but not London. He was very much his own man.

3

Priestley's journey took him first to Southampton, for reasons that are not entirely clear. It's as far south as he went, indeed it's about as far south as you can go in England, but beyond that the rationale seems vague. He says that he begins 'where a man might well first land' but that would just as easily have taken him first to Dover, Workington or Lowestoft. Perhaps he just fancied another trip to Southampton, which he says he knows well, but this time via a new, thrilling and glamorous mode of transport.

He travels to the south coast seated within, for the first time in his life, a modern motor coach and is instantly smitten. 'I was astonished at its speed and comfort … they are voluptuous, sybaritic, of doubtful morality' he rhapsodises with tongue a little in his cheek. But he meant it, I think. Look at the coaches of 1933 online – there are many sites devoted to such things – and you will see that what handsome, stylish beasts they are, all curved lines and futurist elegance. I thought I should start as Priestley did, and the Megabus was our nearest equivalent.

Sixteen pounds in 1933 went a long way. It still does if you go by Megabus. More specifically it can get you from Birmingham to Southampton, half the length of the country, for about as cheaply as it can be done. Priestley doesn't say how expensive his journey was, but then money was little object to the man. He had recently hit the big time with his novel *The Good Companions* and the stage hit *Dangerous Corner*. Nor does he say how long his journey took from West London. But today, from Birmingham, it's just shy of five hours. On my trip, it would be mid evening when we reached the

South Coast, me and my own good companions now assembling in the dirty, grey, damp heat of the city street. There were students with giant rucksacks, African nurses, Indian families with bulging suitcases, young pale girls in plaster casts; a cross section of the modern English people, a varied and diverse crew with but one thing in common; none of them wanted to spend fifty quid getting from Brum to Southampton on a train when they could do it for sixteen on the Megabus.

Late Sunday afternoon is a very English kind of stasis, the sort that weighed heavy on Jimmy Porter at the start of *Look Back In Anger*: irritable, bored, surrounded by newspapers and undone tasks. Douglas Adams caught it well too: 'that terrible listlessness which starts to set in at about 2:55, when you know that you've had all the baths you can usefully have that day, that however hard you stare at any given paragraph in the papers you will never actually read it … and that as you stare at the clock the hands will move relentlessly on to four o'clock, and you will enter the long dark teatime of the soul.'

Something about the English Sunday and the whole notion of a five-hour Megabus trip engenders a melancholy heavy with all kinds of echoes and resonances; school, church, weary travel, the leaving, the coming back. I always feel slightly sorry for Sunday afternoon travellers. They are always burdened by luggage and the inevitability of return, the end of trips to see lovers or much missed families, going back to cold student digs and jobs they hate. This is pure speculation, of course. They may be giddy with the thought of returning to lives of impossible hedonism and glamour; to well-paid, richly satisfying jobs they love and to homes they adore. They may just be hiding it well.

The choleric, shaven-headed driver of the coach in front barks 'This is for Bristol, not Barnstaple!' at a poor Japanese student boy in a natty hat with such curt and unsmiling ferocity that I expect him to follow it up with 'Paperz! Paperz! Ver are your papers!' Happily, I am not bound for Bristol. Not today, anyway; that would come later in my English journey. By contrast our driver Karl, easy-going to the point of a benign Buddha-like detachment, waves me onto the bus without a glance at my ticket. I find my way upstairs to the top deck and settle in for the trip.

The Megabus is essentially the Ryanair of coach travel, and 'essentially', as in essentials, is *le mot juste* here; no table, not even a little pull-down one, no refreshments and my seat won't recline. The more fortunate passenger in front has more luck though, reclining so far back that he is almost lolling in my lap like a courtesan in a Manet study of a Montmartre brothel. This, perhaps, is what Priestley meant by voluptuous, sybaritic and of doubtful morality. Still, at least it's only for five hours.

After the unscheduled halt at Coventry, we eat up the asphalt in the slanting rain. New driver Barry adds that the traffic is easing and we should make the coast by eight-ish. Barry has had quite the day, I'll wager, and I feel for him and the anxious ferry passengers making their angsty phone calls, but all I have to bother me is a slight delay before my fish and chips and first gin and tonic. When, after Newbury, the road signs begin to feature Winchester and Southampton, I start to relax. It feels like the start of something.

I have the night and the next couple of days ahead of me in Southampton. I'd used social media to ask what I should see there and the response had been slightly overwhelming. Much is made of the sour and toxic nature of social media discourse, but it can and is still used for warm, fun, generous things. I must go to the City Walls, to the Dancing Man Brewery and Pub, to the *Titanic* exhibition and to various bars and restaurants, they told me. Being British, of course, some were jokey, partisan exhortations that I should give the whole place a wide berth and head straight for Portsmouth or the Isle of Wight. As we near the coast, a handmade poster on the central reservation proclaims 'Freedom!' Probably an anti-Vaxxer relic, I scowl.

As the Megabus nears its destination, I'm reading in my battered 80s edition of *English Journey* Priestley's account of his entrance here almost a century earlier. We usually regard Thatcherism as the seismic shift that presaged the end of England as a manufacturing nation. But it's clear something was changing even when Priestley's coach hit town. 'These decorative little buildings, all glass and concrete and chromium plate, seem to my barbaric eye to be playing at being factories. You could go up to any one of the charming little fellows, I feel, and safely order an ice cream or select a few picture postcards. But as for real industry with double entry and bills of lading, I cannot believe them capable of it.'

Southampton has one trade and one trade only at heart: the sea. I hope to smell or feel or at least hear talk of it as I unfold my limbs in a painful origami of seized joints out of my seat and alight near one of Southampton's many places of learning, Solent University. Perhaps it's a vague memory of the Hampshire-based 80s boatbuilding TV soap, *Howards Way*, of blazers and caps and pale lemon sweaters loosely knotted around shoulders, of the clink of masts and ice in G&Ts and mild adultery, but I've always considered Southampton to be prosperous, glamorous even, especially when compared to other southern coast ports like Portsmouth or Plymouth. In Priestley's day it was doing reasonably well, certainly compared to many of the other towns and cities he visited. But I veer haphazardly through rain-slick streets that take away some of the anticipation of sundowners on the poop deck and being piped aboard a catamaran. I'm on the edge of St Mary's, the part of town where Southampton FC were born in 1885 and where they returned at the start of the twenty-first century after more than a hundred years at The Dell. Some Southampton fans were upset at leaving that compact and characterful little ground for a new modern stadium. Yet it did reconnect the team to its old roots in one of the city's more working-class districts. It was here that the Reverend Arthur Sole set up the St Mary's Young Men's Association football team to keep the local lads out of mischief. I pass a few of their modern counterparts lounging and laughing on bikes at the street corner, the air ripe with gossip and aromatic herbs. There was nothing threatening here, just kids adrift in those liminal Sunday hinterlands we all know: lads and girls with not much money but acres of time passing the dead early evening hours. I know well enough the sense of life happening elsewhere, the urge to make your street corner a whole lit stage of intrigue and drama. I grew up on a council estate in a northern industrial town and while I never burned with resentment or rage to be away, like Priestley, I always felt the pull of another life. Perhaps that's why he was always sympathetic to urban young folk.

Eventually though, the avenues bloomed greener and modern maritime Southampton was revealed in all its finery, a sudden skyscape of glittering towers and big ships on the horizon. Ocean Village is the naff and meaningless name for the part of the city's seafront I was staying in: 'a busy and lively 450-berth marina ... hopping with activity with private yachts, cruise ships, fine dining establishments and shopping,' according to Tripadvisor. I was a free man in a famous old English port city, and the evening spread ahead in front of me full of seagull cries and southern promise.

I could hear the former from my private balcony (I know) where I took a small glass from the complimentary decanter of sherry (I know, I know). Here was a touch of the sybaritic (I really must look that word up, I thought) luxury JBP had experienced on the motorcoach, unwittingly booked some weeks before in a fit of profligacy. Below me, a spruce flotilla of posh yachts. If I had the first inkling about boats and such, I'm sure there's a better, more illuminating description than 'posh yachts', possibly something about 'drafts' and 'displacement' and 'deluxe flying bridges'. But they just looked posh to me. To be honest, yachts have never 'floated my boat'. I once spent a week in the very upscale Croatian sailing resort of Hvar and the tanned and fabulously rich people I saw imprisoned on their little deck tables, cramped up on even the most monstrous craft, looked silly and performatively on display, like something from a blingy sunglasses advert. I couldn't understand why you wouldn't want to be strolling the streets of the harbour instead, eating and drinking here and there in little quayside bars. But I guess that way, the sunset doesn't catch your Patek Philippe as you lift your flute of Dom Perignon Oenothèque 1996.

There were no expensively attired mariners decorating the drizzly poop decks (I really must look up 'poop deck' too while I'm about it) today. I imagine the owners were all 'below deck' in their 'quarters' having glamorous yacht sex or playing Boggle. I pulled on my Henri-Lloyd (founded 1963 in Manchester, yacht snobs) and headed down to the lobby. I'd intended to walk from Ocean Village up into town and get something at the Top Catch, an out of town chip shop whose reviews were so glowing they were barely believable, but it was thirty-three minutes' walk according to Google Maps and it had been a long day. To settle it, out of nowhere (well, out of the Solent) came a squall of stinging rain, always likely on a June night in England, but so howling and drenching as it skittered across the water that I was driven into the first welcoming doorway I could find. This turned out be that of the Blue Jasmine Chinese Restaurant. Through the glass, a warm and friendly young woman, rather than baulking at my sodden appearance, beckoned me into an interior that was all low pale orange lighting, muted jazz trio accompaniment and expensively dressed Southamptonites. Dripping gently, I was escorted to my table for one.

I promise at this juncture that I'm not going to bang on and on about the places I eat on my English journey, despite the title's indulgent promise. But if I do mention them *en passant*, it is merely in keeping with the spirit of Priestley's original, which is full of roasts and steaks and puddings, if not crispy sweet and sour pork with pomegranates and Cointreau followed by Signature Hampshire Rib Eye of glazed beef garnished with spring onions and black garlic. Yes, that is what I ate at the Blue Jasmine that night. It is, with no exaggeration, the greatest Chinese food I have ever tasted. Should some purist say that it smacks of Westernised inauthenticity and that I should be eating chicken's feet in a bean-curd broth beneath a tarpaulin in a Guangzhou alley, let me say that they didn't arrive here as I did. But with every succulent mouthful, the memory of Coventry bus station was fading. I was definitely the only diner in the Blue Jasmine that night who had come by Megabus. Priestley would have approved. He liked the good things in life and believed 'ordinary' people were entitled to them. I recall that favourite toast of Nye Bevan's, 'only the best for the working class,' as I crunch the last morsel of crispy pork and drain my Pinot Noir.

Southampton's broad streets are quiet and misty after the rain and I'm feeling a little slow and vague myself after the food and wine. I'll get my bearings tomorrow in the daylight, I think, but for now I aimlessly stroll the deserted, glimmering harbour front. The wide streets of the seafront, the tall buildings and sense of space across Southampton Water means the city has none of the huddled, secretive skulduggery of many ports. This feels a large, modern English city that simply and abruptly meets the sea; like Liverpool, but stranger and quieter tonight. But you can sense why people leaving here for new lives in America or Australia, say, might have felt that Southampton was the last of England, a kind of frontier. Behind you, Hampshire in all its comforting solidity. Before you, the ocean with all its allure and threat.

I reach the edge of the Old Town and see that facing the Isle of Wight Ferry terminal is the Dancing Man Brewery and Pub, glowingly recommended by many a local. Naturally, I go in. Or as naturally as one can when having one's temperature taken and sterilising one's hands in surgical anti-bacterial cleanser. Pandemic and weather combine to leave the Dancing Man far from full on my visit. I order a pint of Pineapple IPA, purely for curiosity value, perch in the corner and make surreptitious notes. A hearty, burly young rugger bloke seems to be playing a drinking game with three petite Japanese hipster girls. What's the story there I wonder? An older couple, chatting to the young barman ask 'are you double jabbed?'; another standard greeting in 2021 that would once have seemed absurd and frightening, like something from a J G Ballard short story. Even given the somewhat constrained circumstances, I feel I should throw myself more into gregarious interactions but I'm getting tired and am still uncomfortably damp which probably makes me less than a 'catch' socially. I console myself that JBP would often keep himself to himself on his journey, sometimes preferring to sit and watch. I will more than make up for it tomorrow anyway, though I don't know that yet.

Slightly woozy, stuffed with exquisite Chinese food and Pineapple IPA (basically Lilt with a headbutt) I walk along the seaward side of the city, watching the Isle of Wight ferry workers and all the late Sunday business of a docks: headlights and torches and the swing and clank of crane. Then I walk back along Town Quay and Canute Road to Ocean Village. As I arrive at my hotel, a ziggurat of steel and light, I run into a big group of fabulously glamorous Asian women of different ages laughing, teetering and taking a happily chaotic selfie in the rain outside the hotel. Feeling already out of place, I'm even more self-conscious when they drag me into their giddy throng of gorgeous saris and glitzy jewellery 'to help' with the picture, a request that's almost touching in its optimism. Having probably taken several of my feet and the dockside cranes, I think I get a few good ones of them and they are delighted. 'We've had a lovely meal and a lovely time. Can you tell?' one asks me. 'Oh, a little,' I answer, gallantly. 'Are you celebrating something?' 'Yes. Us!' What a perfect answer, I think.

I go back to my room, peel off my wet clothes, put my sodden notebook and paperback Priestley on the radiator to dry and have my second shower in three hours. Lying on the bed afterwards, having dipped into the decanter again, I notice a small selection of books provided by the hotel on the bedside table. Two to be precise; a book on the joys of walking in rainy English weather by the nature writer Melissa Harrison and an anthology of erotic poetry. At least one of these fits my mood and circumstance perfectly, I think, as I refill my glass and turn the page with trembling hand to the chapter about splooshing through the fens in galoshes, obviously.

4

I wake to find a cruise liner parked outside my window. One of the things Priestley liked most about Southampton is that theoretically a man might walk down the high street until he found himself in a wood-panelled room where he could enjoy a pipe 'only to discover that Southampton had quietly moved away and his smoke room was plunging about in the Channel. For you see you can catch the *Berengaria* or the *Empress of Britain* from the end of this high street.' Like Sydney, and unlike Venice, where they keep the elephantine liners at Maritima or Mestre, until they ban them entirely, Southampton clutches its big ships close to its manly chest.

Priestley's talk of walking in off the Southampton street and ending up in New York was a poetic exaggeration. But a few steps from the town's main thoroughfare could still see you bound in splendour for the New(ish) World. If I were a little younger and lither, and maybe had a hover jet pack to be honest, I could bound onto the deck of the gigantic P&O liner moored outside from my balcony. It is both enormous and enormously impressive, with more storeys than a tower block, port and starboard festooned with pennants and bright orange lifeboats. It's a fitting, resonant sight to be greeted with this morning for I'm off out in search of the city's *Titanic* connection, and other chapters of Southampton's long rich past. *English Journey*'s often light on the history of the places JBP visits. He seemed keener to take the temperature of the times. History as an industry, marketing strategy and media obsession was not as developed as it is now, when the Tudors are as much a part of our national soap opera as *Coronation Street* and prime time TV is Lucy Worsley dressed as Goebbels.

You sure can't get away from history on the streets of Southampton, especially the history of the city's long, intimate, intense relationship with the sea. Having leafed casually through some erotic poetry, I set out with spring in step down Canute Road. Sitting on an upstairs windowsill, two young Southamptonites are having a morning smoke, below them a plaque reads 'Near this spot AD1028 King Canute reproved his courtiers', commemorating one of the most misunderstood incidents in English history. In Priestley's day, most people would have felt that Canute's attempt to defy the tides was an illustration of kingly arrogance. In fact, as we now understand, it was his way of showing that he was merely mortal and powerless over nature. 'Let all men know how empty and worthless is the power of kings, for there is none worthy of the name, but He whom heaven, earth, and sea obey by eternal laws.' Of course, that could have been made up by a twelfth-century spin doctor. And it might have happened in East Anglia. Oh and it's Knut, by the way.

Whether Knut got his feet wet here or not, Southampton was known to both the Anglo-Saxons and Romans as Clausentum and Hamwic respectively. But it was following the arrival on the South Coast of a whole bunch of Normans spoiling for a fight in 1066 that Southampton became a powerful and strategic port and the main connection to the new regime's homelands in France. A couple of hundred years on, God's House Tower, now an arts space, was the gatehouse to the city where Pilgrims from Leiden met up with the rest of their party ahead of their voyage to colonise America. Next to the gate was the Butcher's Shambles where they may have bought snacks for the voyage such as dried ox tongues and salted pork. I'd have preferred Pringles but I doubt they would have lasted the eight-week trip. And considerably later in Atlantic crossings, three years after Priestley visited, the *Queen Mary* docked in Southampton after her maiden voyage. This was filmed by the BBC in what was the world's first TV news broadcast. But the most famous chapter in Southampton's long history with the sea is also its darkest. We will come to that.

The High Street heads into town from Southampton Water and along it the council have established the QE2 Mile, a series of plaques set in the pavement that tell the story of Southampton's history in quotes and stories. There's an anonymous townsperson of 1592 complaining about the 'verie quick trafique'. Another from four centuries later marvels fearfully as the sky darkens with bombers and fighters and ships setting out on D-Day. A deliciously 'period' quote from the *Times* concerning the 1969 launch of the *QE2* reads: 'From the moment you step on board, you get a feeling that this is something special. This is quite simply a swinging ship.' And look! Here's JBP himself and that sweet bit of *English Journey* about hopping on the *Berengaria* at the bottom of the High Street.

Oddly, this small civic initiative has its own Tripadvisor page. I browse it as I stroll, stumbling across a review from one Hampshire seasider that is pretty unarguable in its brisk factuality: 'This tells the story in brass plaques along the pavement from the Pier up to the High Street, of the seafaring history of Southampton.' But then I make the mistake of digging deeper into the comments section where the permanently angry swim.

435sSmudger in a post headed 'A Footpath Of Beggars' opined 'I thought it would be an interesting walk through the heart of Southampton. Alas I encountered 8 people begging all pretending to be homeless but at the end of the day I saw them again, pooling their money and then entering a pub!' Sexagenarian of Wolverhampton was equally blunt: 'Why? This is obviously the idea that earned a pay rise for someone working for the local authority but putting a red heading on the street signs and setting a few brass plaques into the pavement doesn't make an attraction. There is nothing at all special about the QE2 mile it's simple (sic) another high street with the same shops that you will find in any random town centre in England. If it were possible to give a negative score I would do.'

Were we always like this, the English, I wonder? So joyless, so suspicious, so quick to judge, never happier than when carping and finding fault? Perhaps we were. Priestley always railed against this mean, shrivelled cast of mind, and does so many times in *English Journey*. So I shall take my lead from him. I thought the QE2 Mile was an interesting minor addition to the city streets of Southampton. Furthermore, if I could give you a negative score, Sexagenarian of Wolverhampton, I would. As it is, I looked around for a beggar to give some booze money to, but finding none decided to head up to the 'smelly fast-food stalls' (Fusspot 43, Yeovil) in search of breakfast.

I turn into the High Street as the sun begins to beat down, last night's murk and drizzle having burned away in that climatic quick change act that is a mark of coastal towns. A good vantage point to observe Southampton's street life would seem to be Sidewalk South, an Iranian café with a faux Yankee name. Perspiring gently, I ask to sit outside and the waiter looks queryingly at me and shrugs. All along the street, other pavement tables are full, but not here. Patrons are sweltering inside. Not me I think. Let me enjoy an al fresco breakfast on this glorious Hampshire morning.

But then with the slow inevitability of a comedy sketch from a 1970s Benny Hill show, a dusty workman in high viz emerges from the alley, stamps out his breaktime fag, clamps on his ear defenders and proceeds to fire up a pneumatic drill with which he carves and chews up the pavement at brain-juddering volume. Of course, as a stubborn Englishman reluctant to admit defeat, I stick it out until the whole right side of my head is ringing and vibrating with pain. The waiters look out pityingly and they usher me wincing and stumbling inside just as my order, the Full English Breakfast, arrives.

Frankly 'Full' doesn't begin to cover it. A wooden disc the size of a lorry tyre arrives laden with three sausages, three eggs, three hash browns, a mountain of beans, toast, mushrooms and (joy) black pudding. Over the next half hour, I manage as much as I can before, as my notebook scrawl has it, 'The Final Sausage Defeats Me,' which I decide will be the title of my first slim collection of haiku. I pay the bill, which comes to next to nothing, and continue on at a particularly well-fed snail's pace.

Back in 1933, Priestley described the shops as being full of the 'brittle spoils of Czechoslovakia and Japan,' which seems snooty. In any event, they would soon be full of nothing much except broken glass and splintered wood and ashes after the Luftwaffe turned its attention to the juicy target of Southampton. In the Dunkirk evacuations, the *Gracie Fields* ship of the Isle of Wight Ferry company was sunk with the loss of eight lives. Five days later, Churchill gave his 'We Shall Fight Them On The Beaches' speech. But the day after that Priestley gave a BBC radio broadcast about the valour of the 'little ships' on Sunday night which was less bombastic but just as stirring. It had such a profound effect on listeners that he was asked to broadcast every week in what became his enormously popular, influential and controversial *Postscripts*. You can still listen to them on the BBC Archives.*

The Southampton Blitz escalated throughout 1940. Hermann Göring, commander-in-chief of the Luftwaffe, said the city centre resembled 'a piece of cake' from the air and that he was going to 'cut himself a slice.' Twelve bombs were dropped, one a direct hit on the Civic Centre killing thirty-five people, including fifteen children who were having an art lesson in the basement. The huge International Cold Storage was hit in August and, being filled with 2,000 tons of butter, 'burned for weeks like a candle of fat'. When the Pirelli tyre plant was bombed, German planes strafed the fleeing women workers with machine gun fire.

After the war, Southampton rebuilt itself to most people's satisfaction, with the exception of Beryl Bainbridge. In her queer little

---

* https://www.bbc.co.uk/archive/postscripts--jb-priestley/zn9xkmn

80s book loosely based on *English Journey* (in that it shared its title) she moaned about the pedestrianisation of Southampton's downtown shopping district: 'Traffic-free areas are a silly idea. The trick with shopping is to get the whole wretched business over with as quickly as possible – nobody in their right minds would want to sit down in the middle of it.' By that measure there are a whole bunch of mad people in Southampton today, as well as everywhere else in Britain. The High Street, Bargate and Old Town are full of people refusing to conform to Bainbridge's weird dictum, chatting, playing with their kids, actively enjoying the business of commerce like informed consumers rather than just 'getting the wretched business over with' like automata. There is a long and illustrious history of celebrities shopping and 'chilling' in Southampton. Queen Victoria herself would do her 'big shop' here en route to her Osborne House gaff on the Isle of Wight and Jane Austen had her twenty-first birthday in the Dolphin Hotel with brother Frank.* It is not recorded if they 'did shots' or did the rowing dance to 'Oops Upside Your Head'.

I arrive at the Bargate to be as impressed as every visitor by this glorious edifice, standing above Southampton's busy late morning crowd of shoppers not 'in their right minds'. This medieval gatehouse, once the main entrance into Southampton, is a remarkable thing to find in a modern retail street, which makes it all the more noteworthy that in 1899 the civic fathers were going to knock it down, thinking it a gloomy old eyesore (your average Victorian grandee was often highly dismissive of anything they didn't build themselves or pinch from some other country's long standing indigenous civilisation). Happily, the Bargate survived, has been restored and is now sometimes used as an exhibition space by Solent

---

* I love that Jane Austen's bro was called Frank. Frank Austen sounds like the bloke who runs the MOT centre on the corner, not the sibling of the lapidary romantic prose stylist of *Pride And Prejudice*.

University, the former Southampton School of Art. Fancying a bit of art myself, and somewhere cool to sit and look at it, I popped in to the welcoming and attractive shady white marble of the City Art Gallery. A plaque outside 'commemorates the arrival aboard the 'Habana" of 4,000 refugee children from the Basque region of Spain in May 1937 following the destruction of Guernica during the Spanish Civil War and to thank the people of Southampton and Britain who volunteered to care for them.' It's fitting that this plaque should be outside the art gallery, since of course the most powerful and enduring commemoration of Guernica will always be Picasso's anguished masterpiece. Less fittingly, on the same day I read the plaque, the home secretary is in the papers talking about turning back boats of Syrian refugees braving the rough waters of the English Channel, a stretch of which I can see glittering on the horizon.

Southampton knows well the bounties of the sea. Priestley attributes its prosperity to what he called 'fathoms of luck … an odd narrowing of the English Channel between Portland bill and Cap de Hague in Cherbourg. It is this bottling of the water that gives three high tides a day.' But Southampton knows the cruelty of the ocean as well, and everywhere there are reminders of this. Southampton's fine harbour saw the greatest passenger ship ever built leave in 1912 for the first and last time, never to see land again.

Many places trade on their connections to the RMS *Titanic*, some more tenuous than others. In Liverpool (where the liner was registered, though it never visited) there's a memorial, a museum and even a hotel for those people whose idea of a relaxing mini-break is to be constantly and vividly reminded of one of the most terrible leisure-related tragedies ever. There's a whole new tourist complex in Belfast on the slipway where the *Titanic* was built. There's even a blue plaque (and until relatively recently a little museum) in Chorley to commemorate the town's eminent son Charles Lightoller, second officer and survivor. But Southampton has the strongest civic connection to the doomed ship. Of the 897 crew, three quarters came from the city. So consider this: the deadliest peacetime maritime disaster in history had happened just twenty years before Priestley visited Southampton. Many in the city would have lost loved ones. Hundreds would have had direct personal connections to the tragedy. The memory of the disaster would still have been real and raw here in 1933. Extraordinary, then, that Priestley never mentioned it.

I have a theory as to why. It seems to me that disaster movies and documentaries, the rise of dark tourism and the fascination with catastrophe, are the product of a relatively safe and peaceful age. Priestley came to Southampton still bearing the physical and mental scars of his time in the First World War. Fascism had already gripped Italy, was rising in Spain and Germany and within a few years, sirens and bombs and death would be the stuff of daily life again. A depression was ravaging the world. Real life was dark and dangerous and precarious enough to Priestley's generation without wanting to fetishise the tragedies and horrors of the past.

This is not to say that the way Southampton remembers the *Titanic* is not entirely appropriate and superbly done. There are echoes all over the city, from the plaque in Canute Chambers where hundreds of local people crowded on that fateful morning waiting for news of their loved ones, to an oak table in St Joseph's church with a plaque in memory of the restaurant workers like 'Luigi' Gatti who went down with the ship. The Titanic Engineers Monument in East Park remembers Joseph Bell, chief engineer officer and the twenty-four engineers, six electrical engineers, two boilermakers, a plumber and a clerk who all perished. At the unveiling in 1914, an estimated 100,000 Southampton residents came to pay tribute and heard how 'they must have known that pumping could do no more than delay the final catastrophe, yet they stuck pluckily to their duty … driven back from boiler-room to boiler-room, fighting for every inch of draught to give time for the launching of the boats, not one of those brave officers was saved.'

But best, if that's the right word, is the Titanic Exhibition at the Seacity Museum which not only reflects the scale and tragedy of the disaster but sets it in historical context. Our vision of Edwardian England has become sepia tinged by period dramas and literature that largely reflect the lives of the middle and upper classes: croquet on the lawns of stately homes, straw boaters, idyllic prelapsarian innocence shattered by the coming of war. In fact, in our towns and cities, life was unremittingly grim and dangerous for the working classes before their menfolk ever set eyes on Ypres or Passchendaele. Southampton had 17,000 unemployed in 1912 and many of these desperate people took jobs on the *Titanic* although they had never been to sea before. The Titanic Exhibition adopts the smart, insightful tactic of following the lives of six crew members from Captain John Smith and Second Officer Lightoller to Mabel Bennet of the victualling staff and Arthur Rous the plumber. A huge display shows portraits of most of the *Titanic*'s crew and, shorn of boaters and taches and the other stereotypical props that convey Edwardiana, these are modern men and women who stare frankly and disarmingly out at you. George the lookout and Walter the fireman are young men whose open, genial faces you could see in the pubs of Southampton today. Until not that long ago you might have done. They were two of the lucky ones. Both survived.

You might think that a detailed inventory of the ship's bills of fare would be quite dull stuff. In fact, it is weirdly compelling; 50 boxes of grapefruit, 7,000 lettuces, 411 cases of shelled walnuts, two cases of tennis balls and four cases of opium. Other elements are downright incredible. I have never seen an asparagus tong or a beef teacup in my life. Neither, I suggest respectfully, have you. The *Titanic* carried 400 of the first and – wait for it – 3,000 of the second. That's 3,000 beef teacups. Whatever they are. It is these details that impress that this was another world, at least if you were travelling first class.

The evocation of the small hours of 15 April 1912 is spare and chilling. A slight bump, felt by a few as when a train passes over the points, presages the disaster to come. There are harrowing, unsensational testimonies from survivors. Eva Heissman, then eight, recalls that 'you could see the ice for miles across the sea. I thought it was wonderful to see the ice like that.' It's a child's innocent delight that now brings a shudder. Eva Hart, a child who escaped with her mother (though not her father) to the lifeboats, watched the huge ship filled still with light, slide below the waves, as her boat just escaped the drag and suction in its wake. 'I saw that ship sink. I never closed my eyes. I didn't sleep at all. I saw it, I heard it, and nobody could possibly forget it ... I can remember the colours, the sounds, everything. The worst thing I can remember are the screams.'*

The aftermath of the disaster is evoked with the same quiet tact and effectiveness. A local man Charles Morgan remembered that 'a great hush descended on the town ... there was hardly a single street in Southampton that hadn't lost somebody on that ship.' But there were other curiouser and kinder twists of fate. All six lookouts survived. The penultimate room of the museum is a striking revelation: you emerge into a dark and cavernous courtroom where actual testimonies boom out on giant screens. Could the lifeboats have taken more passengers? 'Undoubtedly,' says one crew member. But elsewhere easy conclusions are harder to reach and thus scrupulously avoided. The longstanding rumour that third class passengers were prevented from boarding lifeboats in favour of first and second class passengers is discussed but remains just that, a rumour. There are no glib libels of the dead like those in James Cameron's terrible film.

Leaving the exhibition in bright sunlight and a sea breeze, I decide on a whim to jump on a number 18 bus to Thornhill. Partly a whim at least, and partly because I had read online that in that part of the

---

* Hart suffered from terrible nightmares until at 23, she decided to confront her terrors, returning to sea and locking herself in a cabin for four days until the nightmares ended. She died in 1996 and has a pub named after her near Romford.

city 'not even cats will go out after dark.' So going in daylight seems a good idea. I want to see something of Southampton away from the prosperity and glitz of Ocean Village and the seafront. If I don't dwell on my few hours in Northam, it isn't because it's awful or dangerous or terrifying. It was working class and ethnically diverse; the poorer end of these groups too. I probably wouldn't want to live there if I had a choice. But when you read, as I did, that Southampton is the most dangerous city in Hampshire, bear in mind that that dramatic statistic actually means that it has a very slightly higher crime rate than Hampshire's other two cities, those lawless hellholes Winchester and Portsmouth. When I get back to the town centre I drop into a vintage shop in which two nice posh Southampton ladies were discussing fabrics. One of them had a tote bag that read 'Absolute Shit Show Lads'.

I spend the rest of the afternoon walking the town walls and taking in the Old Town, which is the nicest part of the city and full of character especially after the anodyne luxury of Ocean Village. Even here, two different Southamptons rub up alongside each outside a couple of adjacent-ish pubs, the Juniper Berry and the Duke Of Wellington. One's crowd is older, rougher of face and clothes, bristly and bald headed, the odd scar, pale fizzy lagers in meaty fists. The other has Waterstones bags and Solent University sweatshirts, designer specs, trimmed steel grey hair and chinos. Both groups are loud in the way only British drinkers can be, but the latter are hale and hearty, while the former more grumbling, bitter and laconic. Bugle Street is where they would sound the bull horn in times of civic danger and where the wealthy merchants of medieval Southampton lived. Nowadays there's a few council houses dotted among the Tudor timber. In these few Hampshire postal codes, you could avail yourself of every cuisine of the many waves of immigration that has crossed the sea to come here. In the museum was a display called Southampton Gateway To The World, and of course for the world it was the Gateway To England. You can see that in the museum displays, but you can actually taste it here; Ottoman Kitchen, Argento steakhouse, Beity's Lebanese, bierkellers and trattorias, noodle bars and Nepalese cafés. Perhaps the tapas bar is run by a grandson or daughter of the Basques who escaped Guernica and were welcomed by Hampshire.*

The little cluster of streets around Bedford Place, Southampton's clubland, boasting 'nitespots' like Lift, TokyoMilan and the Orange Rooms must be jumping on Friday and Saturday but are sleeping it off on this hot afternoon. Even here the weirdness of the pandemic years is apparent. A poster for Orange Rooms says 'Wash Your Hands You Dirty Pig … Eh Lads She Wouldn't Have Touched Him Anyway But Definitely Won't Now.'

I drop into my hotel to 'freshen up'. Early evening at Ocean Village is when the taxis and the Ubers arrive, disgorging their cargo of tanned young women teetering in implausible heels and even more implausible dresses, the lads in a pungent cloud of Armani Code Red, or at the very least Lynx Africa. The older well-heeled crowd favour upscale French boat chic from Mat De Misaine or Royal Mer, all soon to be splashed with passion fruit coulis and raspberry jus. Ocean Village is as ersatz as its name, it neither being a village or on the ocean. What it is, is a place predicated on the notion of glamour and living well, of making one feel that one is in Paradise, or at least *Howard's Way*. I, never a tourist always a traveller, a free spirited maverick always wanting to immerse myself out in the edgy, real parts of town that the sheep never see, decide to go for a curry on the High Street.

I had promised myself on this trip not to overdo either the curries or the subsequent smugly sated reportage. But several Twitter correspondents had told me that the Bayleaf Kitchen was the best curry house in Southampton and by these small interventions was my will eroded. Also, online it said that the chef had once been responsible

---

* I know. Basques eat pintxos, not tapas.

for the biggest naan bread ever made and it seemed mean spirited not to honour this by eating in his restaurant. I had a bhuna and a normal sized naan bread and it was excellent. So good in fact that my plan to go and give the dancefloors of Bedford Place a whirl while young revellers looked on admiringly was abandoned in favour of convenience. I went in the Red Lion next door and soon fell in with a good crowd.

Snowie used to be a pub DJ. 'Smiths, Stone Roses, that kind of thing. Used to get quite good crowds.' He has a bit of money riding on France in the European championship quarter final and glances anxiously up at the big telly from time to time. Chris is also a big music fan too and the de facto historian of the group. He tells me about the third-century Roman occupation of Southampton and 'the Southampton Plot' to depose Henry V and replace him with Edmund Mortimer 'They tried the three ringleaders upstairs in this pub and beheaded them in front of the Bargate. A lot of people say the trial was actually in the pub down the road but I like to think it was this pub … because I like this pub.' I liked the Red Lion too, so I am happy to go along with this story, commemorated in a plaque by the fruit machine.

Landlady Tish comes over and commiserates with the gnomic and gnomish Charlie about an accident sustained on her behalf which has left him with a terrifying, swollen red weal on his arm. Apparently Charlie had, somewhat foolhardily I think, volunteered to undertake some repairs to a high cistern in the Gents late in the evening after drink had been taken. 'You should ave seen him … Charlie's got his facking leg up on a chair and I was trying to keep him balanced and the whole facking thing came down on top of him.' Charlie sips his lager and speaks for the first time. 'I think I was a bit pissed,' he reflects quietly.

All are big Saints fans, unsurprisingly. This is a one team, football mad city, like Newcastle. St Mary's regularly gets crowds of 30,000 plus which is about 13 per cent of the population. In the immortal words of the pundit Ray Parlour 'Southampton have always been at the top, apart from the seasons when they weren't.' They have only won one major honour, beating Manchester United in the FA Cup final in 1976, but even when times have not been good for them, they have generally been better for them than for their bitter rivals Pompey just along the coast.

Chris has an interesting history angle here too. 'When the new St Mary's stadium was built, they had to do a big excavation and found Saxon stuff buried there. There's another legend of course, that says that a Portsmouth supporting builder buried a Pompey shirt under the centre circle at St Mary's and so the ground's supposed to be cursed.' A chorus of groans suggest this is not given much credence in the Red Lion, and in this they very much concur with former Southampton football club secretary Brian Truscott who, when approached by the *Guardian* about this, offered the blunt rebuttal 'Total bollocks ... I don't read the *Guardian*, so I don't know whether your publication prints words like "bollocks".'

I tell them about my afternoon wanders around Northam, St Mary's and Thornhill and ask whether they think these areas are rough. They are diplomatically vague. Snowie makes a face. Chris is thoughtful. 'They are diverse ... it's working class basically. It's where our Asian community live and a lot of our Afro-Caribbean community.' At this, Tish goes into a kind of reverie: 'I used to go to a lot of shebeens there when I was young,' she tails off dreamily.

The dream is interrupted by a curt obscenity from Snowie as the French fluff their last penalty and a couple of hundred quid slip away from him. In consolation, I order a round of whiskies and leave the pub some time later with my back comprehensively slapped, Snowie and Tish having rounded off the evening with an exhaustive, colourful gossip about other Southampton pub landlords. 'He's a total prick,' offers Tish thoughtfully of one 'but I would never say that his pub's shit. You just don't do that.' Sage nods all round.

'It is shit though,' concludes Chris, an assessment I would never level at the Red Lion, unless of course I'd just been found guilty of high treason there like some of its former passing trade. By the time this out-of-towner leaves, what with the curry and the IPA and the entirely unnecessary round of Laphroaigs, I hardly notice the long walk through the sluicing rain until yet again I splash into the lobby of the hotel looking like the Beast from 20,000 fathoms. If the staff clock me, they are too discreet to comment.

Time for my third hot shower of the day. Padding out onto the balcony in my complimentary dressing gown and mules, I can see between the wooded headland and the towerblocks of Northam and the bristling, crane-silhouetted skyline of the docks, the Solent, and the last ferries of a summer evening ploughing the gentle sea to the Isle of Wight.

Southampton's trade is the sea and yet it is somehow not of the sea. Parts of its old town feel like York or Durham and its new bits like perhaps Coventry, London or Manchester. Despite being in the rough cold grasp of the Atlantic, it has mainly weathered the storms that have battered other UK cities. It still feels solid and prosperous, just as it did in Priestley's day. Apart from those few secretive, scruffy squares around Bugle Street and the Juniper Berry, it is never as raffish or piratical as, say, Bristol. But just to make sure, that was where I was headed next.

2

TO BRISTOL AND SWINDON

In which I encounter the handiwork of Banksy and
Brunel, have a pattie in the People's Republic of
Stokes Croft, give Viscount Bolingbroke a blast of
the hooter and bid farewell to Edward Colston.

Not far from Bristol Temple Meads station, one of Isambard
Kingdom Brunel's most extraordinary contributions to an extraordinary city, there's an area called Finzel's Reach. Once the site of
Conrad Finzel's huge sugar refinery that fed the city's many breweries and distilleries, like Harveys of Bristol Cream fame, it's now an
office complex, whose workers bustle to grab lunch at the boho
street market there. I am hovering indecisively between some wild
garlic salami and the black bean empanadas when one of the small
crowd by the cheesemonger's recognises me. Charming and garru-
lous, he tells me that he was a singer in an anarcho-punk band called
Black Wendy. Onstage, he wore a bride's wedding dress and an IRA
balaclava and sang songs about toxic masculinity, alcohol addiction
and 'modern trauma'. He jots down a SoundCloud link and, before

I leave, insists on buying me two big wedges of really very good artisanal Ogleshield, the West Country's Raclette.

It is, I think, perhaps the most Bristol thing ever.

With a directness Priestley would have approved of, Bristol's airy central promenade, from Magpie Park and the Cenotaph past the Hippodrome to the Harbour is called 'The Centre'. He found it 'a place where trams and coastal steamers seemed in danger of collision.' Nowadays it'll be an electric scooter that collides with you, Bristol having fallen hard for these awful bloody devices. If you can avoid them it's a fine place to stroll on a decent spring morning and as I did just that, headed for the water with nothing more pressing on my agenda than a good espresso, I thought of another who had made this short trip just recently. A couple of years back, one Edward Colston (or at least his replica) had travelled down here with a great deal more urgency, daubed with paint and dragged with ropes, bound for the harbour also. There he was deposited with a sploosh, to the delight of many, the outrage of some and the drooling appreciation of scores of TV cameras. Some still regarded him a great philanthropist and public benefactor and there is no doubt that he donated about £70,000 – equivalent to millions today – to the city, helping to establish many of its oldest institutions. But the money Colston lavished on Bristol was drenched in blood.

Between 1723 and 1743, until eclipsed by Liverpool, Bristol was England's busiest and richest port for the brisk trade in enslaved Africans. From here were launched more than 2,000 ships carrying half a million brutally abducted men, women and children from Africa into bondage to the Americas. This 'trade' in human misery made men like Edward Colston rich. But, as Hazel V. Carby writes in *Imperial Intimacies*, it was not just wealthy traders who profited from slavery. 'Residents working on the docks, at brothels and inns, those handling sugar or tobacco or making goods for export to Africa or the Americas – everyone benefited.' Bristol even did well out of the abolition of slavery. After the 1834 Abolition Act, Bristol's merchants received £158,000 from the Slave Compensation Commission for the loss of their human property.

These dark roots of the city's life and vitality has never been unproblematic, whatever the ahistorical 'anti-woke' lobby say. In 1788, Bristol became the first city outside of London to set up a committee for the abolition of the slave trade. The committee approached the government about it, held meetings, and circulated a petition signed by 800 people. This was one of the first political campaigns that women were actively involved in, particularly in the boycott of slave-produced sugar. Arguments raged in Bristol's newspapers. John Wesley preached against the slave trade in his church in Broadmead, Bristol. In 1774 he wrote: 'It cannot be, that either war, or contract, can give any man such a property in another as he has in his sheep and oxen. Much less is it possible, that any child of man should ever be born a slave. Liberty is the right of every human creature as soon as he breathes the vital air; and no human law can deprive him of that right which he derives from the law of nature.'

Closer to our own time, voices began to be raised in protest and polemical books and articles written when Bristol's 600th anniversary celebrations in 1973 neglected to even mention the city's slave trade history. Similarly in 1996 Bristol's Festival of the Sea failed almost entirely to address this aspect of Bristol's past and so arts groups launched a counter festival. Bristol band Massive Attack announced at this time that they were boycotting major local venue Colston Hall (now the Bristol Beacon) over its association with the slave trader.

When the Colston statue was erected in Bristol in 1895 it was said to be 'by popular subscription ... a memorial to one of the most virtuous and wise sons of their city.' But ordinary Bristolians contributed almost nothing, and the monument was largely financed by a wealthy local publisher, James Williams Arrowsmith. In January 1998, some of this public indifference turned to rage with the first direct action against the Colston statue. The injunction 'Fuck off slave trader' appeared in red paint on the statue overnight. Ray Sefia, a councillor, said: 'It's like having a monument to Hitler … We have to be very clear about Colston's role in the slave trade.'

Then on 7 June 2020, a 22-year-old labourer called Sage Willoughby scaled the statue and circled a rope round Colston's throat. After fastening a noose, Willoughby and others tossed two canoeing ropes to a group below, who dragged the statue to the ground, where it was daubed in blue and blood-red paint. One protestor knelt on Colston's neck, a deliberate piece of symbolism drawn from the Black Lives Matter protests in the United States. The statue was then rolled and dragged to the harbour by a large group and dumped in the water. The splash was heard around the world.

Back in 1933, as Priestley strolled the city and recorded his thoughts, he mused at some length about Bristol's wealth as a city and how it acquired it. He talked about the bustling productivity of the Wills tobacco factory and an economy based on chocolate 'and soap and clothes and a hundred other things.' He even mentions the 'West Indian' trade, but makes absolutely no mention of what that trade might have been. He speculates not at all on what cargos were packed into the holds of those fine ocean-going ships. In other words, he makes no mention of slavery, the real and bloody reason Bristol grew rich. This seems extraordinary to the modern reader (and writer). If it were Evelyn Waugh or P G Wodehouse's *English Journey*, one might understand this omission. But this is John Boynton Priestley, the Bradford humanist and liberal, author of *An Inspector Calls*, that plea for human compassion still taught in every English school. How can he not have thought to mention the chief and darkest reason for the prosperity of this city he warmed so much to?

Here's my guess. In 1933, for socialist and conservative alike, slavery was regarded as something settled and dealt with. Like child chimney sweeps and the Black Death, it was a dire social evil that had disappeared, an old wrong that we had moved on from and come to deplore, just as we did bear baiting or the stocks. Moreover, it was an evil that we had dealt with and addressed unanimously (if not swiftly) by abolishing it in 1807.* By contrast, the United States of America did not just continue with this foul practice; it divided their people so much that they fought a self-lacerating civil war over it. And it remained a burning social issue through the civil rights movement and beyond to Black Lives Matter.

In the immediate aftermath of Colston's downing, the mood of many Bristolians seemed largely supportive of the impulse, if not the method. Ted told LBC radio it was 'really sad that it had to happen this way' but it was 'inevitable ... It is a thing of vandalism, but I feel like it wouldn't happen any other way.' An unnamed Afro-Caribbean man told the same network: 'To see that man with that sort of history, a slave trader, who used to throw black people over-board on ships for economic reasons, to finally see him being put over into the water, I just felt a sense of easing, something to say we can now move forward together united and trying to lead better lives.' He added: 'Earlier on, a lady came up to me and she just said "I'm sorry. I'm sorry for what happened to your people." We were just talking and there just seemed to be a sense of healing and coming together.'

At the 9 June funeral of George Floyd, the African American man murdered in broad daylight by a police officer, Reverend Al Sharpton praised the Bristol demonstrators. US rapper Ice Cube tweeted his support. Local cult artist Banksy raised funds for the accused. Others were more circumspect. Labour leader Keir Starmer said that it was 'completely wrong' to dump the statue in the harbour while equivocating that the monument should have come down 'a long, long time ago.' He felt it ought to have been 'brought down properly,

---

* We have little to gloat about though. Iceland abolished slavery in 1117, Norway in 1274, Poland in 1347 and even Russia in 1723.

with consent,' and placed in a museum. Prime Minister Boris Johnson said the protests had been 'subverted by thuggery.' Bristol mayor Marvin Rees, of dual heritage himself, didn't support the removal of the statue, as it was against the law, but did say 'the statute was an affront to me ... it is possible that Colston had owned, kidnapped and made money off one of my ancestors.'

Four people, including Willoughby, were identified as ring leaders and charged with criminal damage over the statue's destruction. The 'Colston Four' opted to be tried before a judge and jury. This seemed brave as, given the conclusive evidence of CCTV footage, recordings from the defendants' phones and two immediate confessions, an acquittal seemed unlikely. But the tide turned at key points during the trial. One was the expert testimony of the charismatic TV historian and Bristol resident David Olusoga. 'Can't be any worse than *Newsnight*, can it?' he commented to the Four's barrister before taking the stand. An expert on the slave trade, Olusoga put the 'vandalism' into its historical context. Colston's philanthropy was highly selective, was funded by systematic violence and cruelty such as rape, brandings and abduction and was part of a whitewashing strategy whereby slave traders sought to futureproof their reputations. Another crucial moment came when the prosecution asked Sage Willoughby if the toppling of the statue was a violent act. 'It was an act of love,' he answered boldly to an uproar of approval in the court.

In January 2022, all the 'Colston Four', Willoughby, Jake Skuse, Rhian Graham and Milo Ponsford, were cleared. A scrum of reporters and photographers greeted them outside the court. Three of the defendants wore T-shirts designed for them by Banksy. Willoughby wore a suit. Later he would receive a text from David Olusoga saying, 'You've made history.' But by then he was enjoying a large tequila in the Star and Garter in St Pauls, celebratory drinks having been paid for by Banksy. Willoughby had grown up here next door to this famed local landmark and potent symbol of Bristol's rich multicultural mix. His childhood window overlooked the pub's courtyard. 'Open till 4am every night,' he told the *New Statesman* 'blasting dub reggae sound systems out. Caribbean culture was such a big part of my childhood … to not feel some sort of family and solidarity with these people, to not stand up for them, with them – that would seem bizarre to me.'

I'm sitting in that very courtyard reading these words with a half of Speakeasy bitter and a tot of rum, both of which feel very Bristolian late afternoon tipples. This is my second half of beer, since I spilled the first all over the table almost immediately, which at least broke the ice with the other clientele. In the playground that adjoins the pub, kids just out of school play a game of tag under the relaxed, benignly watchful eye of mums.* Two girls are playing table tennis. A flamboyant gay man in espadrilles and a pink leather jacket is making a small audience laugh with a lively account of a recent Tinder date. A Rasta in an implausibly large Tam o' Shanter and shades sits on a grassy knoll smoking and booming out Prince Far I and Horace Andy on a huge ghetto blaster. Perhaps England's last one. The atmosphere is aromatic.

The Star and Garter describes itself as a 'storied neighbourhood pub', and it's exactly that. The neighbourhood in question is St Pauls, a name which, like Toxteth and Moss Side, carries a sombre weight of import not entirely deserved. As I get my second half of Speakeasy, among the kaleidoscopic array of historical memorabilia and pictures that cover the walls and the bar, two catch my eye. One is a yellowing cutting from 1963 referring to the Bristol Bus Boycott, when Bristol's Afro-Caribbean community refused to use the city's buses in protest at a colour bar denying work to non-whites. Sixty days later, the policy was overturned because of this direct purposeful action.

---

* In Wigan, we call it ticky. You may know it as tig, it, tiggy, tips or tip. In India they call it, rather literally, 'running and catching'.

The other is a tiny, framed picture of a grimy, nondescript little property called the Black And White Café. At this establishment, you could pick up Jamaican staples like ackee, saltfish, curried goat and jerk chicken. But it was the other fare on offer that made the Black And White Café the most famous 'greasy spoon' in England. It stood just a few streets away on Grosvenor Road, Bristol's so called frontline, beyond which police were said to be afraid to tread. Tread they did though. Subject to more criminal raids than any other premises in British history, the *Guardian* described it as the 'biggest and most blatant hard drug den in Britain.' On 2 April 1980, the Black And White Café was subject to yet another raid, but this one was to have profound consequences. Somewhat comically the riot, or as many prefer, 'the uprising', that followed was said to be ignited by a patron getting their trousers ripped and demanding compensation. This slapstick analysis is rejected forcibly on the café's Facebook page.

> We owned the Black and White cafe and our story IS NOT YOUR STORY. To set your story straight, it was not because someone trousers got ripped THAT THE RIOT STARTED. I know the person who trousers got ripped and that was when they raided the cafe another time. NOT ON THE RIOT day how do i know. I WAS THERE it was my house. #facts #askdem. The ghetto soldiers from the cafe started the riot because the police kept raiding the café and taking liberties with Cafe and the people from the Café. We the ghetto soldiers started the riot from the café

Trouser damage notwithstanding, everyone agrees there was a riot/uprising. Estimates of numbers involved vary between a couple of hundred and 2,000. Pitched battles were fought in which fire engines and police cars were wrecked and torched. Infamously, a bewildered police chief was heard to exclaim: 'Surely we should be advancing, not retreating?' Some 130 people were arrested. The *Daily Telegraph*'s verdict was '19 Police Hurt in Black Riot.' The *Daily Mail* reported 'mobs of black youths' roaming the streets of a 'riot-torn immigrant area of Bristol.'

The Black and White Café closed in March 2005 and was later demolished as part of a general wave of urban renewal in the suburb. Though some probably yearn for those good old days of flying bricks and Molotovs, the Star and Garter patrons I talked to did not express much enthusiasm for them. They liked Montpelier and St Pauls as it was now, a less tense but still funky place to hang out, work, play and bring up kids. But that doesn't mean there's any shame here or hurry to forget. Many of the people who were part of the events of 1980 are now respected community elders and grannies and granddads who remember justifiable anger at oppressive policing and institutional racism applied via 'sus' laws. This all feels very distant in the sunny, peaceful courtyard of the Star and Garter on this April afternoon. Run for many years by local legend Dutty Ken, it's had a chequered few years. Rocked by a massive tax bill, the pub nearly went under till a citywide crowdfunded appeal saved it. After Dutty Ken's death, another well-known local name Malcolm Haynes, promoter and DJ, has taken over and, post Covid, the pub is thriving.

A couple of the Star and Garter's 'legendary' patties and another half later, I head back through Montpelier to the city centre. For objectivity I should say that not everyone loves the vibe of these streets. Here's a disenchanted newcomer on the Hijack Bristol Music website: 'Well after moving around a few places in Bristol I have come to the conclusion that Montpelier, despite its reputation for good restaurants and baked goods, is a bit of a shit hole. I have so far witnessed my private driveway being used as a regular exchange point for drug deals. Constantly getting woken up by smackheads skulking around at silly o'clock in the morning. Crustafarian motor homes smashing up and down the road at all hours scuffling for parking. General drug/alcohol abuse and homelessness. Regular fighting/antisocial behaviour. This evening in fact a gang of youths attacked a man to steal his bike which he defended valiantly despite his seatpost/saddle being used as a pickaxe to his skull. So basically – don't believe the hype. Everyone swoons when you tell them you live here but I have quickly come to retort how it is essentially an artery for the smacky dregs of society to skulk between Stokes Croft/ St Pauls/Gloucester Road etc.'

I ponder all this, particularly the excellent designation Crustafarian, as I 'skulk' down to Stokes Croft or 'The People's Republic of Stokes Croft' as it is sometimes known. This ironic title is now embraced by a community arts organisation who 'see direct action as a means to move things forward, start discussions, and disconnect it from criminality. Whether we campaign for legal graffiti walls and areas, organise buy or burgle art events, set up a parody of a Stokes Croft Museum: we aim to start a discussion, playfully challenge the status quo, and inspire people to find their voice.' Similarly, confidently loquacious The Bristol Tab is a student guide who 'livestream from protests, expose bullshit and discrimination and tell you which kebab shops are worth your money.' They have a word of caution about Bristol's most self-consciously 'edgy' street 'where even sweet little old ladies probably run meth labs.'

'If you're planning on moving to Stokes Croft next year, you might want to change your mind. New UK police statistics reveal the street was the site of an eye-watering 1,352 crimes in the last academic year. From September 2013 to June 2014, the hipster hotspot averaged twenty-eight crimes a month, nearly one per day. Third year biologist and Stokes Croft resident James told The Tab: "We were questioned by the police about an armed robbery down the road. I never worried about safety before but now I'm considering investing in some heavy weaponry and karate lessons. You can never be too careful."'

It was hard to know if and which bits of this were meant to be funny. None of it seemed to ring especially true, not least from the look of the Cuban cantina offering 'the best Mojitos in town' for seven quid, or the Biblos Lebanese Wrap café or the branch of the Pieminster chain or the minimal and funky modular synthesizer store where serious young men in Boards of Canada T-shirts twiddled nobs and looked gravely sensitive. From this vantage spot, the only accurate part seemed 'hipster hotspot'.

My vantage point was about halfway up (or down) Stokes Croft at the junction with Jamaica Street, first designated stop on the Banksy Walking Tour. Where Bath has its Jane Austen Trail, Stratford its Shakespeare and Hull its Larkin, Bristol has a city walk based around the enigmatic street artist and here was his first public appearance, a spray can mural of a teddy bear lobbing a Molotov at some cowering riot police with shields. It is a highly representative debut as it seems to embody many of the essential Banksy traits: a work that was superficially striking but essentially hollow, a gestural flourish that crumbled under anything like analysis, an 'edgier' but no more meaningful version of those wooden signs you find in posh Cornish gift shops that extol the virtues of hugs and gin and best friends.

To paraphrase the philistine's credo, I don't know much about street art, but I do know what I like. Full disclosure: Banksy's work leaves me a little cold. Even fuller disclosure, I've sometimes been in the past somewhat snarky and northern about what I'd thought of as the Bristolian cultural aesthetic. As an urban Lancastrian with 'casual' leanings, I never felt the call of the 'New Age Traveller' movement or 'crusty' culture, the eye-jarring Peruvian knitwear, the ginger dreadlocks, the didgeridoos. Unthinking prejudice probably, but while working-class subcultures like the Mod scene were smart and aspirational, emphasising looking good even in straitened circumstances, 'crusty' seemed innately middle class in its rejection of bourgeois tropes like showering, living in a house etc. I'd always assumed this was a reaction against the comfortable family backgrounds of the 'actors'. Kind of 'judgy', I know, but maybe a kernel of truth there.

Certainly, Bristol University is infamously snobby and its student body thoroughly middle or upper class. Nearly half Bristol's students are privately educated and only 11 per cent are from working-class backgrounds, compared to a national average of 25 per cent according to the Higher Education Statistics Agency's 2021 figures. Only the University of London, Glasgow School of Art, Cambridge and Oxford have fewer working-class students. Some of the stereotypes of Bristol culture are crass generalisations, but the city does wear its political credibility with the same swagger that Manchester wears its studied cool. Just before visiting Bristol, I'd been to see somebody in BBC management at the new BBC Wales HQ. He told me that inner city parking was a constant headache and source of staff discontent, adding: 'Of course, that only applies to the Cardiff base. None of the Bristol staff complains about parking as they're all vegans who cycle to work.'

That admitted, I've come to admire the city's embracing of protest, activism and political engagement, if not always the clothes and music that go with it. When Priestley visited here, he encountered a Fascist meeting down by the docks. Something of that nature in central Bristol today would get pretty short shrift, I think. The city embodies a defiant progressiveness that we could all learn from.

For the last thirty years, that dissenting aesthetic in this city has been inextricably linked to music. In the 1960s, the city's hit musical exports included athletically digited pianist Russ Conway and bowler hatted clarinettist Acker Bilk, whose mournfully sweet 'Stranger on the Shore' was the first ever UK record to top the US charts.* As you'd imagine Bristol embraced punk and especially post punk, enthusiastically bringing forth angular, funky, rebarbative acts like The Pop Group, Glaxo Babies and Rip Rig + Panic. The city's

---

* In May 1969, the crew of Apollo 10 took 'Stranger on the Shore' to the moon on a cassette and played it in the lunar module during 'downtime'.

rich street culture of hip hop and graffiti crews like the Wild Bunch which begat Nellee Hooper, Massive Attack,* Portishead and what became known, not entirely to Bristol's liking, as trip-hop. No scene ever agrees that it is a scene, and Bristol was no exception. 'Let's get one thing straight: there's no such thing as the Bristol sound,' said Beth Gibbons of Portishead, somewhat tetchily, to one curious journo, while rapper Tricky claimed 'I was never part of the Bristol scene. My sound was a Knowle West sound. Massive Attack wouldn't come to my area because they know they'd have got beaten up there.'

All my previous visits to Bristol have been connected to music, gigs and interviews and festivals. So I decide on my last night in the city to take in the first night of Bristol New Music. This event is basically four days of the kind of 'challenging' music I love, the kind that makes people ask me with pained expressions, 'do you actually like this?' Anyway, ready for some earbashing, I head to the venue via the Christmas Steps, perhaps the cutest corner of a city not especially known for 'cute'. Perhaps the only Grade II listed city steps in Britain, they are crammed full of classy shops and characterful pubs but steep in a kind of 'you wouldn't want to be coming up here several times a day unless you were in training for the Pennine Way' way. At the bottom there's a bustling and very Bristol bar called Chance & Counters offering craft beer and board games. It's absolutely full as I dash by, wheezing, though I didn't see anybody actually pushing a top hat to Coventry Street or accusing Colonel Mustard in the Billiard Room.

The show is in the lovely surrounds of St George's Bristol, a converted church sitting grandly on Park Street. I enjoy a glass of wine in the bar before with Polly the organiser and Andy from marketing. Because of the pandemic, it has been four years since the

---

* A persistent but unproven rumour has it that Robert Del Naja of Massive Attack is Banksy.

last biennial festival and the excitement and anticipation are palpable. But they are keen to hear about my time in Bristol, so I give them a recap. Polly almost moved to Montpelier but was expecting a baby: 'You would not want to be pushing a buggy up some of those steep little alleyways.'

The first performer is a darkly earnest and frankly under-rehearsed acoustic singer-songwriter. She stops every song after a few seconds to twiddle various knobs, looking annoyed at something unspecified but which unaccountably seems to be our fault. She clears her throat continually and mutters to herself. Yet there is something mordantly soothing about her gloomily circular songs. At the end, she starts to pack her guitar away while the last chord is still resonating. I know 'stagecraft' is a terribly fustian notion but merely condescending to face the mike when you're speaking is hardly 'selling out to the man' is it?

Happily, the next act turn out to be one of the greatest things I've seen in ages: three art students from Glasgow who play a crazed avant-garde jazz soul that combines the extremism of Derek Bailey or King Crimson at their wildest with a singer who has the husky pipes of Ella Fitzgerald or Nina Simone. In happy contrast with their predecessor, they look like they are having a ball, tugging excitedly at their zip-up jerseys and sometimes having a little mid song chat about where they should go next. I loved them. There was another act but by then I was flagging somewhat after a long day. Also, during this last ensemble piece, on the row alongside me, a man in a topknot and Day-Glo harem pants kept laughing loudly and knowingly during quiet parts of the music, suggesting some insights into its mechanics we mere mortals lacked. As you can imagine, this was phenomenally irritating and all my old prejudice against his sort, which two lovely days in Bristol had done so much to dispel, started to creep back. So, I slipped down the back stairs and out into a crisp and fresh Bristol night, alive with light and people and music and I picked my way down the Christmas Steps. The Chance & Counter was still full of beery hipsters playing Escape From Colditz and Connect Four.

2

Next morning, in one of Bristol's many graffitied subways, this one by Haymarket, I pass a young man selling papers. He's milky-skinned and ginger-haired and speaks with a softly effeminate Yorkshire accent: 'Pontefract, West Yorkshire. I had to leave. Things went wrong ...' On my travels, I often meet people who are happy, eager even to give you every detail of their biography, but this exiled Yorkshire lad obviously wasn't and I, equally obviously, didn't push it. The paper he's selling is a self-styled 'seditious' magazine printed by a worker's co-op in London's East End. He buys them for one pound fifty and sells them for three. I give him all my change, about five quid's worth, and he's chuffed, as they say in Pontefract. 'I hope you enjoy it,' he calls after me.

When I sit down by the harbour, just about where Edward Colston went for his unscheduled dip, I skim read this slim publication. It is 'published in solidarity' but doesn't specify with what. The masthead mission statement rails against 'the fictions of copyright and patent' and states that 'intellectual property is a legally fabricated monopoly.' As someone who makes a living that way, like a million others in the creative industries and media, I don't warm to this theme. When I come up hard against the word 'cisheteropatri-archy' in a piece about abolishing psychiatry, my patience runs out and I fish out *English Journey* again, ready for my boat trip.

That's right. A boat trip. Once I had found out that a ferry service worked out of the harbour and called at Temple Meads station, I was sold. Before long, two yellow ferry boats chug into view, significantly raising this level of childish excitement. One is headed for Brunel's SS *Great Britain*, moored in the harbour. But mine takes the other route, bound for Bristol Bridge and Temple Quay for Temple Meads station. The young skipper tells me 'this is the less glamorous trip. But it looks like you'll have the boat to yourself, like a proper VIP.' Once under way, he fills me in on the history of the ferry, a proper community initiative with some 800 shareholders. 'Everyone loves us. We're a real part of the community. But Covid hit us hard. We nearly didn't survive that first winter. To pull through we had to encourage the stag do trade. Basically, we still have to prioritise it. I feel bad when there's a nice family who want a boat trip and I have to say, sorry, but we're fully booked with these twats here in fancy dress.'

He came here seventeen years ago as a student and never left; a common Bristol narrative. 'I think sometimes I really should try somewhere else. But I have made so many connections here and there's such a sense of community. When you first come here, you live in Stokes Croft, there in the middle of all the craziness. But as time goes by you quieten down and you go progressively further out, St Pauls, St Werberghs, Easton.'

The ferry winds along the Avon past a floating nightclub called Thekla and then around and under Bristol Bridge. This, or one of its predecessors in wood and stone, gave the city its name from Saxon Brycgstow or 'Brigstowe': the 'place of the bridge.' During the devastating Bristol Blitz of 1941 this city of churches became the city of ruins. Nearly all the buildings along this stretch of the Avon were destroyed and hundreds killed. The biggest bomb, nicknamed Satan, didn't detonate, but was dug out by astonishingly brave disposal officers and later paraded through the streets of London on VE day. This spring morning, the same grassy riverbanks opposite the Left Handed Giant Brewpub are littered with sunbathing office workers. The papers they read are full of bombs falling away to the east, on Kyiv and Kharkiv, Lviv and Mariupol.

In his Bristol section, Priestley remembers his previous trips to Temple Meads. His visits, he says, were always crepuscular and gloomy, skulking around in the middle of the night changing trains, tipping the hotel night porters in the nearby 'dismal streets' to let him snooze by the fire. 'The natural result was that I carried with me for years a vague impression that this was an unpleasant city. Now I know better a great deal better. Bristol is a fine city. They are right to be proud of it.'

I disembark lithely. It is by now the hottest day of the year so far. Spring has not just sprung but exploded in this city full of unexpected heat and life. I find myself concurring wholeheartedly with Priestley's revised opinion. Bristol is a city in a healthy, vibrant dialogue with its future and its past. As I take a last look at it from the water, I realise that many hundreds of others would have seen it recede into the distance this way, but in circumstances far less pleasant.

3

Even if, by the time you read this, tech entrepreneur turned capricious 'defender of free speech' Elon Musk has built Wiltshire's first space station there, there'd still be only one proper way to arrive at Swindon: by train. It's a company town, even though the company has gone, and it's been a long time since they actually made trains here – 1984 to be precise. But diesel and steam course through Swindon's blood like Guinness in Dublin. An unassuming hilltop market town for centuries, modern Swindon was essentially created from scratch by the advent of the railways, and in particular Brunel's GWR. When Priestley visited, it was his first trip and he was excited to see, as he put it, the 'town that makes the best locomotives in the world. Swindon and its engines should be one of the feathers in our cap and it was my duty to look at this feather to report on its shape and colouring.'

There have been many different editions of Priestley's *English Journey* since 1934, but the 1984 version edited by John Hadley contained several unexplained, inexplicable indeed, cuts and changes. Priestley underwent major bowel surgery in February of that year, dying a few months later, so he was presumably in no state to argue. But Swindon was the biggest casualty of Hadley's scissors, excised entirely.

Poor old Swindon. So often the butt of sneers and jokes. In Mark Haddon's *The Curious Incident of the Dog in the Night-Time*, a character calls it 'the arse of the world.' In TV comedy *The Office*, the excruciating David Brent greets the new Swindon intake to Wernham Hogg paper manufacturers with the words: 'I heard they dropped an atomic bomb on Swindon and did about £15 worth of damage.' Even when people try and be nice, their compliments have the backhand of Roger Federer. BuzzFeed once ran an article called '24 Things That Aren't Completely Awful About Swindon.' Hailing myself from a town that was a music hall joke for decades, I arrive determined to restore Swindon to its rightful place in the English Journey.

Priestley's train dropped him at Swindon Junction, from where a loop line took one to Old Town Station, but thanks to the efforts of sinister Dr Beeching, both closed in September 1961. You can watch the final journey on YouTube, accompanied by driver Fred Bennett and a breezy light jazz soundtrack. I change trains at Cheltenham Spa and while I wait I catch a first glimpse of those three letters that made Swindon great – GWR – written in glowing cream Clarendon slab-serif on the deep chrome green of the locomotive, a livery revived in 2015 when the Great Western Railway franchise was restored.

I am by no means a train buff. Not for me the long twilit vigil, waiting with sodden notebook in a dismal siding for a flash of decommissioned Class 52 Western. But even I feel some nostalgic, oddly sensual frisson as I gaze at the sleek flanks of the beautiful machine that pulls gracefully yet powerfully into Cheltenham Spa station. So much so that I spend several minutes taking pictures of it, before watching it glide elegantly away. I realise too late that it was in fact my connection to Swindon and the next train will be another hour. Had I known, I would have left the station and splashed out on a croissant at the extremely well reviewed Green Coffee Machine around the corner. As it is, I plump for an underwhelming flat white in the Pumpkin Café on Platform 2 while time expands sideways.

When I eventually get to Swindon, I find that, like Priestley's, my hotel is in the Old Town. Unlike Priestley, I do not find the chambermaid furtively re-securing the peeling wallpaper with drawing pins. Mine is a briskly functional US chain hotel with a gauzy portrait of the founder J Willard Senior flanked by son J W Junior given pride of place in reception. Though ostensibly a chummy couple of dudes in sports coats and slacks, J Willard Senior has a fixed smile and is clutching what seems to be a baseball bat or possibly some arcane bit of illuminati paraphernalia. 'There's one of those paintings in every Marriott hotel in the world,' says a passing chambermaid with an admirable lack of corporate enthusiasm.

Keen to see all the railway stuff, Priestley skipped through Swindon's Old Town in a couple of lines and with barely a backward glance. I decide to linger a while because everyone will tell you that the Old Town is quite the nicest bit of Swindon. Old Town or New Town, what is not in dispute is that Swindon is very definitely a town. It is, for the time being, staying that way. In what now seems a misguided piece of feel-good hubris, the first New Labour administration posited a scheme called New Cities for the New Millennium. Perfectly contented towns like Brighton, Inverness and Wolverhampton were cosmetically 'elevated' into cities in PR stunts of debatable benefit while across England other towns were left to decay and simmer with the resentment that would eventually boil over at the ballot box in the Brexit Referendum of October 2016.

A leaked Home Office document around the turn of the millennium showed that Swindon's bid had been rejected as 'poorly constructed' and giving the impression of a 'particularly materialistic town, rather than a rounded community.' Swindon was a town, it seemed to say, and should not get ideas above its station, as it were. Even Swindon's civic fathers seem to have gone cold on an idea that never much inflamed ordinary Swindonians. In 2019, the leader of the Borough Council, David Renard said: 'The average person living in Swindon would not care if they woke up tomorrow in a town or city ... the *Advertiser* ran a poll asking readers if they would like Swindon to become a city and almost half (48 per cent) said "no" with a further 16 per cent saying they weren't bothered ... The time and money ... would be better spent on delivering services and projects that will make a real difference to people's lives.'

To be honest – and this is no criticism – Swindon doesn't feel like a city. It has the solid unshowy pragmatism of a big town. Take us or leave us, it seems to say.

Back when Brunel was hatching his plans for the Great Western Railway, commuting on horseback between London and Bristol and dropping in at Swindon en route, the Old Town in which I find myself was really all there was: a cluster of little streets perched on a hill. Passing the ivy clad Goddard Arms, there is a wide and glorious view stretching to what is either the Marlborough Downs, the Cotswolds or the Vale of the White Horse. (I don't have my map and compass.)

It's at Wood Street and Devizes Street that Old Town starts to live up to its pre-publicity as a patchwork district home to Swindon's funkiest, craftiest, most artisanal, bespoke, curated, locavore, street-food, plant-based eateries. There is a Yoga Restaurant, whatever that might be, and also that absolute signifier of the hipster enclave, a shop that sells vinyl records and something entirely unconnected. I have popped into vinyl record shops that also offer pastries (Mansfield), haircuts (Ramsbottom) and pies (Southsea). This one offers vinyl and artisan coffee and I would have popped in but it's closed, as is Head Start Tuition, the Regent Hotel, the dance studios and Blitz craft beer shop. Swindon is not alone in looking this way. I'd encounter sad sights like this all over England in those first years after Covid and Brexit, causally linked or not. Still very much open, happily, is an old-fashioned hardware store smelling of carbolic and varnish and offering washing baskets and mousetraps. Maybe it was here when Priestley came, back in the days when a hardware store was as much a high street fixture as chicken shops are now.

From the Old Town you drop down the hill past the upsettingly named Kwality Stores and the Burkhardt Hall, an imposing building that was once a technical school, until finally you turn the corner at Khyber ('Wiltshire's First Indian Restaurant 1962') into the commercial sprawl of modern Swindon. Apart from the nod to the local hero in its name, the Brunel Centre could be any large, unlovely retail mall anywhere from Denver to Darwin. But in the local library, the one place I visit in every town, there's real Swindon character evidenced in the large and proud selection of local interest books. Histories not just of the fancy stately homes and gardens of Lydiard Park but of the town's rich industrial past. On my way to the New Town, I pass the Gurkha Mini Market, opposite Bismillah Groceries where a chalkboard advertises fresh fish for sale. In Priestley's day it would have been cod, haddock and maybe halibut if the fishmonger was feeling particularly experimental. Today the Gurkha is offering good deals on Golden Pomfret and Rohu, fresh from the rivers of South East Asia, which would have made JB's head swim if not his mouth water. The mango, kiwi and sweet papaya would have done that.

Just as in Blackpool all streets lead eventually to the prom, in Swindon you will inevitably end up by the railway works. I visited the tremendous Steam Museum in a previous book so I won't dwell on that beyond telling you that if you are in Swindon, you really must go. This time I want to see what the railways did for Swindon and for Britain as a whole, so I head for the New Town, GWR's Railway Village. The original idea was Brunel's. Each road was named after the destinations of trains that passed nearby – Bristol, Bath, Taunton, London, Oxford and Reading among them – and was constructed in a grid of parallel lines that would have pleased a draughtsman's mind. Here the company built 280 cottages for its burgeoning workforce and it's here that JB and I part company vexatiously for the first but not the last time. I find the Railway Village charming with its spick and span rows of tidy cream cottages. But this was Priestley's opinion in 1933: 'There was something miniature and monotonous about these houses. Everywhere the same squat rows. It was like wandering through a town for dingy dolls. There was nothing to break the monotony. If a number of bees and ants, cynically working in bricks and mortar, had been commissioned to build a human dormitory they could not have worked a more desolating uniformity ... I felt I had had hours and hours of it. When at last I came to a blank-faced shop labelled *Pang Bros. Chinese Laundry*, I was almost startled. What were the Pangs doing here, and what did they think of it? I ought to have stopped and enquired.'

Well, yes, I rather think you should have JB, if only so that future acolytes like me could assure my readers that you weren't a massive racist. For what it's worth (and wait till we get to Liverpool) I think these glancing and slighting references to immigrant communities simply and sadly reflect the tenor of his times. But Priestley was clearly much more progressive than his times in many ways, so it would be helpful to have had some interactions with real immigrants to prove it. *Pang Bros. Chinese Laundry* is of course long gone, as is the toy shop whose 'innocent' display prompted an intemperate burst of rage in Priestley: 'The only other article offered for sale in that street that I noticed was a present for any good child called Jolliboy II Quick-firing Machine Gun, and as I walked away I hoped that the jolly boys who played with it would never find themselves caught in the barbed wire with a stream of hot lead disembowelling them.' The Great War never really left Priestley. He spent his twenty-first birthday in a frontline trench and lost all the close friends in his

Company in the first winter of fighting: 200 men killed of 270. Thus, I'm guessing Priestley's grandkids never got a Johnny Seven for Christmas. I did. I smashed my Nan's teapot with the rocket launcher attachment. Happy days.

Advice about the New Town and Railway Village had been forthcoming in droves. Tim Dunn pointed me to his excellent TV documentary in which he met Fred Jennings, a 91-year-old who had moved here as a child in 1933. This was the year of Priestley's visit and the youthful Fred was similarly unimpressed by the habitation. There were six different levels of property in the village. At the cheaper end were the cramped 'one up one downs' for the labourers' families at three shillings a week. These might have housed twelve people in one living room and one bedroom, 'hot bedding' as the day and night shift changed, and kids 'topping and tailing'. To save on building materials, there was no division between the lofts of the houses so it was possible to run along a row of houses at this level, which is just what the local rats did. At the classier end was Farringdon Row, or 'Foreman's Row' as it was known, where the houses were twelve shillings a week and are still occupied today. One of these houses has been kept just as it was in the Edwardian era and visitors can squeeze into the neat but tiny interior, done out in what is effectively GWR livery as the houses would often be decorated in paint and fabric 'liberated' from the works.

Fred Jennings worked in the railway works from the age of fourteen, recollecting rather sweetly: 'I enjoyed every minute. Especially the shunting, I thought the shunting was marvellous.' But what he liked best about the Railway Village was the public baths on Milton Road. It's still there but now rechristened The Health Hydro. Another plank of GWR's paternalistic capitalism in action, it's essentially a railway station filled with water. It also housed a doctor, a dentist and even a hairdresser: all part of a holistic approach to workers' health. Paternalistic? Yes. Exploitative? Maybe. Enlightened? Certainly, for its time. And most of it was down to Sir Daniel

Gooch, founder of the Swindon Works and the smart cookie who employed Brunel.

Gooch realised quickly that the hard manual work and a high accident rate at the works was harming his workforce. He persuaded the directors of the GWR to appoint a works doctor and lodge him free in company property, saying: 'The happiness of my men and their families depended much upon the influence I exerted over them, and I have striven to make the influence beneficial.' In December 1847 the Medical Fund Society was founded and Swindon Works became the first and indeed for many years only industrial organisation in the world with compulsory membership of a medical fund as a condition of employment. A century later, when Nye Bevan was looking for a template for his new NHS, he took inspiration from Swindon and its 'cradle to grave' service (literally since the GWR even employed a works undertaker offering free funerals). 'There it was, a complete health service in Swindon,' Bevan said, 'All we had to do was expand it to the whole country.' Local historian Trevor Cockbill notes: 'In looking at the early days of the Mechanics' Institute at New Swindon we are studying a cradle which nursed the direct ancestors of our present welfare state.'

But here it is in 2022: idle and crumbling, its windows smashed, its walls encrusted in scaffolding, entrances boarded and fenced off. This was once a marvel. It housed a library, a theatre, place of education and leisure, a fresh food market, a community centre, a place where workers could share and express grievances, all built by the workers of Swindon themselves for themselves. If this were an aristocrat's stately home like the nearby Lydiard House, would it have been allowed to fall into ruin like this? Or am I being 'an unreconstructed class warrior,' as an old editor of mine Dylan Jones once described me, not unfriendlily. It is hard not to concur with Andrew Thompson's message to me: 'Shame on the local council for their neglect of the genuinely brilliant collection gathering dust at the closed museum and art gallery in Old Town. Other than that, there's not much in my hometown. Its heritage has been allowed to rot – the Mechanics institute a prime example.'

On the hoardings outside are two splashes of graffiti showing the contradictions of modern England: one a wobbly rainbow with the legend 'Thank You NHS For Caring For Us' in a childish hand; the other, a jagged aerosol spray reading 'Fuck Your Vaccine' it says, depressingly.

I am getting cranky and needed to self-medicate, beginning with some food and drink. Priestley's Swindon dinner, consumed in a bad temper while listening to gramophone music on the wireless ('that is, music at third hand') consisted of 'Roast Griskin pork with two veg – one and threepence. It was dear at the price. The pork was nearly all dubious fat, the Brussels sprouts were watery, and the baked potatoes might have been made of papier mâché.' I have Momo Thukpa dumpling soup and a cold Gurkha beer (which disappeared in a couple of grateful gulps) at Yak, the tiny Nepalese Kitchen in the Old Town. I enjoy the background music too: 'Jhamke Phuli' by Kutumba. Check it out. This place is so small and the kitchen so near that I can hear the sizzle through the bamboo wall when my dumplings hit the pan. A group of loud white middle class 'guys' come in and I steel myself for some theatrical masculinity, but they are actually very well behaved. Two of them sport topknots, which I can only think is a misguided act of cultural solidarity with the staff.

The 1851 census, a volume never far from your bedside, I imagine, dear reader, shows that there were some dozen inns and alehouses in the Railway Village. Richard Jeffries in his history of Swindon wrote that 'publicans discovered that steel filings make men quite as thirsty as hay dust.' There are just two now, one at either corner of Emlyn Square. The Cricketers bills itself, combatively, as 'the original Railway Village pub,' presumably an aggrieved 'push back' against the status of The Glue Pot which is by far the most famous and celebrated. Usually, a pub became nicknamed Gluepot with some haughty disdain, a reference to its adhesive hold over the lower orders. Hence one of my old London locals, The George on Great Portland Street, was called The Gluepot by Sir Henry Wood for its vexing attraction for his BBC musicians. But the Swindon Glue Pot is so named, it's said, for the pots of glue the railway works coach-builders would bring with them into the pub at lunchtime, standing them on the central stove to stay warm and liquid. Whatever the nomenclature and whatever the reason, everyone told me I had to go there. So I do. Tragically, so it seems did everyone else, and at the time of publication The Cricketers had closed.*

The Glue Pot is quiet in the warm dusk of a mid-week evening. Only one table sits full and I am soon welcomed by Emma and chums, Swindonians all and each, with a take on their town that I would characterise as realistic but quietly proud: 'Halfway between Bristol and London. Not as posh as Oxford. Railway town or used to be. Thatcher sold it all off in the eighties.' I ask about famous Swindonians and they come up with darkly surly comic Mark Lamarr; Don Rogers, the ex-Swindon Town legend who scored the winner in the town's storied 60s League Cup win over Arsenal; Billie Piper, pop poppet turned actress; and two very British blonde bomb-shells of different eras, the quintessentially 50s/60s Diana Dors and emblematically 90s/00s TV's Melinda Messenger (now a practising psychotherapist). 'The Oasis Leisure Centre is where Oasis the band got their name,' adds a male pal.

'It's a shame what's happened there,' says Emma of the Mechanics' Institute, 'Or hasn't. Apparently, it was sold to some developers for £1 but nothing happened. Homeless people were in it for a while. Now they say English Heritage are doing something. The railway village was all built for the railway workers but now it's half private,

---

* To mark his sixtieth birthday, pop singer Paul Heaton put £1,000 behind the bar of sixty pubs around the country selected for their excellence. The Glue Pot was one.

half council. If you want to buy a house there, you can have one in the east. The west is allocated.' Emma is slightly wistful for the passing of the railways and that source of vigour in Swindon's streets. 'These streets would have swarmed with people once. As a kid, I remember the air horn that would make the windows rattle and all the people would go back and forth to the works.'

If T S Eliot's Prufrock measured out his life in coffee spoons, the people of Swindon measured theirs by the blaring of the railway works hooter – the town's unmistakeable sonic landmark. For over a century, it sounded to a strict timetable: at 6.45am came a seventeen second blast, audible even by sleeping workers in outlying villages; then a further twelve seconds at 7.20am; seven more seconds came at 7.25am; and if the hurrying thousands of workers weren't clocked-in by the final twelve-second blast at 7.30am, they were late and subject to being put on report and their pay docked.

Despite being a deafeningly obtrusive daily reminder of GWR's steely grip on their lives, the Hooter was almost a beloved fixture of town life. 'Swindon would not be the same without the old hooter's clarion call,' said a writer in the (possibly biased) staff magazine in 1960. Lore and legend grew up around it. It was said that the hooter could be heard twenty-five miles away which seems a bit fanciful. But it could certainly be heard three miles away at Lydiard House, the posh gaff of one Viscount Bolingbroke, much to his displeasure. William Morris, writing of the entitlement of the aristocrat, noted that it was 'exemplified in recent times by Lord Bolingbroke … when he objected to the use of a steam whistle for calling the thousands of workmen to their labours on the grounds that its noise might possibly frighten and disturb a few of his pheasants sitting on their eggs a few miles off.'

Hundreds of workers objected to the Viscount's whinging and the hooter continued to blare until 4.30pm on 26 March 1986, the end of the last shift at the works. You can still see the brass domes of the hooter by the entrance to the Great Western Designer Outlet Village (excellent for a cheap, serviceable emergency waterproof and some socks, as I can vouch) and still actually hear it at the start of 1986 single 'The Meeting Place' by Swindon art pop act XTC. It's quite eerie. 'It wasn't exactly pleasant,' says Emma 'but it was a symbol of the town's livelihood and role I suppose. People miss it.'

We finish our drinks and I head back up the hill from the New Town to the Old. It's been a pleasant evening and I share Priestley's mood at the end of his Swindon day when he wrote of 'quietly sinking into that not unpleasant melancholy that comes to a man alone in a strange dark town.' I pass by Rudy's and am tempted, as always, by the pub quiz ('and the next round is quotations') but it is in full, boozy swing. By the door, a woman on crutches is trying to canoodle with a man with a buzzcut who is swearing under his breath in a thick gravelly voice that sounds like tectonic plates shifting beneath shallow pre-Cambrian seas.

Back at my hotel a large multi-generational, multi-ethnic party is quietly winding down in the bar. Ivan, Dmitri and Colin are three of the kids' names. The little ones are up far too late and keep going round to Granddad for a cuddle. Priestley would have approved, I'm sure. Checking my phone, I see I have walked 37,632 steps around Swindon, a town I came to like a lot, if not love breathlessly, and so I head for bed, raising a glass to J Willard Marriot and square-jawed junior, still alert and ready for business in the huge portrait by the stairs. When I get to my room, I see the wallpaper is still very much in place and so I sink into a sleep from which no hooter could rouse me.

3

TO THE COTSWOLDS

In which I find several 'Gateways to', a phonebox
where Graham Greene once sweated and narrowly
avoid the 'Chipping Norton Set' while buying
some burgundy jumbo cords.

The first thing any visitor to the Cotswolds will realise is that it is by far and away England's largest producer of clichés. This is apparent from one's very first experience of its 'idyllic picture book villages,' 'delightful rustic pubs' and 'honey-coloured stone'. Travel writers, marketing copywriters and tourist information guides will find a reliable source of stock phrases to tempt visitors and begin their broadsheet articles. To these, you can now add 'favourite getaway haunt of London's media glitterati'.

When Priestley came to the Cotswolds in the 1930s, the region's now booming stereotype industry was still in its infancy, limited to a few rustic poems and the odd folk song. Even then though it was becoming obligatory for rueful, melancholic writers to put in a few paragraphs about 'England's disappearing rural way of life' or perhaps 'lost pre-industrial innocence'. But they were still actually making things here then. The chief local industry in the thirties was still wool and stone masonry, and mainly stone of the honey-coloured variety. Heresy perhaps, but I think it's more accurate to describe Cotswold's stone as 'yellow' but clearly that is nowhere near as evocative. Only one writer in the history of English letters has managed to write about the region's stone buildings without recourse to the word 'honey'. That writer was J B Priestley. Weirdly, he thought they were grey.

Beginning by calling the villages 'symphonies of grey stone,' he went on 'it has no colour that can be described. Even when the sun is obscured and the light is cold, these walls are still faintly warm and luminous as if they knew the trick of keeping the last sunlight of centuries glimmering about them.' I, however, think 'yellowy brown' does the job of description quite well. As for pre-industrial inno-cence, the problem is that all that unspoiled bucolic simplicity tends to also involve quite a lot of back-breaking physical labour, starva-tion wages, bullying aristocratic bosses and rapacious landlords. If we think that Laurie Lee's *Cider With Rosie* describes the ultimate Cotswolds idyll, it's worth remembering that there was quite a lot of disease, poverty and sexual abuse mixed in with the cider and snog-ging. As Lee puts it, 'Manslaughter, arson, robbery, rape cropped up regularly throughout the years. Quiet incest flourished where the roads were bad; some found their comfort in beasts; and there were the usual friendships between men and boys who walked through the fields like lovers. Drink, animality, and rustic boredom were responsible for most.'

Priestley, disappointingly, asserts in *English Journey* that 'The Cotswolds are the most English and the least spoiled of all our coun-tryside.' This feels both hugely out of character and rankly disloyal. Surely a lad who roamed the high moors of the north must know in his bones that up there is bleak and rugged grandeur that makes the Cotswolds look positively over-developed and domesticated. Also, 'most English'? What exactly does that mean? Is Bradford not as English as Bradford-on-Avon? If by 'most English', you mean 'most white', then that is certainly true. In one aspect though, the Cotswolds shows a rather more outward and cosmopolitan face; c. 51 per cent of its inhabitants voted to remain in the EU, unlike their Eurosceptic neighbours in Stroud, Gloucester and Tewkesbury. This slimmest of majorities is hardly a ringing endorsement of the European project though, which is odd since the farmers of the Cotswolds did rather well out of it.

I like the Cotswolds a great deal, but also feel tremendously conflicted about the place. I love the feel of its landscape; never challenging but always quietly lovely, a mosaic of woods and rivers and splendid little hills. I love the accent, warm as cider punch in autumn. When I think about the Cotswolds, I always begin by recalling how gorgeous it all is, all those scrumptious pubs with lolling dogs, real fires and delicious food made by 'passionate' chefs (with produce from local suppliers wherever possible), in cosy little villages.

But then I remember the snobbery, the innate conservatism, the private schools, the forelock-tugging, the foxhunting, the parson and squire, the agricultural subsidies, the unearned wealth, the Range Rovers, the pink trousers, the preponderance of wankers, and a little shiver runs through me, cold and clear as the River Windrush. But it is nothing compared to the icy torrent of contempt that gushed from Jay Rayner who described Stow-on-the-Wold in one choice review as 'completely and utterly ludicrous. ... A compendium of everything that is wrong about ersatz, up-itself, self-deluding, arthritic, rural Britain.' The late and lacerating A A Gill was terser still in *The Angry Island*: 'the worst place in the world ... a little smug Hobnob stuck in a tin of dog biscuits,' he concluded, entertainingly if absurdly.

The Cotswolds sit in the heart of middle England, spreading gently across several counties like melting butter on a toasted muffin or the soft rise of an ample midriff after a lunchtime pint:

Gloucestershire and Oxfordshire chiefly, with a drop of spillage into Warwickshire, Worcestershire, Wiltshire and Somerset. Essentially, the Cotswolds are an escarpment. In the east, the land swells gradually and gently from Oxford and the Thames Valley. But on the western side, it falls away steeply and dramatically, making for gorgeous views but bringing fast-flowing water down the rivers after rain and regularly putting Tewkesbury underwater.

When Priestley visited, he was plagued by a nagging worry about its future: 'once the Cotswolds are ruined now, they're ruined forever … It could be turned into a sort of national park … a district that, regarded as a national heritage of great value, is controlled by the commonwealth and acquired by the nation itself which would not however turn away the people who work the land. The beauty of the Cotswolds belongs to England, and England should see that she keeps it.' Presciently, Priestley here anticipates the notion of a 'national park' by over a decade. The Cotswolds hasn't achieved that lofty status but was designated, in 1966, an Area of Outstanding Natural Beauty.

Many firmly agree with Priestley's contention that the Cotswolds are the very epitome of a certain kind of Englishness. Most of these people direct TV dramas. Large parts of the Harry Potter and Bridget Jones movies were filmed here, as well as *Downtown Abbey*, *Father Brown*, and the cutesy detective series *Agatha Raisin*. Holst, Ivor Gurney, Herbert Howells and Vaughan Williams (a local lad from the village of Down Ampney) all wrote beautiful, yearning music inspired by its landscape. And, to prove that I stop at nothing in my research, before visiting I diligently and expertly seek out a Channel 5 TV series called, appropriately enough, *The Cotswolds with Pam Ayres*. This looked promising, but when Pam announced that she was 'going on a journey,' as is ever the case, I remembered I had one of my own to be getting on with.

As summer fades, russet as apples, I set forth, sticking closely as before to Priestley's own itinerary of 1933. Like him then, I begin in

Burford: gateway to the Cotswolds. Unless you count Chipping Campden. Or maybe Stow-on-the-Wold. But it's definitely Burford if you're coming from London, which the Cotswolds assume you will be. There's even a Cotswolds Gateway pub, hotel and restaurant, which is where I hang a left onto the High Street.

Turning onto Venice's Grand Canal in a motorboat taxi, looking down towards the Rialto, remains, I think, the single most extraordinary moment of James Bond style glamour available to we wage-slave civilian mortals. But turning onto Burford High Street is, in its own way, a real moment to savour. You don't have to be Julian Fellowes to prefer Burford High Street to, say, Stoke Newington. The famous boulevard sweeps downhill towards the Windrush, a long dip leading to a three-arched medieval bridge and the misty greens and purples of the Cotswold Hills beyond. Every tourist from Oklahoma, Osaka and Oratunga Station must feel as if they have died and gone to Downton Abbey. I'm not being snide – it takes my breath away too.

I still don't agree that it is any more English than the fog-shrouded Cheviots or a frosty Buttermere in winter. But it does have a sausage roll shop and a decent off-licence. In fact, Burford is a shopaholic's dream, perfumed with mouth-watering ripe cheeses and artisanal pasties, scented candles and Barbour jackets, pot-bellied stoves and antique brushes to clean them with. There is the Oxford Shirt Company with its fine selection of pastel-coloured shirts. There is the Madhatter Bookshop with its excellent selection of books and, err, hats. Outside Three French Hens, a shop which seems to specialise in high-end, mass-produced whimsy, a chalkboard sign reads: 'I dream of a world where chickens can cross the road without having their motives questioned.'

By law, the Cotswolds traveller must at some stage find a nice little tearoom – the more rinky-dink the better. 'Rinky-dinkiness' is a hard quality to define and quantify but should involve some element of rusticity and Merrie England, ideally with a nod to that pre-industrial innocence we spoke of earlier. Priestley finds just the place: 'I had tea in a studio café, an amusing little high room decorated with antique knick-knacks.'

I choose the Priory Café, which may or may not have once been a priory, but if so, was certainly a very compact one. It's just around the corner from the Parish Church where Henry VIII's barber-cum-surgeon is buried and Cromwell executed some rebellious socialistic Levellers during another heart-warming episode from the 'good old days'.* The waitress is a German girl who potters about with dishes and trays, helplessly giggling at some private joke, while music plays loudly from a laptop. Specifically, the music of Stormzy, Dave and other proponents of UK Grime. Not just Grime, obviously. There is a soupçon of drill, trap and drum'n'bass too. It is fantastically, hilariously inappropriate for the surroundings. No one seems to mind.

I order a pork and leek sausage sandwich and it is sensational. Three Frenchmen at the next table order the same and when it arrives, butter dripping from the doorstop of white bread and obscenely plump tubes of meat, they fall on it with the ravenous, drooling delight of men from a country with the world's very worst sausages. Brexit has inflicted incalculable losses to our happiness, I think, but I will not be sorry if it keeps from our shores the fatty, underwhelming Toulouse, the weird and unpleasant fromage de tête and the utterly unspeakable andouillette, with its rank odour of the charnel house. As I leave, the French contingent have moved on to the scones with jam and cream with low moans of pleasure and I feel a swell of pride at this small victory for maligned British provincial cuisine.

---

* In fairness to the Cotswolds, each May there is commemoration of the rebellion, Levellers Day, celebrating freedom of speech and human rights.

2

In 1933, when Priestley visited the Cotswolds, he wrote of a 'mysterious hollow land' where 'you saw hardly a soul between the villages.' As you sit in a tailback behind a combine harvester near Lower Slaughter, you will reflect bitterly that times have changed. Perhaps you will then steer into the ditch to avoid someone from Knightsbridge who's paid nearly four hundred quid for the Cotswold Slaughters Circuit Road Trip. 'Is there a better combination than some classic cars and some great country roads?' the bumf asks. 'Our Slaughters Circuit gets you deep into the Cotswolds scenery on some really off-the-beaten track roads in a range of five classic cars.'

But if you're prepared to get out of your infernal machine and pull on a pair of boots, there are good walks, perhaps stretches of the Cotswolds Way, where you can get away from the various traffic: human, bovine and vehicular. Perhaps you might stride the ridge between Broadway and Wood Stanway, take in the Iron Age fort of Shenberrow Hill and go on to Capability Brown's faux-Saxon folly of Broadway Tower. The latter was built for no better reason than that Lady Coventry idly surmised one morning after her devilled kidneys that a beacon on this hill could probably be seen from her house in Worcester, twenty-two miles away, so ordered and paid for one to find out. It turned out she was right, and in fact you can see fourteen counties from the sixty-five-foot summit. It was later repurposed as a monitoring station for nuclear fallout – a task for which it remains happily unemployed. The village which gave the tower its name is so sugary sweet that you can feel your arteries harden and your teeth ache just by looking down upon it. Henry James described it as 'the perfection of the old English rural tradition,' by which I assume he meant picture book cottages rather than not paying taxes, witch-burning and bestiality (none of which are known to be currently prevalent in Broadway, say the lawyers).

In the same way that Burford is 'the Gateway to the Cotswolds' and Bourton-on-the-Water is the 'Venice of the Cotswolds', Broadway is usually described by the guidebooks as the 'jewel of the Cotswolds' or the 'show village of the Cotswolds'. As yet, I have not discovered 'the arsehole of the Cotswolds' and I expect I never shall. Certainly not here. All around Broadway are the equally lovely if less self-regarding villages of Aston Somerville and Weston-sub-Edge, who sound like minor cast members in *Brief Encounter*. Then there is Willersey, Childswickham, Snowshill, Wormington, Saintbury and Buckland, all surely members of a village cricket eleven who perished on the first day of the Somme.

Self-regarding? Absolutely. Broadway, cubic zirconia jewel of the Cotswolds, is as showy and ersatz as its New York namesake. Granted, there is nothing fake about its 5,000 years of rich history, its storied past of Mercian kings and Anglo-Saxon burial mounds, the Benedictine monks breeding fat perch and tench in their ponds on Fish Hill. But just like Dorset after Hardy or Manchester after 'Madchester', one gets the feeling sometimes that the Cotswolds is playing up to an image of itself confected by painters, writers, composers and, latterly, telemarketers. This is no new trend or modern affectation either. Priestley noticed it back in 1933 when, rather than gambol here on wings of delight, he somewhat grumpily recorded 'The guardian spirits have left this place to its own devices and those devices are not very pleasing. In short Broadway is at Ye Olde game. The morning we passed through, it was loud with bright young people who had just arrived from town and the *Tatler* in gamboge and vermilion sports cars.'

Broadway knows just how conventionally gorgeous it is and after a while the effect is more enervating than delicious. Like wearers of dubious seventies aftershave 'Denim', it doesn't have to try too hard – and so it doesn't. Most of the cafés seem to have that irritating 'take it or leave it' attitude that being genial or good value are super-fluous because another coach will park on the high street soon. But let me very definitely exclude Broadway Deli from this generalisation. The staff are pleasant and welcoming and usher me swiftly upstairs to an empty table. Next door to me two posh middle-aged white men conform depressingly to type, the kind of chap the shrill modern leftist dismisses as a 'gammon'. I've never liked this kind of name-calling, but viewed objectively, I suppose, these men are of the pinkly cured variety. It is the trial of the Bristolian youths who toppled Colston that animates them today: 'The thing is these men were great benefactors. They gave a lot of money to make that city great,' declaims one. 'These "woke" people are trying to erase history. That's our history! And you can't judge him by today's standards!' the other affirms.

They turn and notice as with a low groan I place my forehead firmly on the table, narrowly missing my coffee walnut cake. I gather my thoughts for a possible exchange. I mean to ask them whether they'd be happy to see a statue of a goose-stepping Gestapo officer or a Maoist Red Guard down at the golf club just because he'd 'done a lot of work for charidee.' But I don't, because the next comment stuns me into silence. 'Anyway, plenty of other races have done bad things. What about Red Indians (sic.)? They used to come into the white man's wagon trains and steal kids!' A pause. 'Or they do in the films I've watched anyway.' And with that I decide to take my leave.

Though it gets a mention in the Domesday Book, Broadway only really became known beyond rural Worcestershire when a coaching route opened up over Fish Hill in the 1500s, on the road from Worcester to Oxford and London. Soon, enterprising antecedents of the Broadway Deli and The Lygon Arms sprang up to feed and water the passing trade. The 'Broad Way' itself, once the old track from St Eadburgha's to Nether End, is now essentially a parade of eateries and retail opportunities worn with discreet classiness. Should you need a new Caesar Guerini 12-gauge Invictus I Ascent Sporting Over and Under Shotgun, Broadway Guns have one for just under four grand. And Landmark Country Wear has a Pachacuti Ranger's Hat and some Aigle Parcours wellies to go with it. None of these names are familiar to me, but each has the ring and price tag that suggests they might be widely admired at the next shoot.

I am more familiar with quality booze and so I do pop into the Cotswolds Distillery shop. As part of my extensive research, as well as watching Pam Ayres, I'd listened to the Cotswolds People podcast and heard an interview with founder Daniel Szor and been intrigued. A native New Yorker, working in finance in London, he'd fallen in love with the Cotswolds at a wedding and found a weekend home here. Depressed every Sunday evening at having to leave for London, he tried to think of a business venture that could combine two things he loved: the Cotswolds and whisky. Hiring some top minds from the Scottish brewing industry to help him, he bought a derelict site and the Cotswolds Distillery opened in July 2014. Now his botanically intense gins crammed with black pepper, grapefruit and lavender from Snowshill Farm fly off the shelves at Waitrose, Booths and John Lewis. But he's a whisky guy at heart. 'I wanted to make a whisky that reflected the Cotswolds. If you drink a Bowmore or a Laphroaig, you can taste and sense the crags and wind and pounding surf and mountains. But I wanted my Cotswolds whisky to taste of what we make and grow here, fruit and grain.' It's customary to curl one's lip at rich London financiers who come to the Cotswolds for the glorious second acts of their gilded lives. But as I sit with a glass of Cotswolds Signature Single Malt to hand, savouring the custardy depths and hints of barley sugar and strawberry jam, I decide that, you know what, Daniel's OK by me.

Back on the Broadway, the endless tide of people falls essentially into two types: the tourist in their Goretex and rucksacks or slacks and anoraks, and the locals wearing the uniquely awful full dress casual uniform of the Cotswolds posho. Now I should tread carefully here. I once got a very angry letter from a gent's outfitters in

Burford for mildly mocking in print their distinctive clothing range, which if memory serves, I said would suit Rupert the Bear's gay cousin. But come on! What is it with the well-heeled men of Oxfordshire and Gloucestershire that they want to dress in lemonish panama hats and salmon pink jumbo cords, maroon blazers and cherry red loafers, with lime green pastel pullovers knotted over tweedy shoulders? What possesses a grown man not currently onstage in an amateur dramatics country house mystery to wear a cravat? I'm looking at you Nigel Farage. My theory is that the upper-class male likes a uniform. A habit acquired at school or office, it saves you from having to develop taste or style. It comes with a little catechism of rules like 'never brown in town' and at the weekend you can dress like an idiotic toddler. When at breakfast on the first morn-ing in the Cotswolds, I realised that I had forgotten to pack almost all my gear, I asked my waitress if there were a men's clothes shop nearby. She looked me up and down and said 'if I were you, I'd go to Oxfam. I think you'll find something that's more "you" there.' I took this as a compliment.

3

'There is not, I imagine, much distress anywhere in this region,' Priestley mused over a pipe one Cotswolds evening. 'People looked comfortable there. Their children were noticeably in good shape.' Remarkably, he came to this conclusion without even venturing to Chipping Norton. The Cotswolds has three Chippings (from the Old English 'ceapen', meaning market): Sodbury, Norton and Campden. From Burford and Broadway, Priestley made for Chipping Campden only. But we should at least mention 'Chippy', as Norton is known. This is ironic as it hasn't got one. There is nowhere here to get steak pudding, chips, pea wet (for the Wiganers among you), saveloy, gravy, 'scratchings', or any other lovely comforting notions. But you can get woodfired gurnard fillets with a fennel, orange, pickled beetroot and toasted hazelnut salad for a touch under thirty quid.

The phrase 'Chipping Norton set' was first used by *Daily Mail* writer Steven Glover in the late noughties. Essentially it refers to a coterie of celebrity associates from the worlds of politics (David and Samantha Cameron), music (Alex James of Blur), PR (Matthew Freud), journalism (News UK CEO Rebekah Brooks) and having loudly reactionary opinions and driving cars (Jeremy Clarkson). All this glittering band had properties in this corner of the Cotswolds and became emblematic of a kind of countryside elite described by Peter Oborne as 'an incestuous collection of louche, affluent, power-hungry and amoral Londoners.'

The gurnard dish above is on the Jamie Oliver influenced/curated menu at the Kingham Plough, a pub near Alex James' farm where every year – apart from the one that went bust owing a million quid – there's an event called, painfully, The Big Feastival. It is the brain-child of James and Jamie Oliver and described as a 'family-friendly event (that's) a magnet for celebrities, with the likes of TV presenter Kelly Brook, Professor Green, *Downton Abbey* actor Matthew Goode, film director Sam Mendes, actress Amanda Holden, comic actor Simon Pegg, local singer Jack Savoretti and former PM David Cameron frequently seen enjoying the fun. Jamie Oliver, who previously co-hosted the festival, is still a regular visitor, as is neighbouring farmer Jeremy Clarkson.'*

The festival is still with us, but the heady, imperial phase of the Chipping Norton set's reign of soft-power terror and overpriced burgers may be over. 'The Chipping Norton set is dead as a geographical or social entity,' said Peter Jukes, author of two books

---

* There is a TV series about Clarkson's farm called *Clarkson's Farm*. It was quite popular, I think. I did not watch it for fear that I would kick the television in like that London lorry driver did when he first saw the Sex Pistols.

about the phone-hacking scandal. 'These moments of power rarely happen so sumptuously and so visibly.' But bonds forged over ripe bries and awfully good Saint-Émilion are hard to completely dissolve, even when faced with newspaper closures and jail sentences. 'I'm afraid we need to face the terrifying possibility that the so-called Chipping Norton set did not die. It simply ... mutated" said *Guardian* columnist Marina Hyde. 'Perhaps it was retooling and in its newest strain presents a threat for which we may be profoundly unprepared.'

As far as I know there is no Chipping Campden set. I'd imagine 'Campden', as it prefers to be simply and straightforwardly known, rather likes it that way. If there has ever been a 'set' here, it was all a long time ago and comprised stiff-backed types like military man Sir Percy Hobart or Frederick Landseer Maur Griggs, architectural historian and conservationist.

Priestley strides into town and, rather brilliantly, states that 'the whole of this region, although it now seems so Arcadian, is actually a depressed industrial area.' Metropolitan writers often sneer at Priestley for being a sentimentalist. In fact, he is nothing of the sort, being acid-sharp regarding nostalgic tripe and with a very keen bullshit detector, especially regarding any middle-class cant about 'Arcadia' and 'Merrie England'. Priestley saw the Cotswolds for what it was: mesmerizingly lovely, yes, but, for those not up in the big house but out in the fields or at the looms, a place where the days were hard and life nasty, brutish and short. He encounters what we might call an early 'Cotswolds set' member, an artist who has relocated from London in search of a simple life among untainted people – a return to those prelapsarian golden days before the Industrial Revolution. There's still a lot of people like this around in the Costwolds I reckon. Priestley gives this one cordially short shrift. 'As it was of course I opposed him, pointing out that comely objects in a museum or a rich man's house gave one a very faulty notion of the actual life of the past, when most people had to do without nearly everything and were far less merry than he appeared to suppose.'*

The great roaring machine-driven world rather passed the Cotswolds by. In the nineteenth century the textile industries and the weaving sheds all moved north, leaving the Cotswolds to its picturesque industrial decline. Priestley was glad that Campden had been spared the changes that had made northern towns so cramped and smoky: 'If there had been a few thick seams of coal between Gloucester Evesham and Cirencester, the Cotswolds would have been torn up and blackened and built over with brick horrors.'

Priestley notes 'There is no Ye Olde Chipping Campden nonsense about it,' and I like it for very much the same reasons. There is less here of what we might call 'panama hattery'. I even hear a man in plaster-spattered overalls use a swear word: 'They think I'm a fucking double agent. They want to know who's side I'm on. But if it weren't for them, we'd all be unemployed. That's the truth.' I tried to earwig for more of this exchange and unpick what it might possibly be about: machinations and chicanery at the nearby spybase GCHQ in Cheltenham? Intrigue and rivalry in the world of plastering? Sadly, he spots me, and I have to feign a sudden, pressing interest in the vintage brush shop window.

What I'd heard was not your typical Cotswolds village green chat. But then Chipping Campden is a town, not a village. The decline of 'the town' has been exercising many minds these last few years. Many British towns of the North and Midlands have been characterised as 'left behind' as the young flee to our cities while an ageing and unskilled populace who do not espouse the cosmopolitan social values of liberal professionals remain: resentful, overlooked and excluded. But while the wool trade may have gone a couple of centuries ago, it makes little sense to think of Chipping Campden as

---

* JBP would have approved of the view of contemporary Cotswolds poverty offered by Daisy May Cooper's *This Country*.

forgotten. You'd struggle to find simmering resentment or creeping neglect here. Absent are the sights of other English towns who have lost their traditional manufacturing muscle or stock-in-trade: the shuttered shop tagged with graffiti, the jagged glass of the shattered window, the chain link fence around an abandoned, overgrown lot. Chipping Campden is more likely to offer an antiquarian volume, an artisanal biscuit or an understated lithograph. Graham Greene, perhaps the town's most famous former resident, adored walking the High Street for 'the quiet aesthetic pleasure' of its sundry architectural delights, its oolitic stone cottages and the early perpendicular church. But these days, Greene, a sensualist as well as a Catholic purist, would now be distracted by the many women's clothes shops filled with sleek designer jeans and angora sweaters in muted tones of slate and oatmeal, and delicatessens crammed with cave aged cheeses, sourdough and intensely-scented Ethiopian coffee.

Regardless, it still feels like a town compared to its neighbours. There are real pubs. I am staying at one. The Eight Bells Inn has stood on Church Street for 700 years, its name referring to the fact that the huge bells of the magnificent town church were stored here during its construction in the fourteenth century. The masons who built it stayed here too and it's pleasing to imagine them, dusty of smock at the end of a hard day on the chisel and a windlass sinking a few flagons of rough local cider and discussing the big upcoming joust or which heretics had been burned recently. Time lends all this a flippant distance. But there's a glass panel in the dining room that reveals the tunnel to a priest hole so, as you enjoy your breakfast kippers, you can reflect on the fact that some poor Roman Catholic antecedents of Graham Greene had to scurry down there fearful of being burned at the stake during one of Good Queen Bess's periodic spasms of enthusiastic religious intolerance.

Successive waves of triumph and tribulation have beat against the Eight Bells's wonky wooden door: Civil War, threat of invasion, purges and plagues of varying kinds. Through it all it has remained a great little English country boozer with a distinct 'pubbiness'. Yes, the food was smartly-plated and terrific, the gins aromatic, but it had not succumbed to that soulless malaise of the posh country pub – all stripped pine and collars-up rugger buggery. It is The Eight Bells 'in' not 'at' Chipping Campden and it has a restaurant, not a 'kitchen', avoiding both those modish new linguistic tics of gastro-pretension. On a busy weekday evening, when most of the salmon-pink-trouser guys are in the Square Mile overseeing their hedge funds, it belongs to regulars and tourists. I fall into a long and incomprehensible discussion with a very drunk local handyman and his smiling but silent girlfriend, who come back in from their 'quick fag' and order more gassy lager and dry roasted peanuts. We could almost be in Rotherham.

Life begins to imitate art around nine, this being *Midsomer Murders* territory. The local choir come in and order Malbec and real ale and sausages and begin a loud and hearty discussion of their rehearsal which seems to be of some medieval vocal motets (naturally). Brian the baritone, quaffing deep of his IPA, becomes a little too loud and hearty as his wife looks daggers at him. I wonder if he will become one of the implausibly high number of murders I am convinced they have in these cosy shires. On the bar, a newspaper headline tells of a less cosy reality; another MP, David Amess of Southend, has been stabbed to death.

I take a stroll in the gathering dusk. In leaded and lit windows, the interiors pool with warm light falling on book-lined shelves and music stands. Cats curl in front of crackling fires. Campden is a 'left behind' town in the most benign sense, but still reality intrudes. I find a table in a busy little Mediterranean restaurant and listen to a Brummie couple next to me mutter darkly about 'furlough' and 'lay-offs' over their moussaka and Rioja. Saloon bars and offices across Britain rang to those anxious conversations in the months and years after 2021, all conducted in the same tone of stoic English resignation tinged with real desperation.

4

The next day dawns wild but clear and I decide to stomp up to one of the Cotswolds' prime viewpoints, Dover's Hill. Hoo Lane is the kind of old country thoroughfare that has been in use for centuries, once by rickety haywains, now by a John Deere 6250R with AutoPower transmission. I follow in the wake of one of these, trailing silage and lord know what, as the lane rises steadily, flanked by cabbages on either side. Sudden fierce wind brings with it a stinging, tree-bending rain and I'm reminded of Housman's line 'On Wenlock Edge the wood's in trouble ... the gale it plies the saplings double.' From the high escarpment here you can actually just about see Shropshire's Wenlock Edge and those blue remembered hills of Housman country. North lies the Vale of Evesham and Bredon Hill. This is an older England now and you may have Dover's Hill to yourself, except on the first Friday after the spring bank holiday when they still hold the eccentric and almost parodically English 'Cotswold Olympick Games'. Some four centuries before Baron De Coubertin, and a long time before doping and testosterone and boycotts, Robert Dover, who gave the hill its name, inaugurated a quirky kind of sports event involving the tugging of ropes and the kicking of shins. When Priestley came, it was just a memory shared over whisky with the old farmers. But now it is back, marketed by the National Trust and part of the tourist itinerary sandwiched between the music and literary festivals.

Coming back down the lane, I pass a property nestled in Back Ends. Orchard House is now a posh B&B but when Graham Greene and his wife came to live here in March 1931, there were rats nesting in the roof and the light and heat came from paraffin rather than electricity. It was just the place for a struggling young writer to knuckle down to the pressing business of coming up with a hit. His first two novels, *The Name of Action* and *Rumour at Nightfall*, had flopped. So he decided to try his hand at an explicit crowd pleaser, a spy 'entertainment' called *Stamboul Train*, essentially a classier, more cerebral *Murder on the Orient Express* involving communists, lesbians, anti-Semites and scientists.

It worked. It was chosen by the then influential Book Society as their Book of the Month for December, guaranteeing it some 10–15,000 sales. This would have been a lifeline for the penurious couple. However, with copies printed, bound and ready, he received a panicked call from his editor at publishers Heinemann. One J B Priestley, a rather more successful Heinemann author, had been sent an advance proof of *Stamboul Train* and had surmised (rightly I think) that the character of the pompous hack writer Q C Savory was a thinly-veiled, somewhat cruel caricature of himself. Priestley threatened to sue. As Greene recollects in his memoir *A Sort Of Life*, 'My suggestion that we should fight the libel action was brushed aside. Evans made it clear to me that if Heinemann were going to lose an author, they would much prefer to lose me. Thirteen thousand copies of the book had already been printed and bound. Pages would have to be substituted, and I must share the cost. Alterations had to be made at once, on the spot, without reflection.' All advance copies were recalled and Greene was told to amend the text within the hour. He dashed to Chipping Campden Post Office and made the necessary changes, having to make the new text fit exactly into the spaces left blank in order not to upset the pagination. Then he was forced to dictate these changes from the public phone box on Campden High Street, thrusting in coins, as the pips went continually, presumably in a lather of anxiety. Only a handful of copies with the original offending text survived the cull.

Now, I love Graham Greene. My late dad bought me a tranche of his books to take with me when I went to college and they are still some of my favourite novels: *The Heart Of The Matter*, *A Burnt-Out Case*, *The Power and the Glory*, *The End of the Affair*. All are masterpieces of a very English darkness and humour; of love, lust, faith and duplicity in murky wartime and sour peace. On a very human level, who could not feel sorry for him, the starving novelist in his rat-infested (if delightfully situated) garret, feeding in his few coins and perspiring at the thought of the wrath and power of rich, successful pumped-up John Boynton Priestley?

Nope, I'm still on JBP's side. The ruling class – of whom Henry Graham Greene of Berkhamsted School, scion of the Greene King brewing giant and brother of BBC Director General Hugh was certainly a part – always have the defence that they were merely 'ragging' or 'joshing'. They declare that we oughtn't to be so touchy or 'chippy'. So, much as I love Graham Greene's writing, I find the idea of him sweating a little anxiously in his Oxford bags, having had his snobby joke rumbled by a burly Bradford lefty, rather delicious. Incidentally, Q C Savory (changed to Quinn Savory to avoid the first initials 'nod') is a cockney in *Stamboul Train*, not a Yorkshireman. For me this implies that Greene suspected all we provincials were alike really: philistine, materialistic, dim.

I pass the infamous phone box on my return. There's a blue plaque back up at Orchard House but none here. Maybe the J B Priestley Society should erect one. I spot a second-hand bookshop and it feels appropriate to pop in. Draycott Books has seemingly been a beloved Campden fixture for thirty years. It's run by Duncan and his dad and hardly ever closes. They don't have a copy of *Stamboul Train*, but Duncan did read it last year without knowing anything of the little human drama played out on Chipping Campden High Street. He takes down a huge second-hand book bible and runs a finger down a page in the middle. 'Here we are. Q C Savory becomes Quinn Savory in the second edition. The uncorrected first edition is the rarest of all Greene's, currently fetching £8–12,000.' He gives a low whistle, 'I'll keep my eyes peeled.' I ask whether Priestley himself is a collectible author. 'Not really. An excellent first edition *Good Companions* maybe but even so nothing remarkable.' We do a little online check and I'm disappointed to learn that even a first edition

English Journey only fetches £3.99 on eBay. Even-handedly, I buy a nice first edition *Festival at Farbridge*, Priestley's satire on the 1951 Festival of Britain, and also *A Gun For Sale*, one of Greene's slight crime entertainments. I dip in before turning the light out that night. It's no *Brighton Rock* for sure.

I check out into an autumn morning filled with whistling post-men and apple-cheeked children in pushchairs. Swifts dart over thatched roofs against azure skies. I can see why people lose their heads over the Cotswolds. I can appreciate all this loveliness. But it's just not me. I would never feel at ease or at home here, among the tweed caps and bounding dogs, the 'casual cotton jackets' (£299.95) and locally sourced pheasant (£18). I find myself secretly pleased to find a generic Co-op and a quite ordinary looking Indian takeaway, with chicken tikka masala rather than fusion-style venison pakora. I stand in the former soaking up the ambience of dishwasher tablets and bin bags, the granular everyday stuff of the uncharmed life. This is all England too, which is why Priestley's comment about Englishness seems so odd, lazily straying into the soppy romanticism his critics accuse him off. Broadway is no more quintessentially English than a disused railway siding in Bacup or a lock-up garage in Bow.

By the chapter's end, though, JB has pulled himself together. He parts amicably with his artist friend but still at odds. 'He asked me to share his contempt for the new urban mob, the products of indus-trial towns and free education at council schools and cheap books and so on and so forth; but as I consider myself one of these very people, I had to decline.'

I was one of these very people too, and the time had come to go in search of cities full of us.

4

TO COVENTRY, BIRMINGHAM AND THE BLACK COUNTRY

In which I meet Yam Yams and Peaky Blinders,
see the beauty of Tile Hill and witness the city
that rose from the ashes.

Had Priestley been writing *English Journey* forty years later, its most
unwieldy chapter title would have been much more concise. In
1972, with the stroke of a local government officer's pen, Coventry,
Birmingham and all of the Black Country became subsumed into a
vast region called the 'West Midlands'. Not everyone was keen on
this. Some ardent Anglo-Saxon loyalists felt West Mercia was prefer-
able. It's certainly more evocative. But like Cumbria and Merseyside,
the name passed quickly into the vernacular, being a bold, even fool-
hardy attempt, to corral a whole spread of very different places, some
of them fierce rivals. Generally, the people here are so genial and
self-deprecating that they don't make a fuss about trivialities. But
woe betide those who think Noddy Holder is a Brummie, or Ozzy
Osbourne a Yam Yam. Bad impressionists and second-rate actors
may not be able to tease it out, but there is a world of difference

between Walsall and Worcester, Sutton Coldfield and Handsworth, Bournville and the Balti Triangle. Perhaps Priestley's title was better, then. This is a place with a big heart, broad shoulders and a proud and diverse people.

Like Priestley, I head from the Cotswolds to Coventry. But for entirely personal reasons, I hop off the tiny clanking tram-like West Midlands train at Tile Hill. I want to see the vistas and landscapes that have inspired some of my favourite works of art. These were not haywains but derelict garages; not watermills but flat-roofed estate pubs. Tile Hill is a suburb a few miles west of Coventry. Historically it was part of the Forest of Arden, immortalised in Shakespeare's *As You Like It*. Now, it is a huge open plan estate, enshrined in the paintings of Turner Prize shortlisted George Shaw. Shaw is a true 'Cov Kid' – the affectionate, cheery designation those born and bred here give themselves. At the age of two, in 1968, he and his family moved into the Tile Hill estate. It was built a few decades after Priestley visited, but it's not fanciful to suggest that it, and estates like it, were built partly because of him. Books like *English Journey* and his wartime *Postscripts* broadcasts, along with Orwell, the Jarrow March and the visionaries of the post-war Attlee government, fostered a great public hunger for change, and with it the sense that a 'New Jerusalem' could be built. The squat maisonettes, the high-rise blocks, the Costcutter, Toners Hair and Marrs Domestic Appliances may not seem like what they had in mind. But families like George Shaw's, and like mine in Wigan, came to these new estates – modern, centrally heated, with gardens and garages – and were elated to be here after cramped terraces and gloomy tenements. In the quiet of the afternoon Tile Hill goes about its suburban business with not a hint of the feral or abandoned. Health visitors and delivery drivers do their rounds in the sunny stolidity of the Bevan estates. Listen hard and there's the occasional angry yell from an upstairs window, you might find the occasional door that could stand a lick of paint. But you can have a bad neighbour anywhere.

Many critics have misunderstood Shaw's work, taken it to be a respectable salon version of the rancid old trope 'it's grim up north', or north of Watford anyway. But these images are not clichéd signifiers of urban squalor; they are loving, celebratory, mystical. Painted in a hyper-realist style with Humbrol model paint, Shaw's images imbue the places where he grew up – the estate shop, the football pitch, derelict garages – with numinous light and significance. They are entirely without figures, which Shaw attributes self-deprecatingly to a lack of skill, but that only adds to the sense of mystery. Priestley, a fairly decent amateur watercolourist, would have liked them, I think.

Coventry is very good with its hands. For centuries, the city has made stuff and made it well. As Priestley delineates: 'In the thirteenth century it was making cutlery: in the fourteenth, cloth; in the fifteenth, gloves; in the sixteenth, buttons; in the seventeenth, clocks; in the eighteenth, ribbons; in the nineteenth, sewing machines and bicycles; and now, in the twentieth, motor cars, electrical gadgets, machine tools, and wireless apparatus.' The skilled artisans of this Midlands city have always been able to turn their hands to the changing demands of trade and industry. Weavers and watchmakers became engineers and bike manufacturers. In 1897, the first British car was built here, essentially a motorised cart called the Owl, made by Daimler. From the turn of the twentieth century to the slow receding tide of deindustrialisation, Coventry was one of the world's major car-producing cities. Priestley complains that in the pubs and restaurants they talked of little else but gears and magnetos and crankshafts. It was our Detroit. Motor City UK.

Unlike Detroit, Coventry is weathering its long climate of economic storms. A few years back Jaguar Land Rover's managers went to the bank on a Friday to draw out the cash to pay the workers' wages. As of 2021, they were turning a billion-pound profit and embracing electrification though no local industry has been having it good of late. Several specialised artisanal engineering companies are still based in the city. At the university, the engineers of the future are being trained, many of them female and people of colour. Coventry has gone from the riot-ravaged, out of work Ghost Town of local band The Specials' spectrally gloomy 1981 single to, exactly forty years later, UK City of Culture 2021. 'The hotels are full, the city centre is buzzing once again, and the feeling of civic pride is almost tangible at every event,' was the verdict in the *Coventry Telegraph*.

I arrive in Coventry with this cultural jamboree in full intoxicating swing. The city seems particularly alive with poetry, as is fitting for the hometown of lugubrious genius Philip Larkin. Characteristically grumpy, Larkin turned down the laureateship, but on my Coventry sojourn I witness the current Poet Laureate Simon Armitage read his own work to a packed, laughing, crowd among the street food vendors and cocktail bars of ultra-hip FarGo Village. I listen to brass band settings of poems in the sunshine at Coombe Abbey Park and see the wonderful Midlands poet Liz Berry hold a class in the gothic beauty of the cemetery grounds. At this event, I chat with another poet, Jonathan Davidson, a long-time Coventry resident now based in Brum who told me that Cov 'has always been at ease with itself and its different communities. There are divisions, of course, but they don't seem to have flared up as they did in Brum or Bristol, maybe because it's small and there is no one dominant community. Well, apart from the white one. The city centre feels like it belongs to everyone. It's always been an optimistic and forward-looking city. Even the ring road, which is a nightmare, was designed to be ambidextrous for when we started driving on the right like the rest of Europe.' That day, of course, is further off than ever now.

Some of Coventry's civic rebirth was forced upon it. On 14 November 1940, 16,000 Nazi bombs were dropped on Coventry in one fiery, rutilant night. Some 1,400 people were killed. A third of the city's factories were destroyed or severely damaged, along with two hospitals, two churches and a police station. War artist John Piper was dispatched to record the damage, but he found the rubble, fires and charred bodies just too distressing to sketch. Then he came across a row of untouched houses next to the cathedral. In an upstairs room, 'there was a girl tapping away at a typewriter,' he recalled 'in a seat by an open window, as if nothing had happened. I said: "Good morning. It's a beastly time, isn't it?"' She let him borrow her desk, and the painting he produced from his sketches there, a lurid symphony of acid yellows, blood reds and funeral blacks, became the defining artistic image of the Coventry Blitz.

Modern Coventry, then, was forged in flame and tears, and nowhere bears testament to this as vividly as the cathedral, or rather cathedrals. On one side is the original fourteenth-century St Michael's, left in ruins as a permanent reminder of the horror of war. On the morning after the bombing, the cathedral stonemason noticed two burned timbers lying across each other in the shape of a cross. He strapped them together and now The Charred Cross, blackened and twisted, sits atop an altar of rubble. Adjoining this bare and devastated wreckage is the new cathedral, designed by architect Basil Spence. It was Spence's idea, a brilliant one, to leave the wartime ruins just as they were and the effect is gravely moving. Opened in 1962, the new cathedral is a modernist masterpiece, a space of affecting starkness combining solemnity and a certain youthful 60s optimism. Its stunning architectural highlights are well-known and bring the faithful and the tourist alike. There's Epstein's striking 'St Michael's Victory Over the Devil'; Graham Sutherland's staggering Christ in Glory in the Tetramorph, reputedly the largest tapestry ever made in a single piece, depicting the risen Christ in glory on the north wall behind the altar; and the Chapel of Unity, a narrow circular space that leaps to dizzying height, with the crucifix seemingly suspended in mid-air.

I'm shown around by a young woman who works here. I ask about the dramatic spiky design of the choir stalls: clearly intended to evoke the bloody crown of thorns that pierced Christ's brow, yes? 'Erm, most people think it's birds or flowers actually,' she replies politely. That's me. Ever the grisly lapsed Catholic, I guess. Music has always echoed here. Benjamin Britten's stunning War Requiem was commissioned for the cathedral's consecration. At its premier here it was intended that there should be soloists representing the nations most affected by the Second World War: the great German baritone Dietrich Fischer-Dieskau, Britten's partner the English tenor Peter Pears, and famed Russian soprano Galina Vishnevskaya. Ultimately the Soviets would not let the latter leave Russia and Heather Harper took her place. Then, in the mid 1970s, the German electronic trio Tangerine Dream were invited to play here in a gesture of healing and reconciliation, a superb concert that you can find on YouTube. When the group's leader Edgar Froese arrived in Coventry for the gig, the first thing he saw was a newspaper billboard proclaiming, '35 YEARS AGO THEY CAME WITH BOMBS! NOW THEY COME WITH SYNTHESIZERS!'

It courts offence to even suggest that a catastrophe like the Coventry Blitz might have any 'upside'. But fans of British Mid Century Modern design and Brutalism may feel that way. When Priestley visited in *English Journey*, the city still had a well preserved medieval 'centre'. But the Luftwaffe changed all that. Faced with the task of rebuilding Coventry from ashes and rubble, a 29-year-old called Donald Gibson was appointed city architect and planning officer. The plan he came up with was radical, and very much not to the liking of traditionalists. It was boldly modern, involving thousands of tons of concrete and acres of clean, solid geometry. As it was, the money ran out before Gibson's total transformation could be achieved, and so King Charles and the likeminded will still find Hay Street, Bayley Lane and Spon Street delightfully and anachronistically Tudor.

Me, I'm a sucker for a bit of British Mid Century Modern. Modest. Functional. Stylish. Festival of Britain. G Plan. The Skylon.

Ercol. Ernest Race's Springbok chair. Robert Heritage's Hamilton sideboard. No? Well, if all this means less than nothing to you, for a brilliant primer in British Mid Century Modern, take the train to Coventry, perhaps with a copy of *The Making of a Modern City, 1939–73* by Jeremy and Caroline Gould to read on the way. The station itself is a perfect place to start. Opened in 1966, its airy Scandinavian design has met with the approval of modernist maven Owen Hatherley, who admires its 'unassuming but generous modernism, a simple concrete box beautifully finished in wood and marble, clear, spacious and achingly hopeful.' If you've time you could take in the Market, the precinct, the uni (once the old Lanchester Polytechnic) or the swimming baths. But you must head for Belgrade Square. Anyone who has played Pictionary with me will know that I am not by nature one of the world's great artists. I may not know much about design. But I know what I like, and, for me, this corner of downtown Cov is as architecturally ravishing as Bath's Crescent or Brighton's Royal Pavilion. It's flanked by two of my favourite buildings. The Belgrade was the first civic theatre to be built in Britain after the Second World War, the masterpiece of Arthur Ling, who took over after Donald Gibson resigned in 1955. It's a symphony in Portland stone, brass, copper, glass and beech timber donated by the city of Belgrade. If there is a more beautiful bar in England than Nineteen 58 (named for the year the Belgrade opened), I've not had the pleasure. At the risk of sounding philistine, whatever the play, it's worth coming here and, for the price of a G&T, feel that you have stepped straight into an episode of *Mad Men*.

Even better awaits. For fifty years, the building across the plaza was the HQ of the *Coventry Telegraph* and rang to the clack of type-writers and the clatter of presses bringing out four – four! – editions of the local paper a day. At this point, we should rightly lament and bemoan the death of the regional print newspaper, living on now sometimes only on the most incomprehensible, migraine-inducing websites there are. But, as with the unwelcome attentions of the Luftwaffe, there's a 'plus'. The offices of the *Coventry Telegraph* are now a hotel. My favourite city centre hotel in England in fact. According to the for-once-entirely-accurate blurb, The Telegraph 'invokes the famed mid-century architecture of the city and reflects the building's former life as a thriving newspaper and print works.' Sometimes it invokes this a little clunkily. The 'Do Not Disturb' sign reads 'On A Deadline' and 'Chasing A Scoop' depending on whether you're having a lie-in or are out and about. But I'm willing to forgive this place almost anything. All the elements of Mid Century style are here: curving sleek wood handrails, heavy glass doors, moss green leather and deep amber brass. Late in the evening, after his triumph at the FarGo Village, I chance upon the Poet Laureate here, refreshed and vivacious, trying to assert his identity to the security conscious receptionist, having locked himself out. 'He's the Poet Laureate!' I chip in brightly as I pass and leave them to their discussions. Perhaps a quick villanelle sorted things out.*

Next lunchtime, I go in search of a sirloin. Steak for lunch would normally be a bit rich for me, in every sense. But while in Coventry, I'd decided to follow not just in Priestley's footsteps but his mouthfuls. JB ate steak in a Coventry grill room and did not enjoy the experience. Too tough and too many fried potatoes, apparently. In fact, the whole underwhelming experience brought forth a diatribe against the way that steak in England 'is venerated and idealised. When an ordinary English waiter mentions Steak his voice is low, hushed, reverent ... It is Steak personal, *your* Steak. How will you have your steak, sir? He's just doing your steak, now, sir. Here's your

---

* On another night of my Coventry trip, The Telegraph being full, I stayed at a Premier Inn on the outskirts of town. Across the road from this was a fabulous establishment called Binley Mega Chippy. As I was writing all this up, it became an unlikely social media sensation, perhaps because of its alluring name, with pilgrims coming from around the world. I like to think I was 'ahead of the curve' here.

steak, sir. It is as if he were talking about your wife. Name any other item on the menu that is discussed in this fashion, that is even treated with the merest hint of respect. It cannot be done. We live in the empire of the steak.'

This imperial phase has lasted quite some time, buoyed by periodic fads. There was the revolution occasioned by the coming of the Berni Inn of the 70s, which introduced a generation of nervous British diners to Fino sherry aperitif, carafes of plonk, prawn cocktail and Black Forest gateau. Medium was rare and rare rarer still in these establishments. Nearly everyone ordered their steak 'well done', which makes it all the more curious that the Germans call a bloody steak an 'englisch'. In the 80s, an Aberdeen Steak House could be found on most city streets, especially in London, where it was sometimes said that the whole rationale behind them was that they were safe and dependable places for young northerners to take visiting parents.

By the turn of the twenty-first century, according to the *Guardian*, 'foodists did not get excited about steak: the only people who ordered it were people who didn't really like food. It was a boring menu staple for risk-averse diners. It was what your dad liked, welldone, and preferably topped with a little rosette of garlic butter.' But then in the 90s came Cao and Josper and Mash and Hawksmoor and a host of other opulent, macho eateries where the onion rings cost seven quid and the Chateaubriand was affordable only by Premier League footballers and Britpop royalty. Even now, in our new sackcloth era of jackfruit and aquafaba, steak houses are still bloody (ho ho) popular with the English omnivore.

I find one between The Belgrade and the cathedral, part of a chain with a punning name which bills itself as 'the most recognised casual steak dining restaurant in the UK.' A niche accolade, I thought, but a tempting one. My waitress approaches with a brisk, friendly air and a notepad. 'I have a few questions,' she says with a smile and begins to grill me (ho ho again!) about cuts and sauces and preparation and sides. Priestley, offered with a straightforward choice of sirloin, rump or fillet, would have been bamboozled by the chimichurri and tempura prawns, possibly even by something as prosaic to us as coleslaw or corn on the cob. He would, one imagines, have been appalled at the idea of eating 'dirty fries', at least until he realised it was just chips with melted cheese. (He'd have thought that a poor sense of the word 'dirty', I reckon, and so do I). Priestley does not mention whether his grill house was full; mine certainly isn't, but then all of the front pages that month were about the worsening cost of living crisis. With endless talk of stagflation, low productivity and recession, with ABBA holograms on stage in the Docklands and Danny Boyle's Sex Pistols drama on the TV, England looked to be on the verge of a full-scale 70s revival in the early 2020s.

Eventually the place fills up a little, with two unusual diners occupying the next booth. They are lads of about twenty, both wearing shades, whose excitable chatter hints at a long night of 'refreshments' enjoyed. 'Can you suggest something exceptional?' asks one of the young waitress, who finds this as funny as I do. 'Try the fillet mignon with onion gravy,' she answers, and from the slurping and ahhing that emanated from their corner, I surmise that their steak is a lot nicer than was Priestley's. Mine is too, if not quite exceptional, and I leave quite prepared for one last bit of sightseeing.

The Transport Museum is a tremendous place which vividly tells the story of the city – of boom and bust, famine and plenty – through a social history of the car. There is a good deal about gears, crankshafts and magnetos, but there is thankfully more about immigration and industrial relations, picket lines and people's lives. I feel a little better about my architectural musings when the excellent voiceover states that 'the blitz might have been a disaster, but it was also an opportunity.' It compares the reconstruction of Coventry's with that of its twin town of Dresden, which suffered even worse at the hands of the RAF than Cov did from the Luftwaffe. Dresden was rebuilt in a revivalist style in keeping with its eighteenth-century architectural glories. Prince Charles would have approved, but for me Gibson was right. His vision was about progress and innovation not just restoration. And, for better or worse it acknowledged the turbine that was driving Coventry's booming economy. By 1950, the UK was the world's second biggest car exporter and Coventry was at its heart. Half of the city was employed in this mighty endeavour. Even by the early 60s, Coventry still built more than 1.8 million cars a year. But it couldn't last. Stiff competition, bad management decisions and poor industrial relations – you can walk uneasily through a reconstruction of a picket line at the museum – brought about a sharp decline. Between 1975 and 1982, 520 jobs a month disappeared and unemployment ran at 17 per cent. This town was coming like a ghost town.

It doesn't feel that way now. Coventry feels young and hopeful. It has two universities and the whole of downtown feels like one giant campus. The piazza between the Herbert Gallery and the cathedral is filled with skateboarders, inept but mustard-keen. Coventry has increased its student numbers by 24 per cent since 2014–15, when there were 27,600 undergraduates and graduates. Many of these students flock to Coventry from all over the world to engage in the urgent business of inventing the future; a future of driverless vehicles, electric engines, hydrogen powered cars and drone deliveries. A cleaner, quieter post-oil world. That's the theory anyway.

But in the Future Moves displays in the Transport Museum, I hear a woman with family in tow, say wistfully, peevishly even, 'Oh, this country used to be great! We could be great again!' Now of course I want her and her son and quiet husband to prosper. I want them to be happy. But when I hear talk like this, my heart sinks. What is this illusion, this phantasm of greatness these people chase? Is it the one where we trampled on the lives and rights of people all over the world and exploited them to death? Why do we yearn for some imagined greatness when right now England can't feed its kids, heal its sick or run its trains? How about forgetting about being great? How about being happy? How about being competent? How about being sane? Maybe the bright new Cov kids can help us with that.

2

Priestley left Coventry for Brum in high dudgeon, having become vexed about shaving. Apparently, he'd lost his razor, brush and soap somewhere between the Cotswolds and Coventry and had splashed out on some replacement kit which wasn't very good. Rarely quoted, never anthologised, no one is ever going to single out these few paragraphs of lubricious angst as the absolute cream of *English Journey*, but they're strangely illuminating, nonetheless. 'The razor I learned was destined to revolutionise the practise of shaving; it was designed on a new principle and after the most superficial trial I would never want to use any other.' So, nearly a century ago, those red braces and big specs advertising guys were already coming up with the weapons grade guff they still peddle, promising shaves of barely believable smoothness utilising technology as advanced as that which would surely one day put a crisply-shaven man on Mars.

Sadly, Priestley's new kit turned out to be some way from 'the best a man could get.' He arrived in Birmingham half shaved, nicked and bloody, once more in a simmering grump. Astonishingly, though nearly forty years old, a veteran of the Western Front and a hugely successful author, he had never before visited Birmingham. He's not at all sheepish about this either. In fact, he's positively bullish. 'I knew very little about it. The little I did know, however, was not in its favour. I had always thought of the place, vaguely, as perhaps the most typical product in civic life of nineteenth-century industrialism, as a city of big profits and narrow views.'

A pugnacious product of the muck and brass of Bradford himself, this sounds a bit rich to be honest. But worse was to come later in the chapter. 'I saw nothing, not one single tiny thing, that could possibly raise a man's spirits … Possibly what I was seeing was not Birmingham but our urban and industrial civilisation. The fact remains that it was beastly. It was so many miles of ugliness, squalor, and the wrong kind of vulgarity, the decayed anaemic kind.'

Priestley scholar Lee Hanson once attempted to ameliorate possible bad feeling about this ahead of an event about *English Journey* I chaired in Birmingham. 'I'm not sure he could be described as nasty. I think it was actually Priestley just trying to be honest. He was the kind of writer who told it as he saw it. He came from Bradford, which has a strong industrial background, just like Birmingham. So he didn't have an aversion to looking at heavy industry. However, I think he was surprised by the meanness and bleakness of the landscape around Birmingham, and also the Black Country. And he certainly didn't like the idea that people were used as machines and pawns for wealthy industrialists, who then went to live in nicer areas themselves.'

Whatever Priestley's intentions, it doesn't seem to have upset Brummies as much as his traducing of the North East did the Geordie folk (more on that later). Frankly, Birmingham can take it. Rarely fashionable, a city that *does* rather than *talks*, it has borne a constant tide of jokes, sneers and trolling with wry, droll perseverance. This is the default Brummie position, developed over decades of listening to Manchester, Liverpool and London boasting loudly about trivial things like pop groups and nightclubs while Birmingham was the workshop of the world and the city of a thousand trades, originator of everything from the electric kettle to the Pacemaker, the bicycle bell to the postage stamp.

I'm teasing, of course. I like pop music and seem to remember, through the mists of time, that I used to like nightclubs. But I also very much admire the way Birmingham has always gone quietly about its considerable business without inventing cheesy self-regarding slogans or going in for bumptious self-promotion. There is something distinctly Brummie in the fact that, until the triumphant 2022 Commonwealth Games opening ceremony, possibly the city's two most celebrated pieces of PR, in a heavily ironised and self-deprecating way, were Cliff Richard's 70s movie *Take Me High*, the romantic tale of a pop singer/canal bargee who invents a new fast-food sensation called the Brum Burger, and *Telly Savalas Looks at Birmingham*. This latter is the most famous example of what were known as 'quota quickies', kitschy travelogues about UK cities shown before cinema main features and required by a law that said cinemas must show a British film for every US one. In this one, from 1981, the gruff, dome-headed tough guy actor, best known as lollipop-sucking New York detective Kojak, extols the virtues of the Bull Ring and Dale End from a voiceover studio in the West End. As the *Independent* remarked, 'Savalas also "looked" at Portsmouth and Aberdeen, but the Birmingham film is a kind of Dadaist masterpiece that sucks you in.'

Savalas never got to experience the thrill of Birmingham's buses – a rich, complex network woven into the fabric of city life. Older Brummies, moist-eyed, will tell you that they had the best buses (and trolley buses) in the land, either those owned and operated by the city itself, resplendent in its distinguished livery of dark blue and cream, or the dashing scarlet of Midland Red. Now, post-privatisation, some of the city's routes are now presumably operated by a hot dog consortium in Albuquerque or an Uzbek gas company, but the 'iconic' routes remain. The most famous is the Number 11 (all in good time), but the grandest way into the city is on the Number 9 from Stourbridge and the Worcestershire countryside. Serenely, it moves in like a battleship from the green edge of the city where, as Caroline Hillier put it, lies 'the gleaming misty presence of the Shropshire and Welsh hills that all West Midlanders must be aware of.' Down the asphalt river of the Hagley Road it comes, and if you sit at the front on the top deck you can watch the towers and crenelations of this second city's skyscrapers loom before you. Even Priestley was impressed, if grudgingly. 'There was a sudden access of civic dignity in the place. Here in Colmore Row you could imagine yourself in the second city of England ... So long as you keep within a very narrow limit in the centre, Colmore Row, New Street, Corporation Street, Birmingham has quite a metropolitan air, and on the fine afternoon I first explored them, these streets had quite metropolitan crowds in them too, looking at the windows of the big shops and hurrying in and out of cafés and picture theatres.'

I jump off the Number 9 just before this, though, so that I can stroll into the city centre via its celebrated canal network. Just as every pub sage knows that one blow of a swan's wing can break a man's arm, everyone knows that Birmingham has more canals than Venice. As yet, there is no Birmingham vaporetto, sadly. But a chap can still feel positively Venetian as he strolls into the city towards Gas Street Basin, the hub of what is one of the most intricate canal networks in the world. These waterways and junctions were the nervous system and circulation of Victorian Birmingham, that workshop of the world. They were essentially watery autobahns, gas lit to allow 24-hour traffic, subject to bores and tides thanks to the endless passage of barges and narrowboats. Now, this is the heart of Brum's night life – the restored canal architecture framing and complementing teppanyaki bars, taquerias and the signature restaurants of world-class chefs. You can eat well in Brum at any price, from the finest curry houses in England to Wagnerian-length tasting menus, wine flights of orgasmic indulgence and heart-stopping bills. In 2022, Manchester finally achieved its only Michelin star after years of dicing and flambéing. Birmingham has twenty. By the time you read this, it will be more. Low and high culture rub along famously in downtown Brum. On Brindley Place there's one of the best modern art galleries in Britain, the Ikon, hard alongside Broad Street, a thoroughfare that is, at 3am on any weekend night, as energising as it is terrifying, almost medieval in its lust and mayhem.

Many English cities have enjoyed a renaissance in the last thirty years. But Birmingham's transformation has been more complete and satisfying than most. Its built environment grew in the same hardscrabble, entropic way most British cities do: a bit of planning here, a lot of war there, successive bouts of carmania and then pedestrianisation. But modern Brum has made its peace with how it looks. The eternal white marble of the Hall of Memory nods at the priapic 60s futurism of the Rotunda; the glittering, new Bull Ring reflects the chrome swoop of the huge Grand Central/New Street Station; the barbed wire arabesques of the new Library glitter across from the burnished statue of Birmingham's founding industrialists Matthew Boulton, James Watt and William Murdoch. Both of these flank Centenary Square, an airy piazza of fountains and passing trams. And on its south side lies Symphony Hall, the stately modern edifice where twenty-first century Birmingham was born in music and built on the passion of a curly-haired Scouser who became the city's favourite adopted son.

'There's absolutely no doubt that Simon Rattle was a huge part of the creation of modern Birmingham,' says Stephen Maddock over the froth of a cappuccino in pretty Brindley Place. 'There was a visionary civic leadership at the time, too, who saw that with the decline of manufacturing, the city had to reinvent itself. But Simon completely drove that change. He took over at the City of Birmingham Symphony Orchestra just at the height of the CD boom, and turned the CBSO from a very good regional orchestra, perhaps akin to Cleveland's, into one with a first-class international reputation.' Such was his influence that people and things dating from before the Rattle revolution are referred to, wryly, as Pre-Rattleite.

Stephen Maddock is the head of the CBSO. I've got to know him through us both being team members on Radio 4's impossibly erudite *Round Britain Quiz*, one of the world's longest-running radio shows. He is a lovely man with a compendious knowledge about both classical music and modern Birmingham. He also supports Manchester City, but let's draw a veil over that. Simon Rattle was the Liverpool-born wunderkind who, talent-spotted at an early age, had worked with the Philharmonic in his home city and the Bournemouth Symphony Orchestra before joining the CBSO in 1980. It was this savvy appointment that elevated both of them to world prestige and fame. One Christmas at the end of the 1980s I spotted Rattle and his fabulous Einsteinian barnet on a late-night train from London and, having had an eggnog, buttonholed him about how brilliant some recent CBSO recordings had been, especially Nicholas Maw's epic *Odyssey*. He was funny and gracious with someone he didn't know from Adam, and you could see immediately why Birmingham was keen to keep hold of him. 'He was very clever,' says Maddock. 'He really wanted a world class concert hall for his orchestra and he was very shrewd about not renewing his contract until the city had promised him it.'

Symphony Hall is an astonishing space, arguably Europe's finest modern concert hall, boasting some of the world's best acoustics. It is a symphony in red, cream and gold, equal parts grand hall of Mitteleuropa and People's Arthaus of one of the more progressive Soviet republics. Its neighbours include the Rep Theatre and the grand neo-classical colonnades of the Municipal Bank 'built by Neville Chamberlain, probably just post Wall Street Crash and just before Priestley came. No one trusted banks anymore so he built a local bank for local people. It's ridiculously over the top architecturally inside, like the bank in the final act of *Mary Poppins*, huge safes and steel walls to deposit boxes.' Centenary Square has the dreamy utopianism of a planner's idealised imagining. 'It's almost our Lincoln Centre,' says Stephen proudly.

Rattle may have left town, but his democratising spirit lives on. A magnificent new CBSO school is being built, the first in Britain to be established in collaboration with an orchestra. And it's being built not in leafy Edgbaston or snobby Sutton Coldfield but in West Brom, the heart of the Black Country. 'A state comprehensive and a curriculum in which music will be totally embedded. So you will learn about science and history through music. Ten-year-olds studying Steve Reich and Webern! Amazing. Our soloists will be giving tuition and our ensembles will be in residence there.' Just think, if you have to budge up on the tram for a woman with an unwieldy case between the Jewellery Quarter and Handsworth Booth Street, she may be one of the world's greatest tuba virtuosos.

This is my second sunlit stroll along the towpath to Symphony Hall in as many weeks to catch one of the CBSO's lunchtime performances, and both I and the orchestra have mercifully avoided the ping of the Covid app this time. Where once the pre-concert ritual might have been the slurp of house red, the programme purchase and a last minute dash to the loo, this time it's a squirt of hand sanitiser, a temperature check, and the track and trace form. Nevertheless, there's an expectant hush in the socially distanced audience. As the harpist tunes up, a man several metres away from me sighs, 'Oh, I've missed my live music.'

They liked it. A broken string mid-adagio adds a jolt of drama but the joy of being back in a room listening to real live music is excitement enough. When Stephen takes me backstage to meet the players, the excitement is still in the air among a gaggle of players and whatever the collective noun for composers is (a score?). 'Did Radio 3 take that?' 'They recorded it?' 'Good 'cos that was the best.' If you heard that broadcast, you might have heard the strings snap. But you will not have heard the trains to Wolverhampton that thunder beneath the stage because the whole building rests on rubber pads to absorb every shudder and clank. Another touch of Rattle perfectionism.

'People come to me from all over the world and say "show us how we can regenerate a city on culture,"' reflects Stephen. 'Now the challenge is to take that out to the towns all around us.' I hope they do because a daring, brilliant wave of cultural and social regeneration might be happening here.

But if the music they play at Symphony Hall isn't for you, head across town to Digbeth, as I do. Looking out across Brum from a rooftop bar at a skyline alive with neon in the setting sun and pulsing with dub reggae, house, metal and pop, all rising from the clubs and arts spaces below, I reflect on the thrill of experiencing music in real time as it happens: evanescent, cerebral, visceral. I cannot wait to be in Symphony Hall and hear a brilliant young soloist announce that they're going to play a Górecki harpsichord concerto or a Debussy prelude in broadest Black Country and afterwards get the tram back to West Brom.

3

Nicholas Jones, aka Nicky Wire, is the bass player in Welsh band Manic Street Preachers. They are one of the few righteously angry rock groups still around. Their songs offer a coruscating, white-hot, clinical critique of a broken world. But I have rarely seen him as angry as when the news broke that Cadbury's chocolate, every Briton's adored taste of childhood, had been bought by Chicago's Kraft Foods, later Mondelez of Ontario. 'Cadbury's chocolate is the best in the fucking world,' he raged to me, 'and we have sold it to the makers of the shittiest chocolate known to humanity.'

He was not alone. Public discontent rumbled for over a decade after Kraft's takeover of Cadbury's until, in February 2021, Mondelez International, Cadbury's new giant owners, announced it was bringing production of its 'iconic' Dairy Milk chocolate bar back from Europe to the UK following a £15 million investment in Bournville. This move united a wide and disparate range of quite different people in approval – Brexiteers and chocolate traditionalists, yes, but then also trade unions. Cadbury's, like football, had come home, albeit in the control of Canadians.

I'm no stranger to large scale sweet and confectionery manufacture. Like all kids in Wigan, I used to hang around the Santus factory begging the production line girls to 'chuck' us a few mint balls out the window, which we would catch in our untucked T-shirts. Furthermore, I once went round the Tunnock's Caramel Wafer factory in Glasgow with Britpop trio Supergrass, for reasons too complex to go into now. I'd also once visited the Cadbury World site in Bournville and had a vague recollection of some people in hairnets stirring giant vats of silky brown molten chocolate. But, unsure if there was any actual chocolate manufacturing going on at Cadbury World now, I emailed their PR person. The replies were gracious but framed in the tone you might employ with a toddler: 'Hi Stuart. Chocolate is made at the Cadbury factory in Bournville but not at Cadbury World as it's not a chocolate factory, it's a tourist attraction. Mondelez International would be able to help with any history/ factory enquiries you had, hope this helps.'

Finally, I understood. Yes, Cadbury World had once been part of the Cadbury factory, where chocolate was still made, but it had outgrown and put aside all thoughts of chocolate production and concentrated on other stuff. Stuff less cocoa extract-related but maybe more fun on a bank holiday, such as the African Adventure Play Area, the Aztec Jungle and Advertising Avenue.

Priestley's tooth was as sweet as Nicky Wire's. He'd hardly arrived in Birmingham before deciding to visit Cadbury's, ostensibly to see this famous model of paternalistic capitalism and Quaker civic morality at first hand, but mainly I think to feed his habit. I was amazed to find that even in 1933 Priestley could have enjoyed a Crunchie, Milk Tray, Dairy Milk or even an early prototype of the Crème Egg, all being made in Bournville long before what we think of as their definitive 60s and 70s heyday. To be fair, as the football pundits say, I can take chocolate or leave it. But strict accuracy to

Priestley's itinerary demanded I follow him to Bournville. It also gave me a chance to ride the famous Number 11 bus, one of the few bus routes in the world to have inspired a state-of-the-nation eponymous novel, penned by Birmingham-born novelist Jonathan Coe. The title is multi-layered, literally, referring obliquely to the Dantesque megabasements of London's super rich and, of course, to the Downing Street residence of the chancellor. But for generations of Brummies, it's the much-loved circular bus route around the city, where bored teenagers can spend long afternoons in flirtatious, gossiping motion for a few pence and, as Alex Clark pointed out in her *Guardian* review, 'providing a haven for those who might not want to go home because, for example, they can't afford to put the heating on.'

Nearing Bournville the bus passes some well-known Birmingham suburbs. Leafy Edgbaston resounds to the thwack of willow on leather; comfortable, prosperous Harborne and its funkier neighbour Bearwood; bustling Selly Oak with its superstores and storage units. Then, an appropriately chocolatey brown sign for Cadbury World. I step down just four miles from the clamour of central Brum onto a village green straight from, well, a chocolate box. When George Cadbury built Bournville at the end of the nineteenth century, it really was rural. The 14.5-acre site he bought was all little hills and hedgerows and trout streams. It was no place to build a factory and he was mocked by other harder-headed industrialist peers. But Cadbury was no ordinary industrialist. A Quaker of humanity and principle, he delivered thousands of Brummies from urban squalor and poverty, and along the way, made the best chocolate in the world. Even Marx and Engels surely concluded if we must have capitalism, then let us have this kind, with decent houses, health care and delicious crumbly Flakes and Wispas, wiping chocolate from their fulsome beards.

It's the last day of exams and the green is full of clusters of schoolkids, laughing and canoodling, buzzing and bored and all the stages of youthful freedom between. On the other side of the green, every table outside the café is full, of retirees and young mums and of bearded hipsters on Macbooks. Next door, a white-aproned butcher stands beneath his awning, a glistening mise-en-scène of chops and steaks and sausages behind him. This is the kind of idyllic, relaxed vibe that we are conditioned to think of as 'continental'. But here it is in suburban Brum in the centre of uptight, costive Blighty. No pastis or Pinot though. The Bournville Village Trust (BVT to the justifiably smug residents) is dry and has consistently voted against as much as a garage shop selling blue WKD.

'People just don't want it,' says Pat, the volunteer in the little visitor's centre, 'and it really has meant that we've kept a quiet character that's not like a lot of other Birmingham suburbs.' This quirky little circular building, built in the Arts and Crafts style like much of the BVT, was gifted as a 'rest house' for George Cadbury and his wife by grateful employees. 'Can you imagine that now?' asks Pat. No, I won't hold my breath for the Jeff Bezos Memorial Summerhouse built by overworked delivery drivers on zero-hours contracts. 'I think it was genuine gratitude for what he did, which as well as making money for himself of course, got a lot of Brummagems out of slum housing and into decent jobs and homes. Every house had a vegetable garden and four fruit trees! Apple, plum, cherry and pear!'

In case any comrades are fuming at this point, we should remember of course that this paternalistic capitalism was still capitalism. The Cadbury family made handsome profits and were classically patriarchal. Cadbury would not employ married women as he felt their place was at home with the children that would inevitably follow. But the difference between a worker's life here and in the factories of the Black Country in the early 1900s must have been jaw-dropping. Even now, a sylvan hour in Bournville will test the ideological ardour of the most committed revolutionary.

Nowhere in *English Journey* does Priestley talk more nuanced good sense than in his thoughtful discussion of this suburb. 'Their workpeople are provided with magnificent recreation grounds and sports pavilions, with a large concert hall in the factory itself, where midday concerts are given, with dining-rooms, recreation rooms, and facilities for singing, acting, and I know not what, with continuation schools, with medical attention, with works councils, with pensions … Once you have joined the staff of this firm, you need never wander out of its shadow.' But you can detect the unease in that last sentence. 'It has rather too many public halls of religion and too few frivolous meeting places for my taste … I for one would infinitely prefer to see workers combining to provide these benefits for themselves … to see them forming associations far removed from the factory, to see them using their leisure, and demanding its increase, not as favoured employees but as citizens, free men and women.'*

The employees, though, did pay for the little rest house which is now technically the Carillon Visitors Centre. A carillon is a curious musical instrument which produces a clamorous peal of bells from a baton keyboard. Cadbury installed the first for his workers' amusement in 1908 and its forty-eight bells weigh a hefty 17.5 tons. There are still two performances every Saturday. Booking advisable. Those locked out can enjoy a CCTV relay to the visitor's centre and a recording of one is playing on a screen. Pat notices my interest. 'There's Trevor, been here since 1965, our resident Carill … Carrol … Carillioneur.' On the screen a white-haired man is furiously thumping out a deranged tintinnabulation at breakneck speed in a performance that recalls Jerry Lee Lewis at his most unhinged. Before I leave, I buy a few books and a slab of salted caramel chocolate. 'Made by a Cadbury. George's great grandson. Not a single Cadbury down at the works now,' Pat concludes darkly.

---

* In her rather sketchy *English Journey* retread Beryl Bainbridge is less circumspect and more snobbish: 'If I had to choose between private patronage and State Welfare, Bournville versus Castle Vale, I know what it would be, even if it meant dropping a curtsey and signing the pledge.'

I stroll around the fine sports and recreation ground – yet more paternalism – where they are setting up Ferris wheels and assorted rides for the village fête this weekend. Glimpsed across the canvas roof of the Dodgems is the grand and handsome factory itself, more like an Oxford college than a works. The signage, all in Cadbury purple, seeks to direct you to the pulse-racing excitements of Cadbury World, still adjacent to the factory but separate. I mooch around the works itself though, somewhat awkwardly, feeling like someone doing an exposé on the declining circumference of the Crème Egg for *Newsnight*. A turnstile marked Mondelez bars my way, and beyond several men in overalls are having a fag in a little smoker's shelter. They eye me a little suspiciously, quite reasonably. I decide I ought to say something and so shout 'are you making chocolates in here then'. This is perhaps the most asinine question I've ever asked in what we might laughingly call my journalistic career (and competition in this category is stiff, believe me). One gives me a thumbs up, generously I felt.

4

When Satan stood on Brierley Hill
And far around he gazed,
He said, 'I never shall again,
At Hell's flames be amazed.'

It might have worked as a Slade single, belted out by Walsall's Noddy Holder. I can hear West Bromwich lad Robert Plant singing it too, somewhere on side two of *Led Zeppelin IV*, backed by the industrial pounding of John Bonham and the incandescence of Jimmy Page's electric guitar. No royalties to pay either, since no one knows who came up with the above scrap of balladry, but it must have been soon after the Industrial Revolution, when a rolling damp green swathe of middle England turned black and pitted, lit by belching fires. Brierley Hill, Quarry Bank, Rowley Regis, Cradley Heath, Netherton, Gornal, Coseley, Oldbury, Smethwick, West Bromwich, Dudley. Sleeping hamlets and Norman strongholds alike were swallowed by the soot and ash of the new foundries and factories of what became known as the Black Country.

'There, smoke trailed on the ground and lurked in hollows, and fumes leaked from fissures in the earth … It is a barren wasteland, riddled with fire and ash and dust, the very air you breathe is a poisonous fume.' That was how another local lad J R R Tolkien put it. Not about Brierley Hill, admittedly. He was describing the wastelands of Gorgoroth surrounding the dark citadel of Barad-dûr, realm of Sauron in *The Lord Of The Rings*. But it is widely assumed that Tolkien drew on the fiery, vaporous industrial hinterland of the Black Country for his depiction of the noisome lands of the Dark Lord. Harsh, perhaps, but probably accurate back then in the early years of the twentieth century. If, as the young Tolkien was, you were headed south-east from the shire of leafy Warwickshire, then Mordor begins at Tividale.

But then again, listen to W H Auden, coming this way too, 'Clearer than Scafell Pike, my heart has stamped on/the view from Birmingham to Wolverhampton.' Perhaps this line came to him from the top deck of the 126 from Colmore Row Birmingham to Dudley Interchange, which is my means of travel. This is the way Priestley came too, though in grander upholstered style. 'I went from Birmingham through Smethwick and Oldbury to Dudley, which seemed to me a fantastic place. You climb a hill, past innumerable grim works and unpleasant brick dwellings … There was the Black Country unrolled before you like some smouldering carpet. You looked into an immense hollow of smoke and blurred buildings and factory chimneys. There seemed to be no end to it.' In 1887, Elihu Burrit, American consul to Birmingham said, 'the Black Country, black by day and red by night, cannot be matched for vast and varied production by any other space of equal radius on the surface of the globe.'

Dudley styles itself as the capital of the Black Country, a collection of about twenty towns each with their own specialist industries and proudly separate identities. I heard quite a lot about these towns as a kid and I liked the Black Country before I ever experienced it. When I was a teenager, my dad was an inspector for an engineering firm in Wigan that made hydraulic pit props, the great mechanical jaws that held tons of rock secure above the toiling miner. Needless to say, that company, Gullick Dobson, is long gone. Back in the early 1980s though, it was still just about a viable concern and most weekdays my dad would drive his little works van to the places Priestley sketches as 'so much alliteration: Wolverhampton, Wednesbury, Wednesfield, Willenhall and Walsall. You could call them all wilderness, and have done with it.' In these small, proud towns of the area, he'd 'liaise' with little independent firms, forges, foundries, tool-makers of various arcane specialisms who supplied Gullick Dobson with parts. 'There are hundreds of them,' he'd tell me, all crammed into this tiny, crowded, dirty, busy part of the English Midlands. And the reason I was enamoured of them was that around the middle of November every year the bosses of these firms would start to send back 'a Christmas bottle for the family,' a sweetener to keep Gullick's custom into a new and precarious year. By December, we had enough to stock a medium-sized pub, certainly enough to supply my illicit parties till spring.

Most of those little workshops and engineering companies are vanished now, victims of a changing world and the abandonment of British manufacturing in the 1980s. Nearly one in four of all British manufacturing jobs disappeared within Margaret Thatcher's first term, as the government turned its affections to the City of London and low-paid service jobs. Of course, as well as silicon chips, dry cleaning and sandwiches, the world still needed dirty, oily, useful things like fan blades, crankshafts and chains. But from now on they would get them from Shenzen not Smethwick, and at half the price. Even so, some companies remain, like Thomas Dudley providing 'the complete, end-to-end solution for high quality grey iron castings and ductile iron castings.' The flag of the Black Country still proudly features a thickly resolute length of chain on a striking red, white and black background. There is pride in this, and rightly so, even if an uncomfortable truth is that some of those chains were made to shackle humans. Henry Waldram of Brick Kiln Lane, Wolverhampton advertised his trade as 'Negro Collar and Handcuff Maker'.

They are a proud, separate folk here. Brummie neighbours call them Yam Yams for their use of 'yow am' rather than 'you are'.* The vernacular is rich and singular too. 'It's a bit black over Bill's mother's' means it looks like rain. Hands are 'donnies', short for 'donniebands' (hope that's cleared things up) and, best of all, 'never in a rain of pigs pudding!' is a brilliant expression of disbelief. 'Going all round the Wrekin', as in the nearby Shropshire hill, means taking a long time to get to the point or a circuitous route to a destination. No such peregrinations for the 126. Within half an hour I am at my destination. Dudley Zoo and Castle, easily England's finest one stop combination zoo/castle attraction. Like Marmosets and Motte and Baileys? You'll love Dudley!

Ansculf De Picquigny, a conquering Norman, built the castle in 1070. Later the castle was expanded and developed by the lords of Dudley, who got themselves mixed up in affairs of state a great deal in the 1500s. First John Dudley, lord protector, encouraged the dying Edward VI to put ill-fated Lady Jane Grey in line for the throne, thus effectively condemning the poor girl to death. His son, Robert Dudley, became a favourite of Elizabeth I and their 'did they, didn't they?' relationship continues to fascinate, played out with varying degrees of sexual tension on screen by Joseph Fiennes and

---

* They use a similar linguistic badge in South Yorkshire for Sheffield people, 'Dee Dars' as in 'nah den de wat da doin ere?'

Cate Blanchett, Jeremy Irons and Helen Mirren, and Glenda Jackson and Robert Hardy. After a fire in 1750 that raged for three days, the castle, as the literature lyrically puts it, 'was allowed to settle into the role of romantic ruin.' When Priestley came to this ruin in 1933 to smoke 'a pipe or two sitting by the remains of the Keep,' the main attraction was Parisian Follies at the 'ridiculous, terra-cotta music hall' below. But even while Priestley puffed, the then Earl of Dudley was scheming and holding meetings about his new project, and in May 1937, he opened Dudley Zoological Society with exotic animals from across the world. Within eighteen months of opening, it had attracted one million visitors.

Roughly that many people are here today, I reckon. The long tail of the pandemic and a cost of living crisis has made Palma Nova prohibido and Vienna verboten for most mere mortals and so we are seeing a consequent boom in what some people are calling, infuriatingly, a staycation. Let us be forensically clear about this. Going to a five-star hotel on a private Cornish cove is not a staycation. Nor is taking your ten-berth motor cruiser for a summer's boating on the Norfolk Broads. These luxurious holidays are not some dreadful, constrained ordeal. They are, quite simply, not going abroad. A staycation is taking a week off work to clear out the garage, go to the tip, watch old Ealing comedies and then have a barbecue. Part of an authentic staycation may entail going for days out. And that is what these working-class people here in Dudley Zoo are doing. They are having 'a day out'. All one million of them. Every picnic table is full and some have brought parasols and portable gazebos. One family unwraps parathas and pakoras, prising the lids from Tupperwares of dahl and raita and tamarind chutney. Nearby a woman drinks a plastic glass of vivid orange lager as she thoughtfully assesses one of Earth's sole remaining Sumatran tigers, languidly eyeing her from a raised platform in Dudley.

As with all zoos, I spend a great deal of time peering through smudgy glass into the sepulchral gloom of a straw-strewn pen wondering whether that thing over there is a log or a tapir. But I have not come for the wildlife but for the radical zoo architecture. The same year that JBP came to Dudley, a young émigré artist was headed to London from the Georgian capital Tbilisi. Priestley never met Berthold Lubetkin, as far as I know, but, modernists, experimentalists and socialists both, I think they'd have got along splendidly. Lubetkin was the founder and leading light of the architectural practice Tecton, whose dazzling work introduced Britain to the Modern Movement. Their first stunning hit was the landmark buildings of London Zoo in 1932. In 1938, Finsbury's Labour council, major patrons of Tecton, commissioned Finsbury Health Centre, embodying Lubetkin's modernism credo that stated 'nothing is too good for ordinary people.' Sadly, Tecton's plans to replace Finsbury's slums with radical social housing were halted by the onset of war in 1939. But in between times the far-sighted burghers of Dudley asked Tecton to build their new zoo, a symphony in reinforced concrete, the zoo as a microcosm of a well-ordered society: safe, harmonic, pleasing.

In the words of Jean Genet, I really like animals, I just don't like people who like animals. A zoo is not my ideal day out. But Dudley Zoo is, because of those radical modernist Tectons and their daring new futuristic designs. The dozen or so elegant buildings, six animal enclosures, entrance, cafés, restaurant and kiosks, had dwindled into various states of dilapidation. But a million-pound restoration programme funded by the Heritage Lottery Fund, and the hard work of Dudley College students and the Twentieth Century Society saw the restoration of many of the original structures. The Bear Ravine and the Zoo entrance are truly fabulous again, the former a concrete canyon, the latter a wave of sky-blue canopies. The restored shop now houses an exhibition for Tecton heads and the Safario café is back in business. The young woman at the kiosk's level of engagement with the practice of food retail suggests she'll never give Rick Stein any sleepless nights but then, like everyone else, I should have come prepared with a whole roast chicken, a gallon of Vimto and a hammock.

But if you really want to experience what the Black Country was like when Priestley came, there's an even better reason to visit Dudley, and it's very near. The twenty-six acres of the Black Country Living Museum is a record of what it was like when, though the region was at the peak of its industrial power, poverty stalked every street. There are streets, canals, workshops, large industrial and public buildings, shops and houses, all recreating the authentic Black Country of decades gone by. It is a wonderful, enlightening, chastening place.

Let's stop here for a moment by the handsome red brick Workers' Institute. In 1910 the National Federation of Women Workers of Cradley, led by Mary McArthur, went on strike in support of those being forced to work for less than minimum wage. Support was high and donations poured in. By 22 October, the women chain makers of Cradley had won and all the employers had agreed to pay new higher rates, a huge victory for the British labour movement. There was a surplus of £1,500 in the fund and McArthur proposed that it should be used to build a centre for workers' education and leisure in Cradley. In 2004, when this beautiful arts and crafts building was threatened with demolition, the Black Country Museum moved it brick by brick to where I sit now, raising a pork pie from the excellent café in silent tribute.

At the schoolhouse I do a class in 'writing and sums'. The 'teacher' tells us that in the period it is set in, circa 1912, most children would go to school for just two hours a day because of the need to work in the factories. A woman with vermillion hair is enjoying hugely the discomfiture of Dwayne, her paramour I assume, who apparently was late for class because he was spotted by teacher buying sweets. 'Oh, he loves sweets!' shrieks Vermillion Haired Lady, entering into the spirit of things enthusiastically. Dwayne is dragged out of the class and after what was patently a show trial, is sentenced to the cane. 'Hand or bum?' asks teacher with disconcerting relish and so, like *News of the World* reporters back in the day, I made my excuses and left.

Outside the cottages on Station Row, a woman in a bonnet is collecting for the Titanic Relief Fund (the chains for the doomed ship were made in Netherton). In one tiny 'one up, one down' cottage lived, according to the 1911 census, eleven children, two parents and a lodger. Yes, they took in a lodger. It is quiet now, obviously, but then it must have been a maelstrom of noise and chaos and tears and laughter; a harder life than I can possibly imagine. Down at Anchor Forge, Steve is making chains in real time. It's sort of fascinating but never going to challenge the Premier League as a mass spectator sport I fear. 'Don't go,' he says forlornly when he spots me slinking away. I feel bad, but time is pressing. There is still a decent crowd anyway, and as I leave, I hear Steve tell one of them 'I've got a forge at home,' in the same way you might tell someone you had a gas barbecue.

I love this place so much with its passionate, rigorous, dedicated commitment to the lives of ordinary people that I could spend most of the rest of this book delineating and extoling its virtues. Just go. You won't regret it. Get some chips at Hodges done in beef dripping and call in at the Bottle and Glass Inn. I once saw a man here ask for a burger and a coke for his daughter to be told gently but firmly that Coca-Cola didn't come to England till the 1920s and burgers not till the 50s. 'She can have a cheese cob and a sarsaparilla,' he was told, and she did, demolishing both with gusto.

Naturally, as enigmatic 'activist' spray painter Bansky once opined, you 'exit through the gift shop'. This perfectly reasonable sales tactic seems to have annoyed Banksy and his ilk, being viewed in some way indicative of the rapacious shallowness of 'the man'. I don't really mind. I like gift shops. In this one I picked up a bottle of Black Country charcoal gin. 'It goes red when you add tonic,' I was assured – and it did. But this was but a diversion from the main stock-in-trade of the shop.

Up until quite recently, the Midlands on TV meant a scant few hugely unglamorous, decidedly unsexy shows. Two of them, *Crossroads* (suburban motel proto-*Dallas* soap opera) and *The Grimleys* (cartoonish period piece comedy) were set in an eternal conceptual seventies gulag of terrible acting, sets and plotlines, the difference being that the latter could claim this was irony. Then, in 2013, came a TV show that would not only make Brum and the Black Country emphatically cool but entirely change the way great cohorts of British manhood would dress at weddings and on trips to the races.

Because I spend my rare hours of leisure reading slim volumes of challenging modern verse while listening to Bartók's astringent string quartets, I have never seen *Peaky Blinders*. But I am aware of its popularity and aesthetic impact. Blinders, as I'm sure its devotees call it, is a fictionalised, violent crime drama created by Brummie Steven Knight and loosely based on the exploits of real Birmingham razor gangs and gangster families in the late nineteenth and early twentieth centuries. Stylishly filmed and soundtracked by some anachronistically groovy alternative rock, it has been a huge global success, making the once mocked Birmingham accent trendy and introducing a whole 'dressy' look for young (and not so young) males going out on a spree: peaked newsboy caps; tweed three-piece suits; short, tapered trousers; and, for those going for real verisimilitude, razor blades concealed in cap band.* Dressed thusly perhaps, you can now try a Peaky Blinders escape room, or read Peaky Blinders books while drinking from a Peaky Blinders mug resting on a Peaky Blinders scatter cushion. Creator Steven Knight admits to being irritated by the money being made from unlicensed merchandise but oddly says that 'it wouldn't

---

* If you want to see 500 blokes dressed this way, hang around New Street station Grand Central concourse on the first day of the Cheltenham Festival.

be a very Peaky Blinders thing to do, to close them all down.' Surely it would, and as ruthlessly and bloodily as possible?

The Black Country Living Museum gift shop was crammed with 'merch' anyway (all fully licensed I'm sure) and with some justification as much of the series was filmed here on the cobbled streets and canal tunnels of the museum. Priestley wouldn't have approved of the glorification of gangsters, since the real Peaky Blinders were not revolutionaries but thugs who terrorised the poor. But he was after all a jobbing hack with a strong nose for a good saleable story, so I think he'd probably wish he'd thought of it.

Before I left the region, I wanted to see a place, the only place in his travels, that Priestley gave a fictional name – and a famous one. 'Rusty Lane', as he called it, inspired the most impassioned section of *English Journey*. 'I have never seen such a picture of grimy desolation as that street offered me. If you put it, brick for brick, into a novel, people would not accept it, would condemn you as a caricaturist and talk about Dickens. The whole neighbourhood is mean and squalid, but this particular street seemed the worst of all. It would not matter very much – though it would matter – if only metal were kept there; but it happens that people live there, children are born there and grow up there. I saw some of them … They need not have run away from me, because I could not blame them if they threw stones and smashed every pane of glass for miles. Nobody can blame them if they grow up to smash everything that can be smashed. There ought to be no more of those lunches and dinners, at which political and financial and industrial 'gentleman' congratulate one another, until something is done about Rusty Lane and West Bromwich.'

I suppose something has been done. What has been done is that Grice Street and Spon Lane, the streets that he conflated into 'Rusty Lane' no longer have people living there. There is one house here now and it would have been quite a nice one, had it not been in the same squalid mess of industry that has been there since Priestley came. No one would want to live here, among this tangle of razor wire and cars with ripped-out engines and corrugated iron and rusty skips. And no one does. But at least this place is still working. It hummed with diggers and clanked with crushers and rattled with scooped aggregate and paid a wage that might be spent on one's family in one of the brilliant desi pubs that symbolise West Brom and the new Black Country. Pubs like The Vine, The Red Cow and The Soho Tavern; old-school working men's boozers now family drinking and eating haunts hosting huge tandoors and grills, serving great beer and stunning Indian food to the whole community, mostly in the hinterland of West Brom on streets with tight little row of terraces, cars parked bumper to bumper, union flags and Sikh Khanda, satellite dishes tilted to catch the last of the evening sun.

5

TO LEICESTER AND NOTTINGHAM

In which I walk the New Walk and England's most
diverse street, head for Meadow Lane and refuse
to mourn the passing of 'Hooters'.

Viewed from Highgate or Halifax, the English Midlands are our
own miniature version of what Brooklyn and Cupertino dismiss as
America's 'flyover states'. They are an English Iowa, a comfy
Kansas, a skein of sclerotic motorway junctions that lead to
baffling ring roads and then to underachieving football clubs,
comedic accents and huge strip-lit Ikeas. This, at least, is the long
practised, sneer of a largely southern media. To be fair, Midlanders
like it this way because it leaves them to their busy, happy lives in
fine cities and sturdy market towns; lives lived in peace and prosperity while London becomes unaffordable and Cornwall chokes
with traffic and second homes.

Here, the schism is not North/South, but East/West. The West
and the East Midlands are, as the solid folk hereabouts know, as
different and distinct as Stilton and Balti; as Spaghetti Junction and

Sherwood Forest; as Alton Towers and the National Space Centre. They have their own accents, their own culture, their own landscapes. But where does one end and the other begin? Where does bap become cob and bab become duck? Somewhere within sniffing distance of the breweries of Burton or the monkey house at Twycross Zoo, I'd suggest. Somewhere around the sleepy pubs and village greens of Sheepy Magna and Ratcliffe Culey, the plump midriff and dark heart of England.

Somewhere around here nasal Brummie and coarse Black Country softens to a blander, more even tone. The late Mark Fisher, austere modernist thinker and native of Leicestershire, wrote in *The Wire* that 'lacking any urban glamour, lilting lyricism or rustic romanticism, the East Midlands accent is one of the most unloved in England. It is heard so rarely in popular media that it isn't recognised enough even to be disdained.' One local linguist Matthew McVeagh, posting online, adds: 'Unlike other dialect regions there is no major distinct urban accent, in the manner of Scouse, Cockney, Brummie etc. Instead, the accents of the bigger cities like Nottingham and Leicester are just continuations of the rural ones around.' There seems truth in this. There's more of a country burr in Nottingham, Derby or Leicester speech than you hear in Manchester, Newcastle or Liverpool. In the local vernacular Leicester comes over as 'Lestoh'. The people are known as 'Chisits' for their habit of wandering around the Market saying, 'I'm A Chisit, I'm A Chisit' (say it aloud). That market by the way is in the city centre or 'Tahn', not to be confused with 'Tarn' which is Barnsley. I hope you're writing this down.

If you've read your Wikipedia, you'll know that Leicester is one of England's oldest cities with a rich history stretching back a couple of thousand years. If you've played the brilliant Valhalla edition of the Assassin's Creed franchise and piloted your longship around this section of Anglo-Saxon England, you'll also be aware that it was once known as Ledecestre and was an important Mercian settlement on the River Soar. If you've read your Geoffrey of Monmouth, an early historian who like Prince and Madonna was cool enough to be known by just his first name, you'll know that around 1136, a King called Leir ruled here with a daughter called Cordelia, a tale to inspire neighbouring West Midlands writer William Shakespeare. And if you've read *English Journey*, you'll know that Priestley, once again, entered this new city in a lugubrious frame of mind. 'The town seems to have no atmosphere of its own. I felt I was quite ready to praise it, but was glad to think I did not live in it. There are many worse places I would rather live in. It seemed to me to lack character, to be busy and cheerful and industrial and built of red brick and to be nothing else. Such was my immediate impression.'

He'd been before, actually, convalescing here after injuries sustained at the front in the First World War. Perhaps that was why has was less than upbeat and vivacious on his return. And I too had been to Leicester a couple of times. The first time, I'd visited a health retreat with Carl, the singer in Britpop footsoldiers Cud, for a humorous feature for the now defunct *NME*. We played tennis and stayed up drinking booze smuggled in by a couple of female legal secretaries from Coalville. Then, in 2016, I stayed in both Leicester and Nottingham on my retracing of the Jarrow march.

Despite this rich prior experience, I seek advice at the Tourist Information Centre. The lovely and helpful Samantha tells me that there is in fact so much to do in Leicester that 'people who come to the city for just one thing, say the football or Richard, wish they had a week.'* Richard is Richard III, the infamous King of England who perished at the Battle of Bosworth and whose remains were found under a car park in 2012. He is now the 'star' of a terrific new exhibition centre. But I've been before so I follow Samantha's advice to 'Start at the Clock Tower. Take a stroll up New Walk. Go

---

* This prompts me to think of a brilliant new tourist slogan: 'Leicester is More!' You're welcome to it, Leicester.

and eat on the Golden Mile. Look at the German expressionists in the Art Gallery.'

Every town has the places people use to meet, to navigate by, worn into the built landscape by love and use like the shine on an old chair arm. This is where friends collect to begin an evening's revels or anxious courting couples arrange to start a date, awkward in best clothes, checking watches or phones, fearful of being 'stood up' or even 'ghosted'. Here, generations of 'Chisits' have congregated by the Clock Tower. You can't miss it. Built on the site of the town's former haymarket in 1868, it has the glamourous distinction of being Britain's first traffic island. I sit and rotate my map, checking the biro points Samantha made for me. I think of famous Leicester folk who may have passed this way. Among them, perhaps, murdered experimental gay playwright Joe Orton and primitivist glam rock teddy boy recidivists Showaddywaddy. Did they ever meet here, Joe in either the distressingly tight 'budgie smugglers' or those jeans with the stupidly massive turn ups he sports in his most famous photoshoots, Showaddywaddy in their eccentrically coloured drape jackets, enormous crepe-soled brothel creepers and quasi-Tudorbethan helmets of hair? I'd like to think so.*

No one could accuse Leicester of being coy about its past. Signage and information boards sprout and proliferate like chickweed, advertising various trails, routes and stories in and out of the city – Roman Leicester, Richard III's Leicester, Thomas Cook's Leicester, Edwina Osborne's Leicester – each colour-coded and carefully mapped. I plan a vaguely circuitous route taking me to the places I want to see, starting off at the Market. Some 800 years old, it claims to be the largest covered market in Europe. But then so does La Ribero in Bilbao and the Kirkgate in Leeds. Down the years, many meetings, demos and passionate speeches have been delivered here

---

* I'm aware Joe met his untimely end some six years before Showaddywaddy came to national prominence on *New Faces*, but I'm sure they'd have hit it off.

by orators and activists like the Suffragettes Emily Pankhurst and Alice Hawkins, whose statue stands nearby. Future England football hero Gary Lineker once worked on his dad's fruit and veg stall here as a lad.

Priestley came here too but was unmoved: 'Though it was doing good business in everything from tablecloths to cough mixtures, it was not amusing. Indeed, I found nothing amusing in these streets.' Tough crowd. I, on the other hand, found much to amuse, at least if you like your humour broad. 'Look at the size of my melons, missus!' bellowed a portly fruiterer, unsubtly, to his audience of two women in headscarves. They forced the weary smiles of those who have heard this several thousand times before, but nevertheless fiddle in their purses and come away cradling a couple of said melons. At the next stall, the trader is having to work with less innuendo-friendly produce. 'Strawberries. Pound a Punnet,' he mutters rotely to no one in particular. Though only just lunchtime, the market seemed to be finishing up, as has every market I have ever fetched up at. There was an overwhelmingly briny smell of fish in the air – perplexingly so, as the Fish Market was now a bank.

The Lanes area around the cathedral is much pleasanter. In the tiny, cobbled ginnels of St Martins East and West you can almost hear the clattering of carts pushed by ruddied men in smocks and smell the horses and their doings and hear the cries of hosiers and silversmiths who worked this patch. At the end of a lane, incongruously, is Leicester Simulations where, for a fee, you can pretend to be taking part in a Battle of Britain dogfight in a Spitfire. A Vegan café offers, in a sparky tone that suggests I should be both surprised and grateful, a bowl of rice for £12.

As I walk up Bowling Green Street to the Pork Pie Chapel (so named for its shape not avant-garde communion fare) I ask myself again 'When did every corner of England start to reek of dope?' Is it just more acceptable and so smoked more openly by more people? Is there a stronger, far more aromatic strain being imported?

Whatever the reason, I am always surprised at its popularity among teenagers, a grouping whose natural state, let's face it, is one of intense, studied lassitude already. I clear the fug and head for New Walk, which looked intriguing on the map and is even better in reality: a tree-lined avenue that's a rare example outside London of a Georgian promenade. Promenading – from the French se promener, to go for a walk – became a fashionable activity among Georgian high society as a means to show off their clobber and cop off. By the end of the eighteenth century, there were hundreds of these promenades in the capital but fewer elsewhere, possibly because folk in the 'provinces' had work to do. Promenades became seaside fixtures in England, but Leicester's is virtually unique in a working provincial city.

Laid out in 1785 and almost a mile long, New Walk was an early example of 'pedestrianisation'. In 1840, one resident described it as 'the only solely respectable street in Leicester.' Ironic, then, that when it declined sharply in the 60s and the grand houses became lodging houses and bedsits, it gained a reputation as a red-light district. Then the short-sighted planning blight that ruined much of Leicester and Nottingham meant that the antique stuff was demolished and brutalist concrete office blocks erected in its place, of which one remains: the IBM building. I'm partial to a touch of brutalism as you know, but here it looks grimly out of place. Happily, the tide turned at the end of the 60s when the city woke up to what a treasure it had here. It has been a Conservation Area since 1969, with many signs reminding you that 'New Walk has been a traffic-free promenade for over 200 years. Please respect its unique character.' This is no civic froth. Strolling amiably under its cooling, green canopy of rowan and silver birch, my first thought was 'I could be in Paris.' But this was fatuous. Apart from Debussy, Ravel and Poulenc, I've never been much of a Francophile. So, better to say next time I'm on the Champs Élysées, 'I could be in Leicester.'

As a modern-art-mad teenager, cruelly without any talent of my own, my favourites were the German Expressionists: haunted individuals with gaunt stares and asymmetric beards whose work's intense psychic ferment was absolute catnip to a pretentious seventeen-year-old. Leicester Art Gallery, halfway up New Walk, houses one of the best collections of such work outside Germany. The paintings of artists like Karl Schmitt Rotluff, a man so severe and angst-ridden he makes Edward Munch look like Alan Carr, were considered degenerate by the Nazis and many were saved by the farsighted curators of Leicester. Looking at these anguished brilliant works, I remember that, though Priestley was a gifted amateur watercolourist himself, he never visits a gallery in *English Journey*. Nor does he mention the rise of Nazism, which was gaining grim pace as he strolled the streets of Leicester. There's one brief mention of a Black Shirt meeting in Bristol, which he scoffs at. But perhaps no one in England fully grasped the darkness gathering in Munich, even as the Reichstag burned. By the autumn of Priestley's English Journey, Germany would be in the hands of the Nazis and refugees were beginning to make their anxious way to England. Over the next century, the people of many lands would make their way to English cities for all kinds of reasons. Thousands would come to Leicester.

2

Local papers don't often make national headlines, but the *Leicester Mercury* of 3 February 2016 became something of a sensation, featuring across national press, television and radio, most notably by Chris Evans on Radio 2's hugely popular breakfast show. Sales of that day's edition leapt by over 2,000 copies and it became a collector's item. The cover showed the flags of twenty-two different nations and the headline 'A WORLD IN ONE STREET' was the 'splash' for a story which began: 'It is said we are a nation of shop-keepers. Today those shopkeepers come from all corners of the globe.' Research from the London School of Economics had revealed that Narborough Road in Leicester was the most diverse and multi-cultural street in Britain. And the tone of Lee Marlow's piece – and the striking design by chief sub-editor Matthew Sulley – is refreshingly different. It's a story about Leicester made by Leicester people, reporting the reality of vibrant life on an extraordinary street in a changed and changing English city. As Dr Suzanne Hall, lead researcher from the LSE, said: 'What we found in Narborough Road was staggering, really, and we didn't interview every owner of every business. There will be more people, from more countries, undoubtedly. What is interesting about Narborough Road is that it's not a Little Italy, it is not Chinatown, it is not Belgrave Road. It is the world in microcosm; all these people, from all these different places, different cultures, living cheek by jowl, working with each other and living in harmony.' Belgrave Road or 'the Golden Mile' is on my itinerary too, but first I must head to south-west Leicester, Narborough Road LE 3, to see 'the world in one street.'

It is Wednesday afternoon. Priestley would have thought me mad to expect to find anything of interest happening at this time of the week, given that was the day that most of England closed for half a day, enforced by the Shops Act of 1912. Given his diatribe against the Americanisation of English culture at the close of *English Journey*, I doubt he would have welcomed our 24-hour lifestyles and all that has come with it: the gig economy, zero hours contracts and twelve-hour shifts. Narborough Street never closes, I imagine, and once on it, I decide to play a little game with myself. I think randomly of a nation and see if I can find a corresponding business. Hungarian? Too easy. A few strides from the Metal Monocle heavy rock pub and past the library I find La Un Pas De Casa, the not-entirely-fitting name for a Polish/Romanian/Hungarian grocers. Peruvian is my next task, but I walk the mile of Narborough Road without finding any Ceviche or Lomo Saltado. I could find pretty much everything else, though: Portuguese pastel de nata; Filipino tea; Lebanese flatbreads; and a Sri Lankan accountant. I am disappointed to find the Tin Drum bookshop closed because the Canadian couple who run it were singled out in the LSE report as significant, as 'anchor immigrants', longstanding residents who help others with paperwork and in return maybe get a free haircut or lunch.

Many of the newer residents of the road come from London, priced out by the gentrification of areas like Bermondsey and Hackney. But gentrification will be a long time coming to Narborough Road. It is rough around the edges and even rougher down its gritty side streets. But it is not threatening, at least not on a sunny Wednesday afternoon. Faisal had come here from Coventry and told me that while he would never use an ATM there at night, he would happily do so in Leicester. 'It's quite a relaxed place. I'm not saying there's no racial tension. But you just don't feel like you do in some places. It feels to me a lot safer than Cov or Brum. I don't think they've had riots here, have they?'

They have, actually, back in 1981 when much of England burned for a while, even leafy Cirencester and placid Shrewsbury. Skinheads were mainly blamed for the violence in Leicester, which was largely confined to the city centre. Since then, the city has been relatively quiet, although it did experience an atypical flash of sectarian unrest involving Hindu and Muslim youths in the late summer of 2022 after an Asia Cup cricket match between India and Pakistan. Before all this, a little light Googling will tell you that Leicester's most high-profile civic disturbance was the Balloon Riot of 1864 in Victoria Park. At the test flight of a new hydrogen balloon an irate mob destroyed and burned said balloon because they didn't think it was the best or biggest aeronaut Henry Coxwell could have come up with. A salutary warning to us all – Leicester is clearly not a city to be fobbed off with second-rate inflatables.

Faisal's a taxi driver. We chat as he takes me from Narborough Road to a street down which Leicester's whole history has travelled. Belgrave Road is as ancient as the city itself, its course roughly following the Fosse Way as it cuts east and north to Newark and Lincoln. After the Industrial Revolution, Leicester got busy and grew prosperous from shoes and socks. Both were made in abundance on Belgrave Road during its early twentieth century boom years. Priestley spent an afternoon at one of the now defunct Wolsey hosiery factories here, then so hectic and noisy he could never have imagined it would ever fall silent. But it has. Its near neighbour on Belgrave Road was British United Shoe Machinery, another colossus that has not survived. The area declined through the 60s and 70s – the machines winding down, the houses falling empty – but the rows of tight terraces that branch off like tributaries from Belgrave Road (many still bearing their stolidly English names of Kensington, Dorset and Doncaster) provided affordable homes for many newcomers from India and Pakistan. Leicester is now home to just short of 88,000 Muslims who comprise roughly 19 per cent of its population and many of them made their way to Belgrave Road, now known to all as the Golden Mile. No one really knows why. Perhaps after the many jewellers' shops here or the wondrous lights of one of the world's liveliest Divali celebrations. But down the years, this has been the traditional cradle and lodestar of Leicester's Asian population. The first came to open a spectacle shop in the 1920s. And, as in Priestley's thirties, many were refugees fleeing the cruelty of a madman.

Explanations differ as to why Idi Amin, unhinged military dictator of seventies Uganda, chose to summarily expel thousands of Asians from his country in August 1972. Former 'insiders' say he acted on a dream in which Allah ordered him to do it. Others claim he fell in love with a married Indian woman whose family's (entirely understandable) rejection saw him turn on the Asian community in spiteful rage. Whatever the reason, within ninety days of his curt, callous diktat, some 27,000 Ugandan Asians came to Britain. And one particular family achieved enduring local celebrity.

Like other suddenly and summarily displaced Asian families, the Lakhanis arrived on Belgrave Road with £50 and a single suitcase. Their property and business had been seized by Amin. After an unsuccessful venture in groceries, disheartened by shoplifters, they decided to open a restaurant offering a taste of home to the disoriented new residents. This is how one of the most celebrated vegetarian curry houses in Britain was born in 1976: Bobby's.

When Enna Lakhani brings me my mango lassi, I ask which member of the family was Bobby. She laughs. 'There is no Bobby. That's Bobby,' she points, indicating a handsome young man in a grainy film poster, one of several around the restaurant. He is Rishi Kapoor, son of the director Raj and the film is *Bobby*, a boy-meets-girl story that was one of the biggest Bollywood films of 1973. Enna's mother and father-in-law, Bhagwanji and Mangla, named it after their favourite date movie. Forty-odd years on, Bhagwanji and Mangla are no longer with us, but their restaurant has become properly legendary. My timeline has been filled with stern injunctions that to eat anywhere else would be criminal, many specifying the delicacies that I must try. In the end I plump for the chana batura, a thick chickpea curry with light puffed bread, a potato and onion dosa the size and shape of a cricket bat, with a crisp and spicy cabbage salad. It's astonishingly good. When I tell Enna that I'm here because I'm writing a book, she smiles again, a little shyly and tells me she's written one as well. As I leave, she fetches and signs for me a copy of *Cook With Love*, a lockdown project that collects most of Bobby's favourites between hard covers. I seem to have ended up with two of them, the chana and sambar, all down my shirt. This is embarrassing as I have one more date in Leicester if I am to follow properly in Priestley's footsteps, and it is an experience we associate with James Bond and tuxedos, not Wiganers with ochreous curry stains down their anorak.

On the surface, with his stolid appearance and bluff humour, his everyman common sense and orotund Yorkshire delivery, Priestley seems more pie, pint and pipe than pina colada. But, like many northerners made good, he enjoyed what are sometimes called 'the finer things in life.' As noted, much of his English Journey was experienced from the upholstered leather rear seat of a chauffeured Daimler. He spent his last quarter century at Kissing Tree House near Stratford-upon-Avon, a splendid Georgian manor. In Lord Snowdon's portrait of him in satisfied late middle age, he sports a fedora with a raffish silk band. It is perfectly in character and perfectly reasonable that he should fancy something a little fancier than a gill of mild on his evening in Leicester.

In the basement of his hotel he found 'a cocktail bar complete with white-coated barmen, salted almonds, and pricelists shaped like cocktail shakers. There was quite brisk demand for cocktails, mostly double ones too, while I was there, and not from guests in the hotel but mostly, I imagine, from young businessmen and their wives and girl friends. I have noticed before that the more dashing persons of both sexes in provincial towns have a passion for cocktails and seemed to be ready to drink them at any time. The cocktail is no longer an *apéritif*, which is what it was designed to be, but a drink for all hours. The taverns offer you cocktails in bottles of all sizes. Perhaps very soon, as the wave of fashion slowly travels outward and enlarges itself, all the landlords of country alehouses and the farmers will be hard at it rattling cocktail shakers and adding dashes of absinthe and spearing olives.'

I have a complicated relationship with the cocktail. As someone who prefers the strong adult taste of a good single malt or decent gin to some sugary carbonated water, I'm not crazy about spending a tenner plus on what is essentially a kid's drink. I invariably panic and end up with something teeth-achingly sweet or repulsively creamy served in a glass Liberace would reject as 'too flamboyant'. Anyway, my initial surmise had been that cocktails would have been a new-fangled trend in the early 30s, but seemingly not. The first British cocktail recipe book, William Terrington's *Cooling Cups and Dainty Drinks*, dates to 1869 and 'American Bars' serving fancy drinks were common in London in the early twentieth century, inspired by the work of the Savoy's celebrity bartender Ada Coleman. So, by the time Priestley fetched up on a Leicester bar stool, even the most entrenched mild and bitter man would have known what a cocktail was, if not exactly au fait with the composition of a Sex on the Beach.

My next stop is St George's Cultural Quarter, to give it its Sunday name, which occupies the eastern district of the city centre and was formerly the shoe and textile quarter. My chosen cocktail bar, Manhattan 34, is just off Orton Square and takes its name, or rather number, from the year prohibition ended. The Manhattan bit is presumably just a bit of clichéd glamour by association. Presumably it was felt Coalville 34 had less cachet. Priestley's cocktail bar had a menu in the shape of a cocktail shaker; this one has a chalkboard list of twelve or so bourbons including one at £23 a measure. 'Please ask for our full bourbon menu,' it says at the foot of the chalkboard. Can there be any more bourbons? Really?

The bar is staffed by two young guys in Hawaiian shirts, pony tails and impractical waxed moustaches. They're a little taciturn, perhaps because a middle-aged man in a curry-stained Helly Hansen kagoule and trainers isn't the kind of dazzling beau monde clientele they're courting. But the dude doing the 'mixology' (a phrase that makes me wish for the swift extinction of humanity) does make me a fabulous Old Fashioned. 'Do you want it smoked?' he asks, confusingly. I reply 'yes' (of course) so he scatters a few tiny woodchips into a sort of pine teastrainer and places it on top of my glass. Then he gives it a good old blast of blowtorch and pops a lid on. 'Give it a couple of minutes,' he says. When he motions for me to 'enjoy', I remove the lid and little fronds of aromatic woodsmoke curl up from the chilly bourbon interior. It feels like drinking bonfire night. Pleasure courses through my cortexes. It cost £12 and was gone in three delicious mouthfuls but, hey, it was a whole lot more fun than a bowl of rice.

3

No Olympics. No Premier League. No Wimbledon. No Proms. No Glastonbury. No Eurovision. No Edinburgh Festival. No Grand National. No Glyndebourne. No Booker Prize. The Pandemic suspended British cultural and sporting life utterly and completely and in a way that would have seemed unthinkable and terrifying just a week or two before. In Nottingham, the most high-profile casualty was the Goose Fair: the boozy, raucous, vinegar-reeking, music-pounding, kids-screaming, lights-pulsing fulcrum of the city's year. For only the third time in seven centuries (the Second World War and Bubonic plague being the other two hiccups) and for two years running, the fair was cancelled, much to public dismay. I couldn't follow exactly in the footsteps of Priestley here, then, as he made quite a thing of his visit to the Goose Fair. Back then, every-one still got a half day's holiday for the event and he enjoyed his visit, despite the paucity of actual fowl being traded. He did have a ride, though, in 'the tail of a ruby and emerald fish which, after I had paid it threepence, rushed up and down and round and round, and mixed the whole fair into a spangled porridge.' Next he went on the ghost train – disappointing again – and then watched a patently rigged boxing match. After that he got bored and walked up a hill so he could look down on the fair and do some ruminating with a fag on this 'crushing mass of gaping and sweating humanity … contrived to attract the largest number of pennies in the shortest possible time.'

Put like that, it sounds like fun. I'd have to find other things to do in Nottingham, though. According to Priestley that wouldn't be hard as 'the city has always had a name for enjoying itself. Among provincial towns it has always passed for the most frivolous.' Now I don't think I would ever call Nottingham frivolous. Hedonistic, maybe. But it's a tough-minded kind of epicureanism, laboriously won at the Raleigh factory or the Boots store – a Friday night and Saturday morning that are paid for by hard graft through a long working week.

Some places have a kind of aesthetic, a look of their own. Whitby and Leeds have their black clad goths. Brighton has its dreadlocked unicyclists. Nottingham has mods, soul boys, casuals, call them what you will. It's a highly distinctive East Midlands look and usually a male one. You don't have to walk very far to see him: a chap of a certain age with crisp jeans, a smart retro zip-up jacket or a Harrington, a Fred Perry, some impeccably buffed loafers or a pair of vintage Adidas Beckenbauers. A certain brand of stylised masculinity – tough, funny, working class, smart in all senses – finds a spiritual home here, from Arthur Seaton to Paul Smith, two famous sons of the city.

Priestley had more to say about Nottingham's young women though. While he didn't think that they were 'any better-looking than young women elsewhere', rather ungallantly, he did seem to like the cut of their jib and their freewheeling spirit. 'Rumour had it that the place was rich with pretty girls who were anything but prudes. There were goings-on in Nottingham … The truth is, I suppose, that in the old days the enormous numbers of girls employed in the lace trade were more independent and fonder of pleasure than most provincial young women; and so the legend began … They seem to accompany their young men into all the pubs, but I am not prepared to accept that as a mark of easy virtue. There are a great many pubs in the place … but that does not necessarily indicate an orgiastic life.'

Nottingham is still a great city for pubs. On my short stomp from the railway station to my hotel I pass a score of inviting ones that I file mentally for future reference, beginning with a little crowded craft bar in the station itself. Nottingham once had five other railway stations, back in the days when public transport was, idealistically, run for the public good and not for private profit. Of course, no one of a certain age ever buys a return to Nottingham without thinking of Peter Cleall's superb and affecting performance as the congested commuter in the immortal Tunes TV advert. I think of him and his breathing difficulties as I make the grim carbon monoxide-wreathed trudge up Maid Marian Way. Much loathed, this is the horrible 60s thoroughfare for which much of the city's medieval centre was demolished, including the sweetly-named, long-bulldozed Jessamine Cottages and Gilliflower Hill. Dubbed 'Europe's ugliest street' by the city's own professor of architecture, it's surely a terrible slur on the legendarily cute Maid Marian to suggest any kind of kinship here. The street was not built without some controversy, but apparently hardly any Nottingham folk bothered to get out and vote against it when they were offered a chance. When you consider the city's proud and pugnacious record of riot, insurrection and arson down the centuries, from Luddite to Chartist to Robin Hood's radical Marxism, this is really most unlike them.

Taking a lead as ever from Priestley, tomorrow is my football day. Tonight, I am off to experience a different kind of performance he loved: the theatre. With any revolution, there will always be unjust, unfortunate casualties. When dramatists like Harold Pinter, John Osborne and Edward Bond revivified British theatre in the late 50s and early 60s, sweeping away the drawing room niceties of Terence Rattigan in favour of a more visceral or abstract framing of life, Priestley's plays also fell from favour. They were, predictably but quite wrongly, characterised as bumptious northern whimsy when they were often, as in *Time and the Conways* and *Dangerous Corner*, daring meditations on time, chance and fate or, as in *An Inspector Calls*, powerful attacks on elitism and hypocrisy. It was Stephen Daldry's magnificent mid-90s revival of the last, an intense expressionist reworking that ended with the comfortable bourgeois home literally in ruins, that prompted a renaissance and a re-evaluation. Since then, productions have boomed and even his lesser-known works have been revived with acclaim.

When the Nottingham Playhouse opened in December 1963 with an inaugural production of *Coriolanus* featuring a young Ian McKellen in a minor role, it was the largest recipient of a regional arts grant ever, courtesy of one Harold Wilson and his newly-created minister for the arts. It soon became a powerhouse of civic theatre, a seedbed for new talent and a beloved fixture of the city. When I notice what is playing today, the coincidence is just too pleasing and apposite to ignore. It is the opening night of a new play by Caroline Bird called *Red Ellen*, about the brilliant, passionate and complex Ellen Wilkinson, that diminutive titan of the Labour movement. She was minister for education in Attlee's extraordinary post-war government but, more pertinently for me, the MP for Jarrow who led the men in that famous 'crusade' to London in 1936. The last time I was in Nottingham I was retracing that march for my *Long Road To Jarrow*. And so, delighted by the symmetry, I buy a ticket.

Beforehand, I pop into a couple of Nottingham's storied pubs, at least two of which claim to be the oldest pub in the city, if not England. Ye Olde Trip to Jerusalem makes this bold claim in two-foot-high emulsion all over the pub's exterior. On my last visit I had a diverting night drinking in the caves – yes, caves – playing a game which involves hooking a ring on a spike on the wall. This time, I thought I'd try The Bell on Angel Row, standing on the site of the old Carmelite priory and perhaps established by the lads themselves after a hard day illustrating manuscripts. Like most of Nottingham, it has a connection with argy bargy. On Goose Fair night 1831, rioters protesting the defeat of The Reform Act had a swift half here before going on to burn down several prominent bits of local architecture, including the Castle. No one here is in that kind of mood tonight. The pub is somnolent. A couple of students flirt sweetly but most are vacantly watching Champions League football on the big telly.

The play turns out to be an excellent, if understandably melodramatic, version of Wilkinson's story. Sitting in the stalls on a spring evening in 2022, though, it is hard to ignore the eerie parallels here. In the early scenes, Ellen is trying to convince the government to do more to prevent the rise of fascism in Europe as bombs fall on innocent women and children in Guernica. As we watch, the same thing is happening in Ukraine's Black Sea port of Mariupol. The appeasers and useful idiots Orwell and Priestley scorned still ply their trade, on the left and the right.

4

Ibuprofen, HP Sauce, the Raleigh Chopper, Tarmac, the VCR, traffic lights, shin pads, the prototype for the Harrier Jump Jet. Now that's a shopping list. Actually, as you'll have guessed, these are just a few of the things Nottingham has given the world, quite apart from D H Lawrence, Alan Sillitoe, Robin Hood, Torville and Dean, Boots the chemist and the Salvation Army. But its world fame rests, or rested at least, on the making of lace. In 1589, an enterprising cove named William Lee of Calverton, Nottinghamshire invented the knitting frame which for more than a century produced hose for the fashionable folk of the East Midlands. But fashions change. By the turn of the nineteenth century hose – all in one tights covering the whole lower body, generally combined with a codpiece – had unsurprisingly fallen from fashion. It has yet to make a comeback, despite the efforts of Max Wall and the front members of agricultural tramp rockers Jethro Tull.

The demise of hose prompted inventive types in Nottingham to switch to making lace on these machines. A remarkable new industry grew up based in the oldest part of the city, the former Saxon settlement that now became the Lace Market. At its peak of trade, Nottingham was the world's lace-making capital, exporting to France, Germany, the United States, South America, Spain, Egypt and India. The global fame and reach of Nottingham and its lace can be seen from the fact that between 1850 and 1950, the city boasted foreign consulates and ambassadors from the United States of America, Germany, Norway, Chile, Argentina, Spain, Costa Rica, Venezuela, France, Colombia, Salvador, Uruguay, Nicaragua, Cuba and Dominica.

Only a lucky few grew rich on this fine fabric, though. For the workers, the vast majority of whom were female, conditions were harsh and the hours long. The knitting rooms were scorchingly hot, disease was rife and tuberculosis and strained eyes just two of the occupational hazards. Standard warehouse hours were 8am to 8pm, six days a week, but workers would be expected to stay till midnight in busy periods and even take work home with them. Prams filled with lace were wheeled through the streets going to and from the warehouses all night long. Every member of the family, from children to elderly grandparents, would be engaged in the manufacture, the spectre of the workhouse always haunting the lives of the industrial working classes.

Now the frames are quiet and, as in Bradford's Little Germany, the quiet tapping of laptop keys is the sound of the Lace Market today. Like Little Germany, the bustle of commerce has gone. But the architecture, largely the work of the celebrated Watson Fothergill, is fine and compact and a gravity and classiness remain here, like an elegantly ageing movie legend or great statesman in their autumn. The old warehouses and knitting rooms, once places of heat and dirt and noise now purr with air-conditioned calm, become luxury apartments or the stylish offices of PR and design consultancies. The Georgian townhouses of rich merchants like the Sherwins, which fell into disrepair with the decline of the lace trade, are now superbly restored. One of them is a boutique hotel, The Lace Market, 'offering 42 fully equipped, luxurious bedrooms (and) a haven for food and drink lovers.'

Beyond his speculations on the amorous nature of the lace-making girls, Priestley didn't delve much into the manufacturing culture of Nottingham. This was deliberate. 'Having seen Leicester at work, I had come to see Nottingham at play,' was his rationale, so having gorged on the Goose Fair, he decided to experience another of Nottingham's big days out – the football derby between the city's two clubs, Forest and County. This is one of the sport's great rivalries, a clash between the oldest and third oldest football clubs in the world, originally billed as the red-shirted Garibaldis of Forest versus the maroon and mustard-striped Lambs of Notts County, and first played in 1866. No exact repeat of Priestley's day out would be open to me, sadly. Forest and County have not met competitively for a long time, being as they are in different tiers of the English football league. The last league meeting was in 1994, and so the two clubs now look to Derby County and Mansfield Town for more regular fierce local battles. However, when the rare opportunity to express this internal Nottingham rivalry through robust physicality occurs, it is never spurned. In 2007, a 'friendly' match between the clubs saw a mass brawl break out after the final whistle. In 2016 another 'friendly' ended with four arrests.

But here's a thing. The grounds are the closest of any two British football clubs, maybe any two clubs in the world. They literally face each other, just 250 metres apart across the river Trent. So, who supports Forest and who supports County? And why? I found it perplexing and so did Priestley. Some say that traditionally County fans came from the city itself with Forest's support being drawn from surrounding towns and villages. This may chime with the theory that County are the posher team; Forest's fan base often hailing from more working-class satellite towns like Gedling, Ashfield or Calverton. Undoubtedly, Forest fans tend to be younger or, less generously, arriviste glory hunters attracted during the club's golden years under Brian Clough and latterly in the Premier League. As with all these things, it seems a mystery, like FIFA's finances or the ergonomics of Ralph Coates' hair.*

Priestley was terrific on football. His novel *The Good Companions* opens with a swooping descent from the heavens to the Pennines and then to the stream of spectators headed for the Bruddersford United game. There follows a famously lyrical passage: 'To say that these men paid their shillings to watch twenty-two hirelings kick a ball is merely to say that a violin is wood and catgut, that *Hamlet* is so much paper and ink. For a shilling the Bruddersford United AFC offered you Conflict and Art … it turned you into a member of a new community, all brothers together for an hour and a half.'

It is a theme he warms to in *English Journey*. Again, he asserts to those who dismiss the game as trivial and vulgar that it is 'no more a mere matter of other men's boots and a leather ball than a violin concerto is a mere matter of some other man's catgut and rosin.' His conclusion seems eerily prescient and modern. 'Nearly everything possible has been done to spoil this game: the heavy financial interests; the absurd transfer and player selling system; the lack of any birth or residential qualification for the players; the betting and coupon competitions; the absurd publicity given to every feature of it by the Press; the monstrous partisanship of the crowds … but the fact remains that it is not yet spoilt, and it has gone out and conquered the world.' Much of this could have been written in 2023 not 1933.

Priestley had little time for those 'gentlemen' who felt there was something crass about being paid to play sport and that amateurism was the only pure and noble calling. In 1955's *Journey Down a Rainbow*, he compared himself to Yorkshire's opening batsman Herbert Sutcliffe, saying that if he could make a living from enter-

---

* The most structurally spectacular of all the 70s 'combovers'. Check YouTube.

taining people, so should Sutcliffe who, he added modestly, brought joy to far more people than the writer ever would. These were skilled men who should be paid for their skill. 'A footballer of genius maybe worth £100 a week to his club and it seems to me that he has a perfect right to demand and receive that hundred a week. His skill may be superlatively rare and valuable and his football life a very short one. Let him earn what he can.' What he would have made of £100,000 a week we can only guess.

I manage to arrange to watch a match between Notts County and Grimsby Town from the press box, exciting in itself for someone whose childhood was filled reading breathless reports in the 'football pink' sold on street corners at dusk in winter, the ink still wet and the scores still raw, followed next day by the more elegant summations of Glanville and McIlvanney in the Sundays. When I tweet about my excitement, one correspondent, Neil Roberts, hopes I shall write it all up in classic 1930s style: 'The big number nine took no prisoners when leathering the orb into the onion bag' etc.

I have an hour to kill before kick-off and so I walk up Lister Gate to St Peter Gate where a little ecumenical Christian band are playing a song even Bob Dylan would reject as too dreary, the wailing harmonica visibly distressing some passing shoppers. I pop into the Rough Trade shop, a little alternative enclave where a gaggle of pale kids with cerise hair are hanging around by the hardcore and skate punk stuff. There's a little section for the city's own Earache Records, now a rock and blues label but once home to Carcass, Entombed, Lawnmower Deth, Boltthrower and many other combos whose music I found relaxing and diverting. I flip through the Ornette Coleman and Sun Ra imports to bolster my waning cool credentials then go and have sausage and chips next door.

Papers in the bin and back on the streets, I notice a big police presence and a febrile atmosphere. I'd chosen County's match with Grimsby purely for convenience in my itinerary, but it's looking very much like this might be a fixture with 'edge'. I sidle up to a policeman (who looks about thirteen) and ask 'Is this a big game then?' 'Oh yeh,' he replies in that characteristic accent, 'Grimsby have brought their full allocation, 2,500. They're all comin' down from the coast and having a day out in the big city.' I reflect that in a career of a few decades I have never had occasion to visit Grimsby (Priestley bypasses it too) and my knowledge of the Lincolnshire fishing port is based largely on a jaunty song called 'Grimsby' on Elton John's *Caribou* album. For some reason I had a cassette of this as a young teenager though for the life of me I cannot remember or explain buying it, the former Mr Dwight's faux octogenarian Alabama sharecropper's delivery being a little rich for my blood. The lyrics are written by Elton's long standing words wingman Bernie Taupin (from nearby Market Rasen) in which he claims to have 'loved every sluice in your harbour' as well as eulogizing the town's pier, the shingle beach and The Skinners Arms. Research told me though that Grimsby has no beach, no pier and no Skinners Arms. Who cares? Olympus does not rise above the Serengeti, but that doesn't prevent 'Africa' by Toto being a masterpiece.

Undaunted by Taupin's many inaccuracies – the pier and candy floss Elton sings of are surely in nearby Cleethorpes – the 'Mariners' fans are in lusty voice as, like the swans on the Trent, we all glide gently towards Meadow Lane, the Notts County home ground. A tide of black and white scarves comes to meet them from another angle but the atmosphere is more boisterous than nasty and there is nothing to disturb the swans' weekend. Ten past two on a grey chilly February Saturday. Floodlights blazing sodium white in the distance. Rich, warm scent of frying onions from the burger van. *Perfect*.

As expected, the people at the ground are hugely welcoming. A young woman in a portakabin checks my accreditation and hands me a lanyard. If I am mildly disappointed that it isn't a ticket marked 'Press' to put in my hatband, I try not to show it. A fine, straight-backed steward of about seventy in blazer and crest greets me at the foot of the stand with a click of his heels and a brisk salute (I may have imagined this last bit). 'First time at the Lane, sir? Come on. I'll show you round.' He ushers me up some stairs into the Media Lounge. There are a few people already there watching a cup tie between Kidderminster Harriers and West Ham Utd. No one here knows where the Grimsby rivalry started. It's no matter. A nice lady puts the kettle on and makes me a hot Vimto. This is the life, I think, fondling my lanyard.

There is something about the sudden shocking green of a football pitch, especially under floodlights on a Saturday afternoon, that will always thrill. It's a terrific ground, Championship standard at least – County are in the National League, three tiers below this – and nicknamed the San Sirrel, a twist on Milan's magnificent San Siro named for County's stalwart manager Jimmy Sirrel. Local musician Jake Bugg's name is plastered around the touchline hoardings as a sponsor of the club. Other notable supporters include former cabinet minister Kenneth Clarke and mass-murderer Harold Shipman. As is customary at time of writing, just before kick-off, the players all take a knee as a gesture of solidarity with black victims of racism. As is also sadly customary, a vocal contingent of Grimsby supporters jeer this loudly. Their away end is packed and noisy and soon after, more entertainingly, they break into one of their anthems 'Sing When We're Fishing'.

It's a good, skilful match in the opening phase, far better than the lower league status of the teams would suggest. After quarter of an hour, County's Callum Roberts scores a tremendous individual goal. Then, just before the half hour a County defender blunders into a challenge clumsily and gives away a penalty to much head-shaking and despair. The keeper saves to huge cheers from the home supporters, who soon all head off to their half time Bovril in good spirits. Yes, there actually was Bovril and I had one, unable to resist. At the start of the second half, a cold rain comes sheeting in and Grimsby come out fighting, literally. It all gets very ugly and bad tempered, and the tide turns against County. Grimsby eventually come out on top 2–1 after a truculent, unedifying second half and I join a group of disgruntled County supporters in the queue for the burger van at the corner of Meadow Lane. 'It was never a penalty. If we had VAR in this league, it would never have been given,' opines one man in a balaclava, mid-cheeseburger, as the drizzle runs down our necks.

The rain comes down harder and I am becoming sodden and miserable as I walk back into town. Peering out from under my dripping hood, I see the welcoming, warming orange lights of a roadside pub and am almost inside when I realise just what it is. This is a building of some significance, in a crap way, for it is Britain's sole remaining Hooters. Back in the 90s, the heyday of ironic laddishness, of Fat Les and 'ladettes' and the other unspeakable horrors everyone is now sheepish about, there were several of these places in the UK. The original was opened in 1983 in Clearwater, Florida. The USP was simple. It was a 'breastaurant' as the original slogan mirthlessly had it, a place where 'the guys' could let off steam by ogling and harassing young women in demeaning little tops and shorts. These were not classed as waitresses but 'entertainers' in order to circumvent discrimination laws based on age, sex, and physical appearance.

Happily, in a rare outbreak of common sense and good taste in the UK of today, all of them have failed and closed. All but this one, here between the Trent and a multi-storey car park. I'll drink to that. But not at Hooters. I'm not being sanctimonious here. But what pleasure can there be in sitting here shouting with dull blokes you went to school with or have to work alongside, drinking pissy lager and eating a mediocre burger, pretending that the smiling, pouting girl laughing at your double entendres doesn't really want to drive that fork between your eyes, deep into your pineal gland.

But not even this grim antediluvian relic of a former age could make me dislike Nottingham. It is a great city: radical, fun-loving, literary. Besides, it had stopped raining. Yorkshire beckoned. Priestley was headed home. I was going on manoeuvres behind enemy lines.

6

TO THE WEST RIDING

In which I waltz across a Todmorden dancefloor
into 'God's Own County', stand downwind of JBP in
'Bruddersford' and Little Germany, get a Kashmiri
Breakfast, and fall in love, hatless, in Ilkley.

Great cities make great breakfasts, each as distinctive as their skylines, their people, their accents. In Austin, Texas you should try chili omelette with tacos on East Cesar Chavez. In Belfast, order farls and white pudding. In Glasgow, head to Wilson Street for lorne sausage and tattie scones. In Yerevan, you should mop up your green apricot jam with hot lavash bread. And in Bradford, take Lumb Lane and climb steadily out of the busy city, all the time working up an appetite for crispy puris and soft, hot paratha, savoury steaming chana and milky chai. These are the delights of the renowned Kashmiri breakfast at the Sweet Centre, a bland kind of name for a joint that is anything but.

Bradford has its curry houses the way Naples has trattoria, the way Fukuoka has ramen bars. But this one is special. The Sweet

Centre was the first of Bradford's many Indian restaurants and remains in many people's eyes (and mouths) the very best of them all.* It was established half a century ago to provide a rich taste of home and warmth and companionship for the new arrivals from Pakistan and India in the 1960s. Now it's a place of pilgrimage for Bradfordians of every colour, creed and class.

'Here for the football?' asks the young owner, Waqar Mughal, and when I mention Priestley and the book, he is instantly, garrulously helpful. 'My grandfather started this place. It's the oldest in Bradford. And this man will tell you everything.' So, on this crisp autumn Saturday morning I find myself sitting with Mazhar Mughal, a quiet, slim, unassuming man in a little kufi hat and brown suit who has become part of the Sweet Centre's extended family. 'I'm not a professional cook. I just help the chef …' he says to a chorus of protest from the young waiters. In fact, he has baked and kneaded puris and naans and waited tables here for nearly fifty years. 'He has magic hands … No one makes them like him!', says a colleague.

Mazhar tells me the long and fascinating story of the Sweet Centre, opened in December 1964 when the first few immigrants were trickling nervously into Yorkshire from the sub-continent, and when the spiciest thing on a Northern dinner table was the ginger in your parkin. 'When I first came here, very few Indian or Pakistani men cooked. Back home men don't cook ever. So, when they came here to work, there was a big problem with food.' Bradford's rapidly growing Pakistani and Indian population had nowhere to get authentic desserts and savouries like the ones they grew up with and so Waqar's grandfather saw both a problem and an opportunity, plunging his entire life savings into a sweet and savouries shop. The Sweet Centre was an immediate success, first with the Asian commu-

---

* The designation is something of a pre-partition misnomer now. Most 'Indian' restaurants in Britain are actually Bangladeshi.

nity but then among the more adventurous and discerning white Bradfordians.

'At first English people were a bit shy of coming in. They did not know what curry was, or samosa or dahl. There were no menus. And we hadn't got the words to describe what the food was. It was just our food. But slowly as well as the Pakistani people, English people came. We soon had many regulars. Lovely, lovely people.'

'Oh, we have had so many lovely regulars,' says Mazhar. 'So many nice people down the years. Robert Swindells, the children's writer, a very good man. Joe Johnson the snooker player. Chuck Berry. Boy George. He hung round here a bit when he was popular …' he suggests, tantalisingly. If Boy George did make the trip up from North London in his dreads, hat and smock at the height of his fame, I can't say I blame him. The Chana Puri Kashmiri Breakfast is a terrific way to start a day. On a misguided whim though I order not what I should have – i.e what middle class people patronisingly call builders tea which would have suited the food perfectly but Kashmiri Tea which is pink, cloyingly sweet and has things floating in it. Soon, a thick skin forms on the surface and I hope my nice hosts don't notice that I haven't touched it. 'Not too keen on the Chai, I see. Have the PG Tips next time!' Much laughter.

'One gentleman,' Mazhar adds as I take my leave 'would take me to Shipley to play squash. I still speak to him on phone. But he moved away …' Mazhar's voice shrinks to a whisper and his eyes drop to the pakora, he looks up at me with real sadness '… to Lancashire.'

If you are looking for proof of how deeply rooted in this place those first Pakistani families are now, how fully woven are those anxious, tentative men and women into the very warp and weft of this damp textile town, then here it is. Mazhar arrived in Yorkshire aged seventeen with a suitcase of thin, unsuitable clothes and not a word of English. Now he is a Bradfordian so dyed in the wool that he can imagine no stranger or more regrettable thing a man might do than move to Lancashire.

My train came the other way, out of Lancashire and at speed, the way most Yorkshiremen and women would approve. The Northern service from Manchester passes through the debatable lands of the East, as in east of Rochdale where the vowels are soft and rolling as the hills. Rochdale is pure 'Lanky' and Milnrow, Littleborough and Walsden too. But then comes Todmorden, 'the Boundary valley of a man called Totta,' and things get complicated. Here is Northern England's Gdansk/Danzig, its Aachen/Aix-la-Chapelle. 'Tod' sits prettily right on the Lancashire–Yorkshire border and was even categorised in both counties until 1888, depending on which side of the Calder you lived. Todmorden Town Hall famously straddles the river and at one time, in the grand ballroom, you could waltz your partner from one county into the other. Nowadays it is officially White Rose territory, but some here about still think of themselves as Lancashire. If those Roses wars of long ago should ever rekindle, there will be fireworks in Tod.

Next comes Hebden Bridge, that little outpost of hipsterdom in hill country, the Portland, Brighton or Chorlton of Yorkshire, the San Francisco of the Pennines. At the end of the 1960s, Hebden, 'Trouser Town' as its old nickname had it, was dying. The mills were closing, the houses falling down, and the local young folk headed for Leeds, Manchester or even, unthinkably, London. Coming the other way though, in camper vans and on BSA Bantams, were the hippies and early eco-warriors, squatting and buying up the cheap weavers' cottages, the actual weavers and their kids having long gone. These hairy, hempish offcomers have permanently reshaped the culture of this dark, lovely little town at the bottom of a cleft of the Calder, where a sluggish canal runs along the high street. In that high street you will find chanting workshops and healing centres (as well as visiting fans of the astonishingly bleak TV cop drama Happy Valley, filmed here). A 2017 local history society exhibition got it right when it styled itself 'how the hippies saved Hebden Bridge.'

Ted Hughes was never a hippy. In fact, he was Elvis Presley, according to a brilliant poem by Barnsley's Ian McMillan: a brooding baritone hunk of love with a coal black quiff and a way with words and the ladies. The great poet is the most famous son of Mytholmroyd, a mile east of Hebden, born in an upstairs room at No. 1 Aspinall Street, a tiny end terrace that is now, inevitably, the start of a Ted Hughes Trail. Ted left young and ended his days a Devonshire farmer who hobnobbed with royalty. But the raw, wet gloom of the Calder Valley never entirely lifted from his work and worldview. In his 1979 Pennine Sequence 'Remains of Elmet' he writes of his home turf that 'for centuries it was considered a more or less uninhabitable wilderness, a notorious refuge for criminals, a hide-out for refugees.'

These were not the hippies of Hebden though. More likely the Cragg Valley Coiners. Led by 'King' David Hartley, this infamous gang of weavers plied a roaring extra-curricular trade in 'coining' or 'clipping', which involved scraping tiny amounts of gold from the edges of genuine coins then milling the edges and returning them to general circulation but using the shavings to make new, counterfeit ones. The conspiracy was so successful that it's thought that at one point coiners came close to completely destroying the British economy. They were only successful up to a point of course. They were caught and King David was hanged in York. He is buried in Heptonstall high above Hebden. But the Cragg Vale Coiners live on in local lore and in Ben Myers' novel, *The Gallows Pole*, and its visceral TV adaptation by Shane Meadows.

Eventually we come to Bradford, as Priestley did in 1933. He didn't arrive without misgivings. 'Perhaps I should never have included Bradford in this itinerary,' he remarks mournfully. 'Obviously I cannot visit it in the same way I visit the other places … I had better apologise now for everything that follows in this chapter.' The reason was that Bradford was Priestley's hometown, his artistic and political motherlode. Like Hughes' Calder Valley, it was always lurking there in his worldview and his work, even if he never lived in the city once he'd left for London in 1922 to try his luck as a freelance journalist. But if he changed his address, for ever larger, leafier premises, he never ceased to be a Bradfordian at heart. He was rooted in its certainties and dynamics, civic and cultural. The Bradford of Priestley's youth was a city with a vibrant and progressive politics and a bedrock belief in self-improvement and class solidarity. The Independent Labour Party was formed here, and it was in this city that Keir Hardie was elected its chairman. As John Baxendale has said: 'From this culture, Priestley took two profound ideological influences: socialism and dissent.' In *The Good Companions*, it becomes 'Bruddersford', a place that is both universally northern but specifically, a distilled, alchemical Bradford.

The Northerner who leaves his or her patch to find fame and success in London forever after 'enjoys' a complicated relationship with home. It's a well-worn trope, a much worked and worried over dilemma, prominent in the fiction of John Braine, Melvyn Bragg, David Storey, D H Lawrence and scores of other working-class writers. Here is the brooding clever lad or bright girl caught between Cambridge and the Co-Op, between Greggs and the Groucho Club. Even now, in an era of fast transit, remote working and high profile 'relocations' north of Watford gap by the BBC and Channel 4, there will always remain an easy 1,000 words for the jobbing columnist in this thorny topic. Mancunians like to say that Liverpudlians who make the big time inevitably leave for the capital while Manchester people stay and improve the city, an observation based largely on The Beatles and Cilla Black that conveniently ignores Oasis, Morrissey, Peter Maxwell Davies, Robert Donat, Howard Jacobson, Richard and Judy, Anthony Burgess and the Bee Gees. It is much easier to stay 'oop north' now. But still they go. Some at least.

Priestley's long-lasting pas de deux with Bradford was complex and ambivalent. The city shaped his outlook just as gales and rain scored the stones up on Baildon Moor. He never forgot or disowned his hometown and was thus called a 'professional Yorkshireman' for his pains. Like 'professional northerner', a phrase I have heard much myself, it is generally used, as John Baxendale notes, 'to alert us to the fact that any identity other than that of male metropolitan public schoolboy was and to degrees still is, regarded in English literary circles as a self-indulgent affectation.'

In October 1958, though, he did return to the city with film crew in tow to make a TV documentary called *Lost City*. This managed to receive complaints from various Bradford institutions before it was even shown. On the eve of transmission the *Bradford Telegraph and Argus* told its readers: 'Producer Richard Cawston emphasises that this is not supposed to be a documentary about Bradford. "Mr Priestley is seen wandering around Bradford," he said, "but we have not attempted to show so much of Bradford as of him."' The more sensitive Bradfordian souls thought that it was a film denigrating the city and were grimly suspicious about a plump rich man with a stately home in the leafy shires, critiquing a city he had skedaddled from long ago. Priestley himself said of it that it was 'an idiosyncratic voyage down Memory Lane', merely the view of a 'grunting, saurian-eyed fatty trying to be nostalgic.'

But in his later years, a lover's rapprochement took place. Priestley was an enthusiastic sponsor and advocate for the University's pioneering new Peace Studies department in 1973, the same year he was made a Freeman of the city. They added a Priestley Library two years later, and in 1986 he was given the most public and visible recognition of all: a whopping great statue on a square plinth just in front of the National Science and Media Museum. Stolid and squat, pugnacious and wry, his big coat flaps behind him with the suggestion of a stiff Yorkshire breeze. Bill Bryson remarked in *Notes From a Small Island*, that it 'makes him look oddly as if he has a very bad case of wind.'

A passing group see me dawdling by the statue, attempting to take a selfie that includes both myself and the flatulent bronze JBP. As is the way around here, we chat. As luck would have it, all three are engaged in an ongoing scheme of civic regeneration in the city, part of which involves putting a new rooftop restaurant on the old Brutalist ice skating rink and making a green walkway that will slice through the car-choked city centre. 'Look down there. At the moment the cars go exactly where they want and the people have to scurry through tunnels full of piss. We're going to flip that and make it the other way round. And when we do that the city's eating and drinking scenes might flourish, we hope. There is nowhere in Bradford where you can have fine dining with alcohol. If you want that you have to go to Manchester or Leeds, which hurts. Yes, we have the greatest curry houses in the world. But it's nice to have a choice.'

But at the centre of this rejuvenation is Bradford Live, a bold new rebirth for the derelict but much-loved and well-remembered Bradford Odeon. When local lad made good Priestley came back in 1933, he bemoaned the city's dearth of live venues and the desolate local theatre scene, noting that the 'sad dwindling of the foreign community in the city, and with it the decline of many things they fostered, notably music ... Bradford has no proper concert hall now – more shame to it. The old Theatre Royal too, where Irving played for the last time, has also been turned into a cinema.'

Unaccountably, he did not mention the recently built New Victoria Theatre, as it was then. Over two million bricks were used to construct what was the largest concert hall in the north of England (eat your heart our Manchester, Liverpool and, yes, Leeds) and one of the biggest venues in all the land. The London Symphony Orchestra played at its opening gala in 1930 and it quickly became one of the city's jewels. In 1963 Helen Shapiro was top of the bill, supported by up-and-coming Liverpool band The Beatles. That same year that The Everly Brothers brought fledgling Kent-based R&B act

The Rolling Stones to support them. Both would return rather higher on the bill in the next few years. In 1968, many pairs of Bradfordian knickers showered down upon Tom Jones on that famous stage. In 2000, the building closed to the public and its future looked uncertain, but the Bradford Odeon Rescue Group and a public campaign to save the building succeeded. Now the Odeon will become Bradford Live, a 4,000-seat venue and entertainment complex. I wangle an invite to the opening night and am pointed in the direction of the old Swan Arcade and Little Germany, where the youthful JBP was once the world's second-least competent and enthusiastic textile clerk. I say this with some confidence, as the very worst was me.

The first part of JBP's 1962 memoir *Margin Released* is entitled 'The Swan Arcadian' and tells of his days as a bookish and not terribly committed clerk. In a memoir published rather later called *Cider With Roadies*, I wrote about my time as a bookish and even less committed young textile clerk in the mills of Bolton and Oldham. JBP recalled 'we used to sit on high stools like the clerks in Dickens. I used to handle a thing called "The Big Book" – or pretend to – and then in the desk below were all the library books I had. It's a tribute to my personality that they had me working there at all. I must have been one of the worst wool clerks that ever existed.' In much the same way, I fancy I might have been the worst sales planner the Courtaulds giant ever had. I would never have the presumption or gall to compare myself to him. But here at least we would have had something to chat and laugh about, some unhappy common ground.

Bradford's brass, and its substantial Victorian might, was made from weaving, warping, wefting and wool; all passing through the fat, full order books and purchase ledgers of Swan Arcade, a palatial Italianate edifice with six magnificent entrances and four linked parades of wrought iron and glass, all filled with sculptural swans of marble and iron. Having this as his workplace must have filled Priestley with at least a modicum of chest-swelling sense of purpose.

In *Margin Released*, writing of Swan Arcade, JBP bemoaned the diggers and 'dozers that were 'clawing it down to spread the glass and concrete monotony from Brasilia to Bradford.' Just as he feared, it would soon be demolished in one of those brutal architectural purges of the 60s It would never be razed so casually now, one hopes. It's cheering to see that Bradford is now cherishing and restoring treasures like the Odeon.

'There's somewhere you must see,' the enthusiastic restoration team urge, as we part beneath the bronzed Priestley's billowing rear end. So, following their directions, I cut through the traffic, through the ammoniacal underpasses, past knots of kids splashing in the fountains in the Peace Square and up to the serene, elegant quarter of the city known as Little Germany. In Paul Morley's fine biography of the Mancunian media dynamo Anthony H Wilson, he observes that the Manchester Wilson grew up in was distinctively shaped by those Germans (like Friedrich Engels) who came to the city to build hugely lucrative, clattering mills and, along the way, introduce liberal political thought and cultural notions like socialism and the Hallé Orchestra to the North of England. 'Manchester was a German town,' Wilson would often remark and much the same was true of Priestley's Bradford. Indeed, you will find that many English cities had their Little Germanies; Manchester's is in Whalley Range for instance. But Bradford's is the best: architecturally striking and home to the business ventures of a particular breed of capitalist entrepreneur – philanthropic, civic minded, politically progressive.

The first of these merchants, Leo Shuster, came to Bradford in 1829. It was the start of what Priestley welcomed in *English Journey* as a 'friendly invasion' of 'men of liberal opinions' coming to his hometown. These energising waves of immigration to the city – Flemish weavers, Irish and Scottish labourers, Basque and Eastern European refugees, South Asians, Afghans – continues to this day. Those German Jews of Priestley's youth were 'so much a part of the place when I was a boy that it never occurred to me to ask why they were there. I saw their outlandish names on office doors, knew that they lived in certain pleasant suburbs, and obscurely felt that they had always been with us and would always remain ... The war changed all that. There is hardly a trace now in the city of that German-Jewish invasion. I liked the city better as it was before, and most of my fellow Bradfordians agree with me. It seems smaller and duller now.'

Little Germany is certainly quieter than it was in 1829 or 1933. I wend my way through and up narrow, steepish streets bisecting fine, imposing buildings still heavy with a sense of past industrial prosperity. The riches may have gone but the grandeur is preserved, echoing in the warehouses and offices now repurposed into apartments and the quieter modern commercial trades: graphic design and accountancy, marketing and online shopping. On the corner of Chapel Street, there's a curious stone clock and a very welcome stone armchair where I sit and make notes under a huge montage of another great Bradfordian, David Hockney. He met and drew Priestley in 1972 but both were born too late to 'hang' with a third artistic giant of the city, composer and adopted Bradfordian Frederick Delius. Delius' best music, 'On Hearing The First Cuckoo In Spring' or 'Summer Night On The River', for example, throbs with a nostalgic ache that is quintessentially English. But Frederick was initially Fritz and he was the gifted musical son of one of the German mill owners who made their fortunes in Bradford. Delius Senior established a business here with Jacob Behrens, another of those 'outlandish names' that you can still see on the plaques that detail the companies of the busy textile district this once was.

You won't get worsted or wool anymore in Delius and Behrens' old block, but you can enjoy rock shrimp tempura in fermented chili and bean paste, roasted bone marrow in parsley sauce or truffle gnocchi. The corner of the grand old wool office is now Cona, which in Urdu means, er, 'corner' and is probably Bradford's finest new restaurant. A young and tired-looking chef is sitting on the pavement having a crafty smoke before the evening rush. 'Is this place good?' I ask. She indicates herself with a mock aggrieved look. 'What do you recommend?' She pauses. 'The steak,' she says, smiling, between luxuriant puffs. This is a little joke. Cona is the region's premier upscale steakhouse, macho as a Sumo dohyo, dark as a Mafia speakeasy, a joint where the meat is seared and bloodied, the prices sting like an uppercut to the jaw. It gets the kind of reviews you have to wipe the drool off to read properly. But, like nearly all Bradford's best eateries, it doesn't serve alcohol. Muslim diners looking for a real treat come a long way to Cona, because it's also the only fine dining establishment outside London that's 100 per cent halal. But if you think the dearth of booze and the absence of costly reds will keep your bill down, think again. A side of Mac and Cheese will cost you £15 and the Wagyu A5+ Pure Bred Japanese Kagomisha Prefecture Sirloin won't leave you any change from a £300 note, even if there was such a thing. I decide to hold out for a Greggs.

A circuit of the Simply Bodiflex Gym (not that kind of circuit), the shisha pipe shop and the disturbingly named Siriporn Thai Massage Parlour leads me eventually to the Bradford Playhouse, a favoured haunt of the young Priestley. Much has changed since JB's time, not least the name. After a disastrous fire in the late 30s, Priestley donated royalties from his hit plays to the rebuilding of what then became, in an act of civic gratitude, the Priestley Centre. For a while anyway. A little ungratefully I think, it then became the Little Germany Theatre (and burned down again) before settling as The New Bradford Playhouse.

I was beginning to feel that the way the city commemorates its most famous son seemed curious and piecemeal. Perhaps because he left early and didn't come back much, Bradford's media were distinctly cool on him for many decades, even excoriating him for his divorce. Eventually some kind of recognition came when they made him a Freeman of the city in 1973 at the age of seventy-eight. Even then this was largely due to the loud and sustained complaints from another popular Yorkshire entertainer, comedian Wilfrid Pickles. To be fair, the Bradford Trades Council stood up for him too: 'J B Priestley is as much associated with Bradford as Joyce with Dublin and Lawrence with Nottingham.'

Today, as well as the shifting nomenclature of the Playhouse (a fading wall sign still bills it as The Priestley), there's the statue outside the Media Museum. But that's about it. Bradford has two stations. One is named Forster Square after W E Forster, the Liberal states-man who advocated the shooting of Irish nationalists. The other is Bradford Interchange. Interchange is an unlovely word, I think you'll agree, and I wonder if anyone has ever suggested Bradford Priestley as an improvement. As it is, there is a drawing of him on the wall, partly obscured by a vending machine full of Kit Kats and Diet Tango.

The one place you would surely expect to do Priestley proud is his birthplace. So, having eschewed Cona's blackened sea bream in favour of a tactical sausage roll, I trudge up the hill out of town to find out. That is, once I've established exactly where he was born. Many scholars and biographers have Priestley down as entering the world at 5 Saltburn Place. It's an understandable error since he grew up here, wrote a lot about it and never mentioned his actual birth-place. But that is actually a few streets away in Mannheim Road. Both are in Manningham, the area of Bradford that most symbolises the change in this polyglot, fractious, boom and bust city.

Manningham, its streets and people, have changed out of all recognition since Priestley's day. The signs are everywhere. There are obvious ones like the Muslim Headstone Company and the Madrassah School, but also subtler signifiers. There's a street called Sylhet Close named after the great city of north-east Bangladesh and many of the cars that pass me are from female-only driving schools: Rose Royce, Pass Girls, Pretty Angels. In 1959, two Pakistani grocery stores opened in Bradford catering for workers from the Indian subcontinent. Ten years later, there were nearly 200

Pakistani businesses in Bradford. Now, it's thousands. In and out of every Manningham doorway families go to and fro, carrying bottled water and crates of okra, phone chargers and bags of rice. Three quarters of Manningham is now of South Asian heritage, a change that has been exciting and dynamic as well as complicated and fraught. Priestley's head would have swum at this new and lively scene, the scents, the colours, the signs like the one in the phone shop that reads 'Back in 10 mints, Prayer Time.' But he would have felt there was no barrier to the new arrivals becoming citizens of England, with provisos. 'Priestley argued in favour of a civic rather than ethnic idea of Englishness,' former chairman of the Priestley Society Ken Smith told the *Guardian* in 2009. 'Priestley assumed that anyone who came here would buy into certain things – Shakespeare, Magna Carta, free speech and so on … He had not envisaged that there would be people who would look beyond these shores for their identity, and he would have had great difficulty grappling with the notion that some people's identity would be bound up in religion.'

Big changes are rarely smooth ones. Down the road in Burnley, the town where the Communist Manifesto was first translated into English, and which boycotted Southern cotton during the American Civil War and opposed the Napoleonic wars, racist groups made inroads into town councils in the 90s and 00s. There was even a BNP councillor ('a glamorous 35-year-old grandmother' as *The Times* styled her) in genteel Haworth, heart of Brontëland and a sepia Hovis ad vision of Albion. Once hotbeds of radicalism and strongholds of socialism, town after town in what became known as the Red Wall switched their allegiance to varying strands of Conservatism, some darker than others.

In Manningham, there had been a suspicious, sullen relationship between Asian youths and law enforcement for years, stoked by heavy-handed policing and far-right provocations that eventually flared into the riots of 2001. Pubs burned, people were stabbed, thousands of youths waged nightly pitched battles with the police. As ever, specific causality was hard to pinpoint in a welter of accusation and denial on every side. But when Wuthering Heights votes fascist, all is clearly not well.

After the unrest in Manningham the right-wing media confected tales about 'no-go' areas where white citizens dare not venture, as it always does in relation to partially black or brown districts. This rabid stuff, though largely bunkum, proves nonetheless dispiritingly resilient. While I was in town, a book called *Among the Mosques* by the Muslim writer Ed Husain, former pupil of right-wing 'thinker' Roger Scruton, raised the issue again, leading to debates in the local press. And once again, Bradfordians from all sections of the community, had to tell the truth firmly. There weren't 'no-go' areas in Bradford and claiming there were was massively unhelpful.

Heading up Toller Lane, apparently the intimidating heart of a 'no-go area', walking through these few tight, compacted streets of Manningham, I did at times feel out of place and uncomfortable. But this was much more to do with the cut of my clothes than the colour of my skin. Some of these streets are poor. Not just working class but grindingly, ruinously poor – much poorer than my old council estate in Wigan. Some of these hidden corners of Bradford have the distinct, sour whiff of desperation and neglect; broken windows, filthy lace curtains, ragged settees getting rained on in overgrown gardens. The divide here feels as much about class as race, as rooted in economics as ethnicity.

But that's a white man writing. Perhaps everything is about ethnicity. On the corner of Keighley Road and Manningham Lane, behind the National Bank of Pakistan, I catch a glimpse of a little lad of about ten tossing a few tentative leg breaks at a wonky wicket aerosoled on a shuttered garage. You'll see this scene down backstreets and across parks all over Bradford, all over Yorkshire in fact. This is cricket country, where some take it seriously, and others are fanatics. Priestley wrote in 1973 'in spite of recent jazzed up one day matches cricket to be fully appreciated demands leisure some warm sunny days and an understanding of its finer points.' We can guess what he might have made of the 'jazzed-up' hoopla of 20/20 or The Hundred, of flashy tracksuits and glaring floodlights. But what would he have made of the scandal and outrage that was gripping Yorkshire as I watched that young lad practising his bowling, dreaming of Headingley?

Azeem Rafiq probably honed his offspin on a garage wall in Barnsley. Born in Pakistan but raised in 'Tarn', as it's known locally, he was a prodigious young cricketing talent, captaining both the England under-15 and under-19 sides, leading the latter to the 2010 World Cup and marshalling future big names like Joe Root and Ben Stokes. In 2012, he became the youngest man to captain a Yorkshire side and the first person of Asian origin to do so. But for various reasons, some now infamous, his cricket career first stalled, then ended. In 2018, his son was stillborn and Rafiq took compassionate leave, during which Yorkshire ended his contract. After spells in Pakistan and Derbyshire, he turned his back on the game to start his own catering business, another of elite sport's 'nearly' men.

Rafiq now runs a chip shop and took time out from frying to give a seismic interview to *Wisden* in August 2020. He revealed the racism he'd encountered at Headingley, talking of a dressing room culture where abuse from senior players was routine, where the P-word was bandied about freely, and where Asian players were told 'there were too many of them.' An enquiry was launched, its findings revealed but not published. Seven of Rafiq's forty-three claims were upheld, but no action would be taken. Racist abuse was dismissed as the regular rough and tumble of dressing rooms, the club's behaviour merely 'inappropriate' and there was no 'proof' of institutional racism. No action was to be taken.

Not by Yorkshire Cricket Club anyway. Others saw it differently. Most British media were united in condemnation. Sponsors deserted the club in droves. Michael Vaughan, former England cricket captain and high-profile media personality, came forward to deny the 'too many of them' remark, while Gary Ballance admitted using racist and offensive language to his teammate while trying to shrug it off as 'friendly banter' between 'best mates'. Eventually senior executive resignations followed, as well as a House of Commons select committee at which Rafiq spoke with a quiet anger that led to inescapable conclusions and very many questions.

Questions like, in a county with towns and cities full of thousands of cricket-mad Asians, why were there no brown faces in the corridors of power at Headingley? In a county whose back streets, school yards and sports grounds were crammed with those cricket-mad Asian kids playing over after over, how could it be that of Yorkshire's twenty-nine squad players, only one came from a non-white background. Awkward questions for Yorkshire Cricket Club, not helped when a leaked letter from club staff, clearly annoyed at the credence given to Rafiq, said that he was a 'problematic' presence in the dressing room and did not share 'White Rose values'.

What exactly were 'White Rose values'? The obvious answer was not very edifying. But where was the root of this problem? Was it Yorkshire Cricket Club, an institution long regarded as prehistoric in outlook by some? Was it Yorkshire as a county? Or was it some national shame. Was it England? The sportswriter Jonathan Liew put it well in the *Guardian*: '"The culture of Yorkshire is stuck in the past," declared Roger Hutton, the outgoing chairman of Yorkshire. But he was wrong. It's stuck in the present.'

I continue my journey to JBP's birthplace on through Lister Park. He would come to this large handsome park as a boy and young man in search of fun. 'We used to go to Lister Park every Wednesday and Saturday throughout the summer and listen to the military band concerts … It was rather a nice scene, there, towards dusk, with the illuminated bandstand, the red uniforms, the brass instruments gleaming, smoke rising from thousands of pipes and cigarettes.' Young Bradford still convenes here, enjoying the dance of adolescence whose steps will never come again; sizing each other up, wary as young horses, giggling and flirting. This afternoon there's culture as well in the shape of events from the Bradford Literature Festival. There was much to divert here; some noisy, energetic bhangra from Punjabi Roots Academy, the Leeds Dance Academy, someone on stilts, a circus skills workshop where small children are being encouraged to juggle and ride unicycles. It's all very lively and jolly. But when a man dressed as a pirate being pulled along in a small cart begins to sing Spandau Ballet's 'Gold' through a megaphone, I know it is time for me to go.

Manningham is still home to Bradford's oldest Jewish population. The synagogue on Bowland Street is a Grade II listed Moorish revival building that may be the best example of an 'Orientalist' synagogue in Britain, and though the Jewish community here has dwindled, they still come here for Shabbat and Passover and Friday night dinner. Here was where the men who built Bradford's economy worshipped with their families. The names of the streets around here reflect their roots; Heidelberg Road, Bonn Place and finally Mannheim Road, where Priestley was born on 13 September 1894.

During Priestley's childhood, 34 Mannheim Road was the modest but respectable home of Priestley's father, a stern but socialistic teacher, his new wife Amy (Priestley's mother Emma, a mill girl, died when he was two), JB and step-sister Winifred. Now it is all rather sad. The houses on Mannheim Road are all good solid Bradford stone, but his birthplace looked abandoned to my eyes. In the garden were a few broken planks and a mattress and, most forlorn of all, a burst Mitre football on the small scrubby front patio. When an *Independent* journalist visited in 1997, they noted that 'there was nothing to indicate that Bradford's most famous literary son had been born there, and the house was for sale at a modest asking price of £24,000.' There is at least a plaque now, erected not by the council but by the Priestley Society. But even this could do with a polish.

5 Saltburn Place, just around the corner, where Priestley grew up feels distinctly more prosperous than the street of his birth. Outside there's another plaque ('J B Priestley, Author and Playwright, lived here') and a car, which at least suggests the house is lived in. Discretely mooching, I glance up at the window where Priestley had slept as a lad and first ventured into prose, as he recalled in the TV documentary about his home town. 'Up there … in the attic of No. 5, I first began writing. I turned it into a bed-sitting room, bought some orange boxes, stained them and used them as bookcases and there I wrote every night … Really, I didn't write very much about Bradford. I can remember a poem I wrote about Atlantis which was about as far away as I could get from Bradford in my imagination.' He was first accepted into print in 1913 and began to write for the *Bradford Pioneer*, a socialist weekly where he developed a chatty column called Round the Hearth, at eighteen. He wasn't paid but he did get free tickets for plays and shows, still very much the modus operandi of many a freelancer today. All up there, in that little room, the typewriter on his knee, the orange box bookcase lit by the flickering little gas fire.

My curiosity satisfied, I take a bus back down the hill and into the city centre. At the bottom of Westgate, a group of young Pentecostal types in goth black or camouflage gear are crying and wailing and rolling around in what appears to be some kind of religious fervour, inspiring the local Special Brew drinkers to do the same. The Asian proprietor of the mobile phone shop stands in the doorway and looks on bemused. Loud and presumably football-related chanting emanates from the darkened, unappealing interior of the Rabbit Hole pub. Outside a neon ticker reads 'No tracksuits. No joggers. No sports shorts.'

At Bradford Interchange I pass by Priestley's painted image again. For several years another station had been promised and planned under the government's HS2 rail update, part of the Northern Powerhouse 'initiative' of the Cameron/Osborne years. As late as

March 2021, this new station, digitally rendered and smoothly futuristic, was still being trumpeted on various websites. But whether they might name it after JBP, as rumoured, became abruptly moot when Boris Johnson pulled the plug on most of the long-promised rail improvements in what looked very like, even to his recent converts up here, a dismissive two fingers waved from an Old Etonian in the general direction of the North. Up here, then, it would still take about twenty minutes to get to Leeds; two minutes longer than in 1910. The Edwardian traveller from Bradford could get to Wakefield by train in half an hour. In 2022 it was forty-eight minutes. England's seventh biggest city is more poorly served by rail in the age of the internet than it was in the age of steam. Some powerhouse.

2

Fortunately, Halifax is just seven miles and one stop away, so you can get there in eight blistering minutes. It's worth the trip. Priestley was billeted here, among 'thickets of mill chimneys,' as he put it, before he was sent away to Flanders in the First World War aged just twenty. Halifax is home to the truly extraordinary Piece Hall. Built in 1779 as a textile hall, a stunning palazzo of three neo-classical storeys frames a dazzling open piazza where fabric was once sold. Today, it's the jewel in the crown of a resurgent town that has been called 'the Shoreditch of the North'. This is bunkum of course. If East London were a hundred times more lovely, it might try and pass itself off as 'the Halifax of the South.' But it would be a stretch.

This autumn week in the West Riding, the piazza is playing host to three bands I know and love – New Order, Richard Hawley and Manic Street Preachers – so of course I am here most nights, among ebullient Yorkshire crowds reacquainting themselves with the simple collective pleasure of going out. As James Dean Bradfield of Manic Street Preachers remarks as he takes to the stage and gazes out across the Piece Hall's magnificent colonnaded quadrangle with genuine wonder: 'Who knew there was a piece of Florence in Halifax?' And as the sun drops behind the roofs of Halifax, Richard Hawley plays his anthemic and uplifting song 'Tonight The Streets Are Ours' and there are real tears in some steely Yorkshire eyes, and at least one Lancastrian pair.

According to Clyde Binfield, historian at Sheffield University, Huddersfield is 'a colder processional city, a foretaste of Edinburgh. The builders may have been hard men but they had a growing sense of responsibility to their surroundings.' A foretaste of Edinburgh may be overegging it, but local Twitter correspondent Bob Melling says: 'I think the processional probably means the long, wide Buxton Road/New Street/John William/St John's axis. Huddersfield does vistas. Also, I reckon before the ring road, the long straight of New North Road passing the mansions, colleges and chapels of the rich, all the way into the heart of the town must have been quite something.' Perhaps, but Priestley was not impressed – at least not by its looks. Huddersfield, he wrote, 'is not a handsome town but yet is famous in these parts for the intelligence and independence of its citizens.'

Here he was bang on. They are smart folk here. From its world-famous Contemporary Music Festival to its thriving poetry scene, Huddersfield is a town rightly proud of its vibrant cultural mix. I go to the Contemporary Music Festival every year and love this week-long celebration of the most challenging, exciting, most outlandish classical music. Founded in 1978 as a weekend event with a budget of £3,000, the instigator was Richard Steinitz, a lecturer at the local university who charmed the biggest and most respected names in the contemporary classical music firmament to come to darkest, coldest Yorkshire in November. We shouldn't overstate this. Huddersfield is not Alaska or Greenland. But if all this squeaking and crashing, bleeping and keening and raging and tintinnabulating were going on in long-haired, dope-smoking Amsterdam or ever-so-slightly-pleased-with-itself, paleo-dieting bohemian New York, it would be completely expected – and therefore also a little 'meh'.

It throws up some delicious juxtapositions too, in this town known for rugby league and Harold Wilson. There is a justly celebrated picture of three titans of modern music Pierre Boulez, John Cage and Olivier Messiaen enjoying a deep pan American Hot in the Pizza Hut on the Wakefield Road. Graham McKenzie, the saturnine Glaswegian who runs the festival, told Radio 3's Kate Molleson: 'We went to that Pizza Hut years later and tried to get them to put up a plaque. They asked head office who said "no". Nobody had a clue who they were.' The people who come every November to HCMF certainly know who they are. 'It isn't remote or random or provincial for them,' says McKenzie of the audience, nearly half of whom come from within an hour of Huddersfield. 'And if it's dark, wet, cold, a bit shit, well that's perfect for the festival. If I programme five concerts per day, I know I'll get my audience coming to all five of those concerts. Because the alternatives? There aren't many.'

The day after I left Huddersfield on this particular trip, Prime Minister Boris Johnson, as he then is, arrives there to give a bizarre and insultingly half-arsed speech defending his decision to renege on promised rail improvements. 'All roads lead to Leeds, really,' he says, bafflingly. 'Because you can either zap up on the left-hand side via Manchester on Northern Powerhouse Rail or ultimately zap up on the right-hand side of the Y on the HS2 trains via Sheffield.' There is a statue of a rather better Prime Minister and local hero Harold Wilson on the windy square in front of Huddersfield station. No one would have been surprised to see its lip curl and eyes roll, bronze or not.

3

I've sung Leeds' praises before, as Priestley did somewhat grudgingly in his youth, so I will not dwell on it here beyond saying that if you can't find yourself a bloody good time in Leeds, it is hard to think of anywhere you will. It is a town that takes fun (and art and learning and politics) very seriously and I never arrive or leave without a sense of anticipation. But leave I must, because I am headed for Ilkley. The train passes through Burley in Wharfedale (which is barely in Wharfedale) and Ben Rhydding (which should surely be in Snowdonia). With each mile, the landscape becomes as pretty as the names: folded valleys and a long blue-green ridge of hills forming the backdrop to tightly packed, delicious villages and towns. 'A country … Thibetan (sic.) in its height and emptiness,' thought Priestley. I doubt, frankly, that Ilkley has ever felt remotely like Lhasa, and it certainly does not now. This is a doughty, busy, quite swanky place, immortalised in Yorkshire's national anthem 'On Ilkla Moor Baht 'At', a salutary tale about courting young women up on the adjoining moorland without sufficiently warm head-covering, leading to one's subsequent death from exposure and consumption by insects. Cheery stuff.

Wells Road leads up to that famously inhospitable moor. On a very normal Thursday lunchtime, not a high day or holiday, at each of its cluster of cafés – the Friends of Ham charcuterie, the Quinto bar and restaurant, the Ikley Café Company – every pavement table is full or reserved with people queuing on the pavement: well-heeled, handsome, older white folk in designer cords and chinos and quality fleeces looking blissfully contented with their lot. In Lancashire we kid ourselves that Yorkshire folk are dour and penny-pinching. But this lot looked like they were having a ball and spending their kids' inheritance with gusto. Some might find these people, having both the temerity and opportunity to pop out for a rich Ecuadorian roast and a slice of mille-feuille on a weekday morning, somewhat smug and self-satisfied. But on this lovely brisk morning in the Dales, I was just very envious. It felt mildly treasonous.

As hard-core patisserie fans will know, there is a branch of Betty's in Ilkley. I would call this famous tea shop chain 'iconic' if I did not believe so strongly that people who use the word 'iconic' outside of discussions of twelfth-century Russian Orthodox art should be imprisoned without possibility of parole. So I shall stick with 'famous'. So famous that I don't even bother trying to get lunch there as, on this showing, I'd be more likely to get a World Cup final ticket. Instead, by wrestling two old ladies to the ground (*joke*) I manage to get a table at Avanti. Over a quite fabulous bacon buttie (hard to get wrong, and yet so many do), I peruse the brochure from the equally fabulous Grove Bookshop and find that some old friends and new ones acquired through Twitter are playing at the first 'proper' festival since the pandemic. I say 'proper' not to disparage the efforts of those who gamely and tirelessly staged online festivals but none of these in my experience ever had the same thrill, except perhaps the Brixton reading 'Zoombombed' by what seemed to be the audio of a gay cowboy porn film. Anyway, there was much to enjoy at the Ilkley Festival, not least philosopher A C Grayling's extraordinary hair.

On the next street corner is a shop called Time Again, 'specialists in formal and highland dress' but also offering several handmade chess sets, comedy tie and braces sets and blue tweed jackets at eyebrow-raising prices. It's a kind of fun version of those 'country shops' which sell gilets, hats with fishing flies in and, on the walls, implements to degut salmon or give sheep a pedicure. Across the way was a restaurant called Avalon specialising in 'Mexitalian' cuisine, which is one of my absolute favourite culinary hybrids alongside Japagentinian and Portulandic.

I've always contended that, despite the generalisations of devotee and detractor, there are many kinds of north. It's neither wholly 'grim up there' nor 'God's Own Country'. Hartlepool has little in common with Alderley Edge. Toxteth is very different from Coniston. And there is more than one Yorkshire, too. More variety than perhaps any other county. Yorkshire takes in both tweedily Tory grouse-bagging Ripon and Richmond and the donkey jackets and picket-line braziers of Rotherham and Orgreave. I now realise there may be even more than one West Riding, Ilkley being very different from Manningham. There is even more than one Ilkley. On Brook Street you will find JoJo Maman Bébé and Oliver Bonas but staring them out with jutting jaw you will find Greggs and Card Factory. Unlike some Cotswolds towns or Chilterns villages, Ilkley is pretty but not vacant. There is a seam of something coldly Northern glittering like coal very near the surface. This is a place where you can have your chakras realigned and achieve closure in unresolved relationship issues but also get your iPad screen repaired in under an hour and pick up some salt marsh lamb, the new Sally Rooney and a tin of emulsion while you wait.

Every one of those folk sipping mochaccinos in the cosy stylish cafés looked radiant and content. Here some of you will be expecting, maybe even relishing, a sneering reference to movies like *Cocoon* or *The Stepford Wives*. But away with that. Why the hell wouldn't you be happy in Ilkley? This is a town with a literature festival, a fantastic bookshop, a clutch of fine pubs to suit every temperament and a shop that sells handmade chessboards. In April 2022, the *Sunday Times* said it was the greatest place to live in England, and it was hard to disagree with this, even from a paper that employs Jeremy Clarkson.

Moreover, if you turn left just after the station and don't mind a bit of a pull, half an hour's good walking will see you on the most famous moor in England, with or without a hat. I stood on the edge of that moor looking down at the town and thought 'I could live here'. I mean obviously, I couldn't. They say 'while' instead of 'until' and they call a fish and chip shop a 'fishery', which is patently ridiculous. But for a second or two, I will admit that treacherous notion was there, until it blew away – over Keighley and Burnley and back into God's Own Country.

But I was not headed there. Not just yet, mi duck.

7

TO THE POTTERIES

In which I learn of saggers and bottle
ovens and share an oatcake with Lemmy
and Arnold Bennett.

So, you're on a first date in that nice Italian everyone's talking about
and you've just been ushered discreetly to a lovely window table
when, abruptly, your possible future paramour flips their plate over
and begins furiously scrutinising the underside. Before you 'remember' that you've left that gas on and call an Uber, hold hard. They
may merely be scanning for the names Dudson, Steelite, Royal
Doulton or Wedgwood. They could just be from Stoke.

Perhaps your companion belongs to the Turnover Club, membership of which entitles you, it's said, to flip over any piece of pottery
anywhere in the world and check where it was made. If you want to
read more on the matter, there's an academic paper stored at the
online archive of the *International Journal of Heritage Studies* enticingly titled 'The Turnover Club: Locality and Identity in the North
Staffordshire practice of turning over ceramic ware'. Tempting, but

a digital version cost thirty-five quid and, frankly, you can buy a lot of oatcakes for that.

'I carried with me to the Potteries a full load of ignorance,' admits Priestley in the typically genial preamble to his own Chapter Seven. In this, we were very much kindred spirits. I'd visited the area only once before, in the early 90s to review a show by an excitable new band called Blur at the Freetown Club which, according to your then youthful scribe's deathless prose, 'nestles beneath the pavements of downtown Hanley. Obviously, a precious thing to its patrons, a cramped subterranean bar … an oasis of subversive *NME*-style fun in the Scampi and Chips end of town.' So, just like Priestley, I arrive 'with a mind like a blank sheet of paper, to be a stranger and a sightseer.' If I were looking for helpful advice in the *Rough Guide to Britain*, whose cover promised bullishly 'full coverage', then I would be disappointed. Stoke is nowhere to be seen. Turn to the index in search of 'The Potteries' and there is nothing between the Potters, Harry and Beatrix, and the Welsh county of Powys. I bring this up over a pint of Townhouse Meridian Mild with a couple of locals in the Congress Inn, Longton who merely roll their eyes and say 'typical'. Potteries people are proud and distinctive, but they are long used to being regarded as a mysterious, smoky lacuna between the Brummies and the Mancs.

Maps out, then. The Potteries are pretty much the dead centre and beating heart, geographically, of England. Frank Swinnerton, in his biography of local laureate Arnold Bennett, has observed that 'if this physical fact should lead you to imagine that the natives of Staffordshire ought to be more typically and peculiarly English than the natives of any other district in the British Isles, you would be warmly supported by Staffordshire men everywhere. It has been their belief, in fact, for centuries past, that they have more English common sense than all the rest of the population put together.'

The Potteries are a clenched fist of tough little towns: the knuckles being Burslem, Fenton, Hanley, Longton, Stoke and Tunstall. These are now collectively merged into a new city called Stoke-on-Trent. But that only happened just over a century ago. Stoke is younger than radio, teabags and the vacuum cleaner. Younger than crosswords, instant coffee and the FA Cup – which neither Stoke City nor Port Vale, the other Potteries team, have ever won. The former have become emblematic of a certain dogged lack of glamour, of a dour and inhospitable grimness. When a creative, flamboyant maverick playmaker from Serie A or La Liga is being praised for their silky artistry, it is now obligatory, axiomatic even, to counter with the humorous question: 'But can he do it on a cold, wet Tuesday night at Stoke?'

These six towns may have once been economically dynamic and world renowned, but they have never been attractive. The strange, surreal beauty of the bottle ovens (like something from a dreamscape by Giorgio de Chirico) aside, not even their staunchest fan would call them pretty. Even their most famously lyrical son could be disloyally cool about them: 'In the Five Towns there was nothing. You might walk from one end ... to the other and not see one object that gave a thrill.' So said Arnold Bennett, as quoted in Caroline Hillier's *A Journey to the Heart of England*. 'The Tolstoy of the Potteries' was a solicitor's son from Hanley who became one of the most prolific and popular writers of his age. His many novels about his home region including *The Old Wives' Tale*, *Clayhanger* and *Anna of the Five Towns* (five, because for some daft, annoying reason, he left out Fenton) were boldly evoked studies of the Potteries' sooty and sinewy glory, revelling in the daily lives of believably real people, particularly women, as well as the towns themselves. 'They are mean and forbidding of aspect,' he wrote in the latter – 'sombre, hard-featured, uncouth; and the vaporous poison of their ovens and chimneys has soiled and shrivelled the surrounding countryside, till there is no village lane within a league, but what offers a gaunt and ludicrous travesty of rural charms. Nothing could be more prosaic than the huddled, red-brown streets; nothing more seemingly remote from romance. Yet be it said that romance is even here – the romance which, for those who have an eye to perceive it, ever dwells amid the seats of industrial manufacture, softening the coarseness, transfiguring the squalor, of these mighty alchemic operations.'

Bennett left Hanley as soon as he had the bus fare to pursue first a legal then a literary career in London. He never lived in the vaporous murk of the Potteries again. But his novels about these 'sombre, hard-featured, uncouth' towns made them famous around the world. In many ways, Bennett had a similar literary trajectory to Priestley himself: hugely successful, adored by the reading public but sneered at by modernist intellectuals, specifically that snobbish bluestocking Virginia Woolf, who publicly disdained them both. She trashed Bennett in a 1923 article which set the critical tone for much of the rest of the mid-century. For her, Bennett was no artist, merely a producer of potboilers for the masses – none of them worthy of serious analysis. This was crudely inaccurate; Bennett loved Eliot, Joyce and Lawrence. But the damage was done. When Priestley visited the Potteries just two years after Bennett's death, he was shocked that 'I do not think I heard his name mentioned once during all the time I was in the Potteries … Why was Bennett not made a Freeman of Stoke-on-Trent? … Why no sort of memorial to him anywhere? and why are third-rate politicians in this country still considered to be far more important than first-rate artists of any kind?' Appropriately, I read on arrival in the Potteries that Gavin Williamson, former fireplace salesman from Scarborough and by common consent the worst education secretary we have ever had, has been knighted.

More recently the tide has turned regarding Bennett's reputation. Margaret Drabble has called his books 'deeply moving, original and dealing with material that I had never before encountered in fiction but only in life.' The writer and broadcaster Samira Ahmed in a Radio 4 documentary called him the Edwardian David Bowie, which I don't follow but sounds good. He is generally regarded as having written the first ever self-help book, a brisk but sympathetic little gem called *How to Live on 24 Hours a Day*, still in print and vastly superior to today's glutinous 'you are a precious and wonderful creature' flannel. Bennett has always been loved by the reading public and the world beyond the Hampstead drawing room. When the writer lay dying from typhoid in his flat at Chiltern Court, Baker Street in 1931, having unwisely glugged tap water on a visit to his beloved France, London's civic authorities had straw laid on the streets to muffle the clatter of the horses. He now has his own statue in downtown Hanley. And Bennett can claim one accolade that surely no other writer can: he has an omelette named after him, basically a nicely fluffy soufflé stuffed with cheese and haddock. You can't get it in Tunstall or Burslem, sadly. It's only on the menu at the Savoy Grill where the Edwardian antecedents of today's chefs made it just to Bennett's liking.

Priestley also observed of Stoke that 'this city has a population of nearly three hundred thousand, but it has no real existence as a city of that size. There is no city. There are still these six little towns [and] unless you are wiser than I was, you will never be quite sure which of the six you are in at any given time.' This may well be fighting talk in Hanley, Longton, and possibly Burslem. But I have to agree. Even before I sample the wares of the Congress Inn, I am similarly confused about exactly where I am. There are no border guards and checkpoints, of course. But the odd bit of signage wouldn't go amiss. There's a huge map in a leaflet I pick up at the station, reproduced on all the big bus stops. But, frankly, I find it easier to get to grips with my battered OS Landranger of Rannoch Moor. Stoke-on-Trent seems to be a mirage, a chimera, an illusion. When you think you are there, you are probably in Hanley. If not, you may be in Tunstall. You are very unlikely ever to be in Stoke unless you are sitting in the station buffet bar. Even then, you're in Hanley.

Like Shangri-La and El Dorado, Stoke-on-Trent is a fiction. Dreamed up by visionary Edwardian planners with watch chains and mutton chop whiskers, it is a mystical, abstract union. Priestley talks of the towns 'quarrelling bitterly' over the arrangements for federation in 1910, but after the toxic schism of Brexit, the fuss over the creation of Stoke seems only the mildest of family disagreements. (Basically, Longton and Stoke were in favour of it while Fenton was opposed. Tunstall wasn't fussed much either way). There was heated debate, though, surrounding which town should be the appointed 'centre' of the newly federated city. 'Beautiful Burslem', the so-called Mother Town, had the handsome buildings, the pretty parks and the rich history. Hanley had all the good shops and the swagger. Stoke had the railway station. But in the end, the arguments faded away, leaving only a 'six towns mentality' as local politicos and business types exasperatedly put it. That's the trouble with people, I guess. Their pesky longstanding tribal allegiances tend to get in the way of consultancy documents and long-term development strategies.

'When Priestley reaches the Potteries, halfway through his book, and halfway between Yorkshire and Lancashire, something odd happens,' according to JBP fan, Margaret Drabble in the *Guardian*: 'They defeat his economic analysis, they baffle and intrigue him, they capture his imagination, they repel and fascinate him. Their "remote provinciality" becomes exotic in his eyes … The faults and virtues of the region strike him as inseparable … It is, as Priestley wrote, unlike any other industrial area. And he found it curiously exhilarating.'

As always in *English Journey*, Priestley is vague about how he arrived in the Potteries, possibly a little coy and sheepish about the old chauffeured Daimler. I changed at Crewe. I was hoping for some of that exhilaration Priestley felt, especially after reading local historian David Proudlove's excellent architecture blog: 'Stoke-on-Trent possesses one of the finest gateways in the country in Winton Square; step off the train in Stoke-on-Trent and you are met with one of the finest examples of Victorian urban planning you are likely to come across, and two great landmarks in Stoke-on-Trent Railway Station and the North Stafford Hotel, both of which are Grade II Listed.'

Built at the height of rail mania in 1848, Stoke station is still a grand piece of Victorian civic architecture. Architecture scholar Nicholas Pevsner was no admirer of the Potteries in general ('the Five Towns are an urban tragedy,' he lamented), but even he was impressed when he strode out of the station into Winton Square calling it 'the finest piece of Victorian axial planning in the County.' Leaving aside the fact that architecture writers certainly do like that 'finest piece/example of' construction, it may well still be the case. I'm not the person to ask really as I had to look up 'axial planning'. But the North Stafford Hotel across the road has seen better days. Its Neo-Jacobean architecture may still excite modern day Pevsners but I am put off from popping in by the gaggle of dishevelled, lairy blokes drinking bottled beer and smoking furiously on the steps. Also, by a review in the *Stoke Sentinel* that contained one sentence that I can never now unread.

I go in search of sustenance instead. Some readers will find it ridiculous, if typical, that my first point of pilgrimage here is not to the excellent pottery museums or the art gallery or the Arnold Bennett statue in Burslem. No, it is an oatcake shop. In my defence, though, it is right up there with their football teams, bottle ovens and their fine china; Potteries people are ferociously proud of, maybe at some ur-level even defined by, the regional culinary treasure that is the Staffordshire oatcake.

Now, I love Scottish food. I admire its hearty (and heart-furring) emphasis on the kinds of pinguid, delicious stuff that will get you through a northern winter, viz. the tattie scone, the Lorne sausage, tablet, Aberdeen rowies and Dingwall black pudding. These are triumphs all. But their oatcakes! Dear oh dear. Dry, rigid and best used for lining a bathroom during a cork shortage. The oatcakes of middle England are very different and vastly superior. They are, in essence, a circular pancake made from a mix of oatmeal, flour, milk and water, cooked on a bakestone often in a terraced house or corner shop, stuffed with cheese, bacon, sausage or eggs to taste, and served to you out of a window. But those mere technical specifications give no idea of their cultural significance. You can buy them commercially in a supermarket and make them at home but, as correspondent Ed Beckett informed me when I asked for guidance online, 'commercial oatcakes are only to be eaten when desperate and on the verge of malnutrition. The real McCoy are usually cooked by a sweaty man in a string vest with prison tattoos, who in years gone by would be smoking a fag at the same time.'

Ed was one of hundreds of people who offered me salient and cogent oatcake-related advice. Long experience on the radio has taught me that nothing exercises the great British public like food. If you want to have the lines buzzing for a couple of hours, ask people what their favourite food is, or their least favourite; what's their ultimate breakfast or hangover cure; what is the strangest thing they have ever eaten, or the most disgusting, or the lengths they have gone to in order to make a snack. In this way, I have learned of people who poach cod in the tiny hotel kettle and who have reheated pizzas in the giant Supertrouper stage lights of the London Palladium, of people who have been offered Quavers as a substitute for fried mushrooms in a Little Chef brunch and who have driven thirty miles to get their favourite fish supper, keeping it warm on the return journey under the bonnet of their car.

So it was that a helpful multitude of correspondents each brought something new and fascinating to impart. Sarah Langan told me that the snack's origins were in India, having been eaten by the Staffordshire regiment there, which means that the left-field modern trend for a curry filling was entirely appropriate. Ken Burt offered a ghoulish detour: 'Having eaten your fill, come west to the former home of regicide Maj Gen Thomas Harrison; though he earnestly forgave his executioner he reportedly punched him in the face after being taken down from being hanged and cut open. We hold to a point in Newcastle-under-Lyme.' Richard Peers pointed out that in an earlier book I had described the delicacy as 'a kind of tortilla with the texture of a flannel.' I was quick to point out that it was an inferior microwaved version served in a weird pub beneath Chester's city walls. The oatcake, like Retsina or the Middlesbrough 'Parmo', does not travel.

Everyone warned that oatcakes are a popular Saturday breakfast so I'd have to be 'sharp'. The best of the shops would be shutting up by midday. Widespread consensus had it that the two best places were Hole In The Wall or Six Towns Oatcakes. The latter was nearest, and thus began a stomach-rumbling race against time in an Uber from the station. My driver was a very recent arrival from the Punjab but oatcake news travels fast on the grapevine. 'Oh, I know the place, it's famous. Always people waiting outside. What is it selling?'

'Oatcakes,' I reply. 'Bit like a chapati. Haven't you tried one yet?' He laughs, 'No, but I promise I will. You enjoy yours, sir but look you will have to wait I think.' He drives away and I take my place in the queue on the pavement outside what is a sort of cross between a terraced house and a corner shop on an ordinary Potteries backstreet. The imposing green signage proclaims proudly 'Six Towns Oatcakes. Oatcake Shop Of The Year for Two Years Running. Winner of 6TR awards' The Oatcake Oscars, presumably.

All Hanley life is here: old ladies in hairnets, middle-aged male cyclists in upsettingly snug shorts and little plastic hats, building site guys in big boots and hi vis, likely lads in hoodies, guys in suits making loud mobile calls to Uttoxeter, and a smart, sweet young couple with a beautiful baby the old ladies coo over. A fairly constant stream of cars pull up disgorging a selection of smug, well prepared people who've had the foresight to ring ahead. They drive away with bags the size of pillowcases full of oatcakes and pikelets, the other staple of the shops. The whole oatcake shop system can be daunting and baffling to a first timer, like going to confession or a barn dance. Inside the spartan interior two blonde women are working feverishly doing some unspecified rolling and folding and frying. Occasionally a head will pop out of a hole in the wall and ask 'what ya having, duck?' at anyone in the queue who takes their fancy, seemingly at random. Eventually this cheery request seems to be directed at me and I panic and order one filled with bacon, sausage and cheese. Then and now, this seems excessive. But it was ignorance not greed that led me to blurt it out. Be aware that I could have ordered The Whopper which had three times as much filling and presumably came with its own defibrillator.

Reader, it was delicious. Just as gloopily tasty and comforting as all the online advocates say. I can see how someone could become addicted to this as a Saturday morning treat, both the food and the ritual. As I leave and cross the busy road munching the hot, steaming, fragrant rolled oatcake wrapped in foil, a man in a passing car shouts 'good choice!' from the open window and gives me the thumbs-up. I walk through Hanley Forest Park with its two grassed hills, former slag heaps. This green space was reclaimed from the Hanley Deep Pit where once upon a Saturday shift one-and-a-half thousand men and boys would have worked somewhere in the dark beneath my feet. Now it buzzes with familial fun, bike tricks and football games, wobbling toddlers and chatting shoppers. I make my way through it all, a little greasy, back into whatever town centre the station is actually in and bound for Etruria by canal.

2

'Soft as the earth is mankind, and both need to be altered,' said W H Auden, a keen student of geology. The people of North Staffordshire have been altering their earth and being shaped by it for half a millenium. The history of the Potteries is built on a seam of coal and clay. This thick subterranean ribbon that runs across North Staffordshire gives up (with no small effort) the long-burning, high flame yield coal that's needed for firing pottery ovens. Add to that the thick layers of yellow clay and red marl just two feet below the surface, all the way from Burslem to Hanley, and Mother Nature has done her bit for Stoke here. This is the perfect geological combination for pottery making, arguably the most enduring art form of the last 5,000 years of human history. To understand why, try drinking from a cave painting. Pottery is human culture's most satisfying blend of aesthetics and practicality. 'Have nothing in your houses that you do not know to be beautiful or believe to be useful,' said William Morris. The best ceramics are both.

North Staffordshire folk were making pots a long time before Josiah Wedgwood came on the scene, but it was his drive and innovation that made the Potteries great and Stoke-on-Trent the ceramics capital of the world. Born into a family of potters, he was not just a craftsman but a savvy businessman and technical pioneer. Wedgwood built a grand home and a technically advanced factory in 1769 and named them both Etruria after the Italian region that was home to the mysterious and artistic Etruscan folk. Here I could possibly outline what little I understand about Wedgwood's technical innovations; how he divided the Etruria works into discreet sections of slip house, clay making workshop, biscuit kilns, glost placing and firing in order to improve efficiency. But unless you have clay in your blood, I fear your eyes would glaze over as smoothly and blandly as one of Josiah's old creamware jugs. Suffice to say that Tristram Hunt, former Labour MP for Stoke, director of the Victoria and Albert Museum, and Wedgwood's biographer has called him 'the Steve Jobs of the eighteenth century.' By this I think he meant a tireless innovator and entrepreneur. But unlike Jobs, Wedgwood was also a progressive radical, an abolitionist, an anti-colonialist and forerunner of the Chartists in many of his egalitarian ideals.

The Etruria works were demolished in the mid twentieth century. But handily for me, the Etruria Industrial Museum on the Caldon Canal, which fetched and carried Wedgwood's output in hundreds of boats a week during its heyday, is firing up the venerable machinery on a rare open day during my visit. First, I have to find it. I make heavy weather of this to be honest, pootling around in the streets behind the University of Staffordshire building with a dodgy connection on Google Maps. In the 30s, when Priestley came, this was Staffordshire Polytechnic, elevated to university status in that great swathe of conversions in 1992 that saw Lanchester Polytechnic become Coventry University and the old Preston Poly spruce itself up as the University of Central Lancashire. An old line came back to me: 'I didn't have any fancy book learning; I went to the University of Life. Course, it was Life Polytechnic back then.'

The new university presents a grand, if grimy, frontage to Station Road and behind is a messy hinterland of commerce and convenience for the many different kinds of newcomers: Middle Eastern grocers, sari shops, a profusion of cheap and cheerful stores for the large hungry, thirsty, penurious student body. When I was a student, a precarious life of frugality was the accepted case for all but the most cossetted mummy's boy and daddy's girl. Now even they must be feeling the squeeze of student loans, rising rents and the overheated cost of living. Students fill our major cities now, thanks to New Labour's well-meant but essentially daft drive to see 50 per cent of the nation's youth at university (in Priestley's day it was 2 per cent). It's a terrific step forward towards equality, for sure, but it has meant England now has a surfeit of debt-burdened, unemployed interior designers and not enough plumbers.

Marsh Street is home to Tribal Images Tattoos and Supplement Junction, one of those terrifying shops that sell angry body builders protein shakes developed in subterranean labs in the former Soviet Union, I would imagine. The owner, standing outside vaping furiously in a tight black T-shirt would seem, by the bursting fabric barely containing his grapefruit sized biceps, to be an enthusiastic user of his own products. Further along, next to each other, are Rubber Soul Records and Terraces Menswear. The former is a Northern Soul records shop calling itself 'a way of life', which was and is true for many hereabouts. The Golden Torch in Tunstall was a legendary Northern Soul club – a squat, ugly building in a back street that looked like a meat rendering plant but nevertheless became a thing of reverence and pilgrimage for thousands, predating the heyday of Wigan Casino.

When I nip into Terraces, the owner pounces on me with news of recently arrived stock. 'We've got Fjällräven, Barbour, Peaceful Hooligan, Away Day sweatshirts …' Above the counter are framed signed shirts of Gordon Banks and Peter Crouch, both former Stoke City legends. I wonder maybe if there's such a thing as Stoke Man, a tribe as distinct as those the psephologists once labelled Basildon Man and Worcester Woman. Stoke Man: an old Mod or Soul boy but with a few Stone Roses records; a no-nonsense working-class romantic with a good haircut; hard but not stupid, leftist but suspicious of what he reads of as 'woke', seeing the kids one weekend and Vale or Stoke the other.

As I turn the corner, a DM from a follower pings on my phone: 'I have left some oatcakes for you at the Bethesda Chapel'. No one with blood in their veins could ignore a sentence like this one from the fine people at the Staffordshire Oat Cake Company, and since Bethesda Chapel is just up the road, I set off for 'the Petra of the Potteries', as one correspondent lyrically calls it. Bethesda was magnificent once, having the widest span of any chapel outside London. Decommissioned in 1985, it fell into serious disrepair but is slowly and painstakingly being restored by people who, as English people do, give up their free time to preserve a little of our past on sleepy branch lines and weedy canal junctions. They're having an open day and one such breathless and enthusiastic lady volunteer urges, 'Go up the stairs first and look down. It's got the wow factor!' And so it had. But I had another open day to attend, and so, popping those generously donated oatcakes into my manbag, I set out once again to negotiate the opaque, baffling geography of Stoke-on-Trent.

This time, I contrive to get hopelessly lost in Hanley cemetery. But by leaping a few fences and pushing Chindit-style through some grim bottle-strewn thickets, I eventually find the canal. I like canals, and I take great joy in leaving a dismal townscape of car exhaust fitters and tired shops and stepping into the urban pastoral of a towpath. This is a greenly-shaded world of dappled light and joggers, plopping perch and silent men in camouflage trousers with roach poles and keep nets, plus the odd weed-choked culvert full of shopping trolleys and nitrous oxide canisters. During the first UK lockdown, when there was little else to do but stomp, I put in a few score miles of canal-walking a week. Indeed, the pursuit became almost fashionable. Added to the usual ruddy men in bobble hats and anglers were scores of presentable young couples in fashionable outerwear. It became apparent to me that, with no pubs, restaurants, nightclubs or cinemas to do their 'courting' in, some were clearly on first dates. It was as if we'd returned to Hardy's Wessex where awkward young farmhands, fiddling with their caps and collars, called on their beloveds to go walking after church. I'm sure there are babies born in 2022 who were made on the towpath, conceptually if not actually.

Not far out of town, I spot my first bottle oven. These strange, lovely things, tall and elegant and, obviously, bottle-shaped would once have dominated the skyline of the area. At their inter-war peak, when Priestley combed these streets, there were 2,000 bottle ovens and kilns in the six towns. Now there are just forty-seven standing, all of them listed buildings, like these 'canalside' on the way to Etruria. If you want to know exactly what went on in these queer stately structures – the weekly coal firing, the saggars and clammins and stints, saddles and thimbles – then it is all online. There's no way I'm up to that kind of technical exposition. I just think they look wonderful and I wonder about the people who worked them when Hanley and Longton and Tunstall were names known all over the world.

Even for a man with a generously filled oatcake in his recent past, Etruria is arrived at in no time at all and the works is abuzz with eager volunteers. The main draw on this open day is the firing up of the steam engine. Until quite recently it was fashionable, obligatory even, among comics and columnists to sneer at people we might call 'enthusiasts'. A disengaged lassitude and cynicism was regarded as the cool and sophisticated approach to life. Happily, this seems to be the unfashionable schtick now, maybe hastened by lockdowns which taught us to value again as precious things as simple as meeting people and sharing our loves and passions. Partly it has its roots in class prejudice. 'Hobbies' have always been viewed as terribly vulgar by the ruling class, whose interests have largely been confined to indulgence in expensive intoxicants and the exploitation of small birds, animals, coal miners etc. Working-class people absolutely love their hobbies. Consequently, when I get to Etruria Junction, it is packed to the crankshafts with cheery, affable folk energetically sharing their love of canals, coal and clanking machinery in all their various permutations. Many of them are dressed in overalls and denim caps and sport little knotted 'kerchiefs. I approve.

The main interest among the cognoscenti seems to be that much-vaunted firing up of the steam engine for the Bone and Flint Mill. A handful of us jockey for position in the intimate, intensely hot engine room. 'Nice and warm in here, eh?' says a lady in her eighties next to me. 'I like it warm,' she winks and digs me in the ribs suggestively. A male volunteer with a greasy rag begins to point things out with appropriate explanations. I try to absorb it all but, to be honest, the cerebral cortex-melting heat and rivulets of sweat pouring down my forehead and into my eyes made it hard to concentrate on the speaker, especially when his material was not exactly zippy. Here's an extract: 'This is what we call a Cornish boiler built in 1903. It wasn't made in Cornwall.' Long pause for mopping of collective brows. 'It was made just down the road. But it's called a Cornish boiler because of the style. As you can see,' he points at something vague in the heat haze with a darkened oily finger, 'it only has one fire tube as opposed to a Lancashire boiler, which has two. Takes a week to heat up …' Some new arrivals in fleeces that they will soon regret comment loudly on the heat as they jostle into the tiny, unspeakably hot room. The guide sighs. 'Ok, I'll start again,' he says, at which the flirtatious older lady moans 'no' and grips my arm to steady herself. It's a bit like a family open day in Hades. But it's a satisfyingly varied crowd, including an eleven-year-old boy, earnest and gimlet eyed, and his dad. There is something a little heartening to see a young lad so pro-actively interested in his region's industrial heritage. A little later, when I've had some fresh air and drunk several gallons of water, I return to the engine room to find the kid on his hands and knees breaking lumps of coal with a hammer to feed into the fiery maw of the engine's boiler. I assume he's doing this of his own volition, but the whole scene is disconcertingly reminiscent of engravings depicting factory conditions we outlawed about a century and a half ago. He seems happy enough as he wipes his calloused, blackened little hands on his boiler suit.

3

From Etruria, I struck out for Burslem along the Trent and Mersey Canal. It was this waterway, completed in 1777, that earned Burslem the moniker 'Mother' of the Potteries. It is, some say, Britain's last real industrial district; a place where the people who work with the kilns and ovens live in the little streets nearby and walk to work as they have done for 200 years.

When Priestley visited, the Trent and Mersey was 'a very dirty canal' that he glosses over in a sentence. Now it is a lovely walk, shaded by trees, chorused by birdsong and gaily enlivened by the stately passing of brightly coloured and raffish canal boats. Recently, one of them was piloted by Gyles Brandreth and Sheila Hancock for one of those twee TV travelogues in which quite sweet posh people of a certain vintage bicker gently and crash their barge/tandem/classic sports car into a bridge before having a slice of cake and throwing a pot badly. (I am of course available for this kind of work).

After a pleasant couple of miles, Middleport Pottery comes into view – pretty and characterful as a film set, which it often is. There are still potters at work here in neat, meticulous studios, like Emma Bailey and Alex Allday. I am drawn to a little gallery named Potteries Images. Inside two men who I now know to be Chris Morris and Richard Howle are deep in pottery-related chat. Richard is a photographer from longstanding pottery worker stock who runs the gallery and Chris grew up in a 'two up, two down' 100 yards away and volunteers in the visitor centre.

'Burslem is really the epicentre of Wedgwood's empire,' Chris tells me. 'He came from a family of potters but when he married into a wealthy Burslem family, he acquired the money that meant he could start his own place and begin experimenting. Then Burgess and Lee came in 1888, one a potter, the other an architect, and they modelled their works on a production line, like the Quakers had done with chocolate-making at Cadbury's. They still made money up until this century when it nearly went bankrupt. The Prince's Trust saved it, essentially. Spent £9 million on it.'

Richard feels there's an erroneous assumption that Stoke's pottery industry has gone the way of mining and steel. 'I live right by the Steelite works that makes plates and tableware for sale all over the world, and I can tell you there's lights on and folk coming and going all day and night, even on Christmas day.' This very week, Meghan Markle was pictured with one of the Burleigh peacock cups made here and sales rocketed. 'They were selling £5k an hour online. Harrods sold out. They had to change their production schedule to accommodate it.'

Richard's granddad worked here, a connection he's clearly proud of. 'See that?' he points at what looks like a brick box full of prints.

'That's a sagger. Pick it up. Feel how heavy it is. When my granddad was a little lad, he would wind his granny's old stockings into a doughnut, put it on like a cap and carry them up on his head to be fired in kilns. His neck were like this …' and he places his hands about a foot apart.

Richard's vowels are pure 'Stewk'. It's an accent I can warm to, since with its flat 'paths' and 'baths' and its 'thissens' and 'woms', it sounds much more like Lancastrian than Brummie. John Ward writing in 1843 noted that the Potteries dialect was 'now almost banished by the schoolmaster's assiduous care.' But like the pottery trade itself, the death of the Stoke accent has been greatly exaggerated. They are friendly folk too; a warm, tough tribe. I buy a lovely evocative print of some bottle ovens reflecting the last golden light of a fine summer's evening and then, with no great confidence as to the route, depart once again.

4

If you like football and quizzes, you soon get to know all the classic quirky questions. Which is the only British football club with a 'J' in it? St Johnstone. Which is the only current English football league club with green in their strip? Plymouth Argyle. And, finally in this round, which is the only English football league club not to be named after the place they are in. The answer is Port Vale, named poetically after the stretch of the Trent and Mersey Canal that runs by Burslem, with many docks for the various pottery works.*

A glummer fact is that Port Vale, the Potteries' 'other club', hold the unenviable record for the most seasons in the League (110 to be

---

* Technically Arsenal is another. But as they were called Woolwich Arsenal before 1912 and merely dropped the locator, I don't count them. And it's my quiz.

exact) without reaching the first tier. Unsurprisingly, there is no plaque commemorating this fact and it does not diminish the ardour of their fans. The most famous is 90s hitmaker Robbie Williams, who was once a major shareholder to the tune of £250,000 and, rather curiously, helped design their current strip. Vale Park, Port Vale's characterful little ground, is the eleventh highest in England and second highest in the Football League. The pitch sits on clay and old mine shafts beneath the stadium prohibit major works below the pitch, which makes it prone to both freezing and flooding. This terrain and altitude, not conducive to the elegant passing game of the mollycoddled southrons, perhaps explains why Vale have never reached the highest tier of the Football League. But there have been some great vivid days.

There was the afternoon in 1988 when, on a pitch made more sodden still by Machiavellian deployment of pre-match hosepipes, Vale put fancy dan North London ballerinas Spurs out of the FA Cup. Seven years earlier, in the summer of 1981, local lad Lemmy headlined the unwisely-named (given his hobby of collecting Third Reich memorabilia) 'Heavy Metal Holocaust' event here featuring his band Motörhead, Ozzy Osbourne and the less lionized Riot, Vardis and Triumph. Those Burslem locals more appreciative of Bach's flute sonatas tried to get the event stopped but were placated by Lemmy's offer of a coach trip to Blackpool on the day in question. It was, according to Lemmy's autobiography, Motörhead's loudest ever show. 'At the soundcheck a guy rang up from four miles away to complain that he couldn't hear his TV.' Over 20,000 head-bangers came, raising £25,000 for the football club. Among them Lars Ulrich, who immediately went off and formed Metallica, unfortunately.

'The Valiants' are away to Bradford on the Saturday afternoon I pass by the ground, so all is quiet. In fact, Burslem town centre as a whole is quiet, apart from a kid on a trials bike, slowly circling on his astonishingly noisy, raspy little machine. In his mind, perhaps, he is a lion on the veldt, his roar asserting his alpha male status as king of the home patch he surveys. Local sub-cultural theorists might contend that he is merely asserting the agency and power that the decline of traditional male working-class identity, family and job status have deprived him of. Both may be true. Still, the urge to heave a brick at him as he passes is almost irresistible.

I arrive in Burslem via Waterloo Road, a trudge up a long, grimy parade of shawarma shops, nail salons, naan bakeries and the occasional grand terraced house. I pass a couple having a loud argument in the street; she, in a skin-tight beige leather dress, pushing him repeatedly into the road by his barrel chest; he, grubby in double denim, unshaven, smiling in a way that suggests his purchase on events is not entire and comprehensive. All of this takes place outside a vacant lot whose hoarding shows a man in a flat cap and reads 'The Little Gold Mine'. This was a phrase that my mum used all the time about any unassuming but profitable small enterprise: a hairdressers, a tea shop, a chippie. Did Arnold Bennett invent it in his short story *The Little Gold Mine*? Did it make its way from Burslem to Wigan? It's a nice thought. Like Hardy, Bennett rechristened real places with fictitious names. Tunstall became Turnhill; Hanley, Hanbridge; and Longton, Longshaw. Stoke was changed to Kynpe and Fenton was inexplicably missed out altogether. Burslem became Bursley and the name has somehow stuck. You can find this literary nod in the most prosaic places, so there's a Bursley Fast Food, Bursley Ale House, Bursley Kebabs. As I crest the long dull climb and turn at last into the heart of the town, I remember another line of Pevsner's: '(Burslem) is the only one of the six towns which has a centre. It may not be up to much, but it is undeniably a centre.'

That centre is a mess, frankly; all picturesque architectural corners then desolation and squalor. Boarded-up shops, manky old signs, graffiti and then a sudden glimpse of spirit and elegance. The two loveliest buildings in town face each other, handsome and graceful as dance partners, across Queen Street: the Wedgwood Institute and the Burslem School of Art. The latter was once the training ground for generations of notable ceramicists like the famed Clarice Cliff, Suzie Cooper and Arthur Berry. Today, it's a small community hub for occasional exhibitions and courses. The Wedgwood is a grand cliff of brick and terracotta and tile topped with two spectacular bas-reliefs; one depicting the signs of the Zodiac, the other pottery workers at their labour. Like the miners' institutes of the North and Wales, it was built to bring art, culture and science to the working man and woman. Most recently a public library, it currently languishes in limbo on Historic England's 'Buildings at risk' list. But it is there, at least. By contrast, there is nothing at all in Burslem to commemorate an overlooked, bloody part of working-class history that the few who know of it sometimes call the 'Potteries Peterloo'. On 16 August 1842, troops drew swords and opened fire on a rally of striking pottery workers and supportive Chartists in the town. One man, Josiah Heapy, was shot and killed outright; others were seriously injured, some later dying as a result of their wounds. To add insult to injury, at the subsequent assizes, 146 demonstrators were imprisoned and fifty-four transported to Australia. So it is a Tolpuddle as well as a Peterloo and yet scandal-ously un-commemorated.

Unlike Arnold Bennett, who lurks everywhere. A street off Swan Square is named Clayhanger Street after his novel and a tiny alley bears a plaque calling it Buggs Gutter, as the novelist did. Swan Square itself is Duck Square in Bennett's novels. It must have been pretty and dashing once and still retains a quaint charm but the defunct and squalid Queens Head hints at a dilapidation not improved by the state of the George Hotel opposite. Bennett fiction-alised it as the Dragon and even relatively recent writers and bloggers describe it as a cosy, busy inn where Thin Lizzy and others played in the 1970s. It is still a fine, imposing building. But its doors are shut and a ragged cluster of rough sleepers and drunks congregate on the steps amid empty bottles and plastic bags.

The Clayhanger was open, though, so I popped into there for a reviving soft drink. Such abstemiousness was met with some amused suspicion by a selection of regulars at the bar who seemed to have been irrigating themselves fairly comprehensively since 'early doors'. No waiting for the cocktail hour or scrutiny of yardarms here. They were cheery enough and one in a Vale shirt obliged me with the straightforward directions to another boozer I was keen to visit – The Leopard. 'But you won't be getting a pint there today, mate,' he drawled as I left. A few minutes later I realised why.

The Leopard's fame has long spread far from the Mother Town, thanks in part to the visit by Yvette Fielding, the absurd Derek Acorah and the rest of the *Most Haunted* team for that fantastically repetitive, wholly unconvincing TV ghost-hunting show which did so much to encourage widespread scepticism about the paranormal among the viewing public. The *Most Haunted* team had come to investigate phenomena like the constant ghostly laughter of children; the spectre of Molly Leigh, the Burslem Witch burned at the stake; and the ghost of a murderer called Richard who declined to give a surname.

The Leopard had been famous long before Britain's most inconclusive 'ghostbusters' staked it out. An inn since the 1760s, Wedgwood ate and drank here and met with the famous canal engineer James Brindley over a pint and a chop to discuss the Trent and Mersey coming to Burslem. Bennett renamed it The Tiger. But after a heyday of nineteenth-century opulence when it was known as The Savoy of the Midlands (perhaps they did a fantastically overpriced omelette too) it went into a decline. In 1956, two floors and fifty bedrooms were sealed off as surplus to the needs of the dwindling clientele. In the early years of this century, a man called Neil Crisp revived it, reopening the shuttered, ghostly bedrooms and commissioning new murals of Wedgwood and various ghosts. But after Neil's early death, the pub struggled and Neil's step mum Sharon closed it permanently. Some enterprising local youths revived it as a successful cannabis factory for a few years until it was bought by property developers. Finally, it burned to the ground a month before I arrived in town. On the day of the conflagration, according to the *Sun*, 'onlookers claimed they saw demonic faces in the billowing smoke.'

Any restless spirits seemed quiescent as I lingered thirstily at the gutted and blackened remains. My Port Vale supporting friend in The Clayhanger was right. I wasn't going to get a pint there today, or any other day soon. Nor, sadly, at the deserted and boarded Duke of Bridgewater, just down the Newcastle Road near Longport station. A pity. It looked the sort of pub where I could imagine Lemmy hanging out; a hairy, gnarled guy in leather and denim putting quids on the pool table – his own cue obviously – and shovelling a fistful into the jukebox, putting on some Zep or Sabbath ('proper music, none of this synthesized bollocks') as he ordered another pint of snakebite.

I imagine the morning shift at the Steelite factory next door risked a pint here at clocking off time. This works is still very much in business; gates open, reversing alarms chirping, vans and trucks passing in and out. There's a bloke on the gate having a break with a fag and the *Mirror* and I spy my chance. 'Busy day?' I ask. 'Allus, mate, allus,' he laughs. 'If you want a job they're tekking on,' and he nods to the poster by the main gate; a classy looking dish of plump langoustine, lemon coulis plated on fine white bone china and beneath 'Steelite International proudly produce over 500,000 pieces of tableware every week and ship to over 140 countries.' Thick coal dust and dark vapours may have cleared from the skies above, but they are still making plates and cups and bowls here for those who care to flip and examine before they tuck in. But I was bound for Longton. Maybe things were different there.

5

The poet, novelist and local lad John Wain said of Longton, somewhat disloyally, that it was 'one of the most squalid and depressing of the potteries towns.' That was in the 50s. When Caroline Hillier came for her 1976 travelogue *Journey to the Heart of England*, she noted that it was 'also known as Neck End and is said to be a bit rough.' Would these damning verdicts still be true? Or would Neck End now be as desirable as Crouch End? My arrival suggested not. As you 'detrain' onto the grimy platform, two large prominent signs greet you across the road. One is for Kebab King, the other for an Adult Store. Fast food and Porn. Like a new civic crest for Britain or a Sleaford Mods album, it sort of sets the tone for Longton. According to the Stoke City fanzine *The Oatcake*, 'even the chair arms in the pubs have got tattoos' here.

Longton's emblematic fictional folk hero is Owd Granddad Piggott, an 'amiable' rogue with a tremendous thirst and an aversion to hard or legal work. Invented by local author Alan Povey and set in the town's 1950s heyday, Piggott spends his days drinking, lazing around ('his last job was milk monitor') and embarking on felonious scams such as robbing chewing gum machines and brewing hooch. He is essentially a Potteries Andy Capp, that very British cartoon figure who nevertheless struck a chord around the world. In Denmark he is Kasket Karl, Willi Wakker in Germany, Angelo Capello in Italy, Andre Chapeau in France and An'Di Capp in Ghana, suggesting that pathetic, if not exactly toxic, masculinity transcends petty national borders.

Owd Granddad Piggott is not the kind of Longtonian that the town's Conservative MP Jack Brereton would approve of. The declaration on his website states that, 'I'm working hard for the area every day and I'm here to help, regardless of how you voted.' I'm standing outside Jack's office on the Strand in Longton which, it's fair to say, is not much like the one in London. The window boasts a large picture of Jack, so open and youthful of face with his broad smile, glasses and curly mop, that it suggests he's being a member of parliament as a Saturday job before he goes to big school.* His office window proclaims him a 'strong voice for Stoke-on-Trent South.'

If you are of a vintage that you might have watched a lot of telly in the 50s and 60s, you would have spent a great deal of time watching a man throw a pot, with great delicacy and skill, while you waited for the return of *Dixon of Dock Green* or *The Woodentops*. 'The Potter's Wheel' was probably the best known of the BBC post-war interlude films made to cover for intervals, studio changes or the frequent technical hitches. The film, a masterpiece of ambient minimalism worthy of Warhol showed the hands of potter Georges Aubertin, never finishing his pot but endlessly remodelling it, like a Stoke-based Myth of Sisyphus.

You can see a classic 1953 'episode' of the Potter's Wheel in the introductory film for the Gladstone Pottery Museum, a slice of Potteries life which I had been encouraged to visit. It had been in the news just a month or so before when, as local paper *The Sentinel* had it, 'One of Stoke-on-Trent's most popular tourist attractions is set to close to the public for five months a year – so it can be used as a filming location. Stoke-on-Trent City Council wants to increase the income from Gladstone Pottery Museum by marketing it as a venue for film and television productions, as well as events, between November and March each year.'

Chief among these shows is *The Great British Pottery Throwdown*, one of a glut of modern TV shows which randomly pair a vogueish stand-up comedian with some craft-related activity. As I write I feel sure *The Great British Brass Rubbing Challenge* with Josh Widdecombe

---

* He was in fact the youngest MP of the 2017 intake aged twenty-six and a Tory Councillor locally since his teens.

is in development in an office in Soho. We are a nation still vacantly watching people throw pots on prime-time TV. Except now it's not when the proper programmes break down; it's instead of the proper programmes.

On the museum's screens, as well as Georges Aubertin's Sisyphean labours, there are wistful monochrome films of backstreets and bottle ovens, courtesy of the even more wistfully named Stoke-On-Trent Cine Society. 'Flushed with success' is a chortlingly titled, thoroughly excellent display on the history of the toilet. Fun scatalogical factoids abound, such as how astronauts John Glenn and Alan Shepard both had 'accidents' in their space suits and that the average person flushes a toilet 2,500 times in a year. Elsewhere, things tend to a more social-historical point of view such as the various attempts to introduce the female urinal or Armitage's 1969 invention of the era-defining avocado bathroom suite, now as fixed in a particular period as a sedan chair. Other exhibits forego the gags and show just how short and wretched life was without proper facilities, with thousands of children a year dying or being orphaned from cholera, diarrhoea, diphtheria and other diseases of insanitary living.

Charles Shaw's extraordinary autobiographical account of child labour in the potbanks, which Bennett used as source material for his novel *Clayhanger*, reveals how as a child of seven Shaw sweated and toiled from five in the morning until eight at night, heaving and pounding clay and lifting moulds onto shelves in the burning hot stove rooms. He tells of unfeeling and indifferent owners and the callous attitudes of 'great' Victorians like Lord Brougham who said 'charity is an interference with the healing process of nature which acts by increasing the rate of mortality and thereby raising wages.'

In the 'surgery' at the museum, there is a genuinely chilling film vignette from the point of view of a kindly but overworked Longton doctor, scanning his waiting room and describing his patients. It is a roll call of ghouls and spectres, actors of course, but unnervingly haunted and sickly. 'Look at these people ... this old boy here, old before his time, years of smoke and clay dust on his lungs ... coughing up blood ... Potters Rot they call it.' Other patients include a woman with lead poisoning from the paints and glazes and a young mother feeding her infant milk from an unsterilised 'murder bottle', risking diarrhoea or something worse. 'Surely we can do better for you, little man?'

We did do better for him, by and large. No thanks to the employers or shareholders of the pottery companies or grandees like Lord Brougham, but by the will of the people and a government acting in consort with them, by the establishment of trade unions, the NHS and the welfare State. The average life expectancy in Victorian Longton among the potbank workers was thirty-seven. What an era! A time of great men and their adventures, of glorious reigns and empires on which the sun never set, of whooping cough and dysentery and five in a soaking, filthy bed and children working all day in hellish factories and dying at thirty-seven and leaving a family in the workhouse.

Arnold Bennett was no Marxist. Once he'd left the Potteries, which was as fast as he could, he enjoyed a comfortable life propped on the twin pillars of fame and wealth. But, while not sentimentalising them with what E P Thompson famously called 'the enormous condescension of posterity,' as evidenced in *The Old Wives' Tale*, Bennett understood the life of the Potteries' people and the towns that held them here in life and in death. 'They are unique and indispensable because you cannot drink tea out of a teacup without the aid of the five towns; because you cannot eat a meal in decency without the aid of the five towns. For this the architecture of the five towns is an architecture of ovens and chimneys; for this its atmosphere is as black as mud; for this it burns and smokes all night, so that Longshaw has been compared to hell.'

Today, daily misery of life at the bottom of the economic ladder is not compounded by smoke and filth but mainly by the grinding anxiety of precarious employment or the remorseless, unworkable targets for warehouse picker and delivery driver. By the end of the twentieth century, the number of workers in Stoke's ceramics industry had fallen from 70,000 in its heyday to about 6,000. Bet365, the online gambling company, are the biggest employer here now. Peter Coates, the millionaire chairman of Stoke City FC started Bet365 with his daughter Denise (now the UK's richest woman) in the very shop, now disused, that was the model for the drapers in Bennett's *The Old Wives' Tale*. What would Bennett make of that? Or Priestley? The sordid, furtive backstreet business of pitch and toss and bookie's runners, now as respectable and institutional in Stoke as Wedgwood, Spode or Clarice Cliff, and now an abstract digital matrix of zeroes and ones, not a grubby matter of coins and dice and betting slips.

Longton's streets don't probably get many flâneurs. But after leaving the Gladstone, I take a leisurely circuit of the surrounding streets. Left on Webberly Lane and up to the works of Hudson Middleton which a flyblown poster on the wall claims is 'one of the only remaining all British potteries.' The broken windows and dirty curtains suggest that claim is no longer valid. I turn up Calverley Street and emerge onto a grim and dilapidated stretch of the Uttoxeter Road where a building called St Mary's Mount Pleasant, a former pottery still owned by Royal Doulton, stands grand if forlorn (Grade II listed no less) above its shabby neighbouring terraces, the pavements crowded with wheelie bins and rubbish bags.

I'd never expected Longton to vie with Lower Slaughter or Broadway for beauty. But even so I am shocked by the bleakness of some of these back roads, such as Baker Street, a hinterland of ruin behind Abigail's Beauty and Plasterworld, both silent and derelict. What has laid waste to these streets? Covid? Brexit? Or just a long receding tide of money flowing elsewhere, to London, Frankfurt and New York? There seems to be one open and functioning shop selling 'exotic reptiles' in a wasteland of old ruined washing machines, smashed toilets, chain fences and alkali scrub – plastic sheeting slapping and writhing in the wind and the acrid smell of god knows what burning in corroded skips. Things improve a little as I walk down Sutherland Street. There are at least signs of activity at Midlands Elements and Tegiwa, though Lord knows of what kind. Two bus stops as well, though it didn't feel as though anyone had needed to catch a bus here in a long time.

The former site of the Aynsley China is now a boxing gym and Talented Nails And Beauty. The china works itself, established in 1775 just as America was being born, closed in 2014 with the loss of the forty remaining jobs. The factory's production has moved, with bitter humour, to China, where it is now possibly known as China china.

I didn't laugh either. We ended the last chapter in Priestley's 'Rusty Lane', West Brom's Grice Street and Spon Lane. Longton's 'Rusty Lane' is down here on Calverley and Baker and Sutherland Street. The last is named for the Duke of Sutherland, who lived not here of course but in the nearby stately home of Trentham Hall in Trentham Gardens.* Unlike 'Rusty Lane', these streets are not full of urchins and disease but rather of very little, of remnants and relics left after successive waves of economic failure. But the Turkish barbers is packed, every chair and bench full of rows of lads, their surly heads bowed over mobile phones, with each identical head being shaved in turn. The image recalls Elvis being inducted into the army, of *Full Metal Jacket*. From the open doorway, the radio crackles with news that the young men of Ukraine are arming. In Longton, the lads – silent and passive over their Instagrams – are getting ready

---

* The Sutherlands, infamous for the family's brutal role in the Highland Clearances, moved south to Stafford Hall in London in the early 1900s, then the most valuable family home in Britain, leaving Trentham Hall to begin a long decline that has seen it derelict since 2015. Part of the estate is now Trentham Monkey Forest, 60 acres containing 140 free-roaming Barbary macaques.

for nothing more dangerous than the skirmish of emotion and testosterone that is a Saturday night in England. That is Longton's small mercy.

8

TO LANCASHIRE

In which I head for the hills of 'Accy' and 'Ossy',
make a pilgrimage to Marcus of Withington's shrine
and try to avoid overdoing The Beatles.

Lapskaus is a hearty, savoury stew of leftover meat and root vegetables enjoyed by sailors and working communities across the Nordic countries. Brooklyn's Eighth Avenue, traditionally home to much of New York's Norwegian American population, was once known as Lapskaus Boulevard. Lobscouse, as it became in loose anglicisation, was one of the favourite dishes of my childhood. It's tasty, hard to get wrong, and even my culinarily-challenged Lancashire nan, whose home cooking was the stuff of nightmares, could be relied upon to rustle up a decently warming bowl of the stuff on a winter Saturday. In my part of Lancashire, we took the first part of the word and called it Lobbies. In Liverpool, they took the second and called it Scouse. From there, it was an easy step of association to call themselves Scousers. It's a term which should simply mean stew-enthusiast, then. But as everyone knows, it implies a lot more.

'Scouse Not English'. If you have sixteen quid to spare and a point to make, you can buy a T-shirt bearing that legend. It's not true, of course. You can be both. But the fact that these T-shirts exist (and sell) tells you a lot about Liverpool. Every time Liverpool FC get to Wembley, the right-wing papers clutch their pearls and reach for the nosegays when their fans boo the National Anthem, something they have been doing since the FA Cup final of 1965. Queen, or King, and country mean little on Merseyside, as it is someone else's Queen and someone else's country. Three quarters of Liverpool claim Irish descent and it's the only British city to have had an Irish nationalist MP in T P O'Connor, MP for Scotland Road from 1885 to 1929. We can look further south for Liverpool's other compatriots. I have previously described Merseyside as 'the Basque Country of Lancashire'. Bootle, like Barcelona, regards itself as a region apart, with a different language, culture and mindset. Liverpool thinks itself funnier, smarter and cooler than the rest of England, relishing a willed separateness, an assertion of cultural difference, even superiority. A Scouse exceptionalism.

Twenty-first century readers might find it perverse then that Priestley begins the Lancashire chapter of *English Journey* in a city which regards itself in all matters as 'exceedingly rare' (as one of Liverpool's many self-celebratory songs has it) and certainly not cut from Lancashire cloth. Lancashire is other; a county Scousers view as a damp rolling upland of cotton towns and slow troll minds brooding under dark hills.

Neither Priestley nor Liverpool felt this way, this separate, back in 1934. These are modern notions. There was never a sense that the Liverpool of the nineteenth or early twentieth centuries was anything other than a proudly English city in the grand old Red Rose County. In fact, it saw itself as the patrician, traditionally English, maritime capital of the north compared to rough, factory-working, non-conformist, socialistic Manchester.

But that was yesterday, when all its troubles seemed so far away. Just as The Beatles' sexy, melodious drawl gave way to *Brookside*'s adenoidal growl, so Liverpool's perceived character and self-image began to alter in the early 80s, with the extinction of industrial Britain and the grim advent of Thatcherism and Militant, twin poles of ideological fundamentalism. In the red corner was Militant, Trotskyite fellow-travellers of mainstream Labour who ironically helped pave the way for the New Labour revolution. In the blue corner was Margaret Thatcher and her government, zealously charged with their mission to disarm and eventually dismantle the northern English working class. Eeyorish Sir Geoffrey Howe was seen as one of the more benign 'wets' of this cabal. Yet even he said this of Liverpool in a secret memo when Chancellor: 'I fear Merseyside is going to be much the hardest nut to crack … I cannot help but feel that the option of managed decline is one which we should not forget altogether. We must not expend all our limited resources in trying to make water flow uphill.' In other words, let the basket case on the banks of the Mersey die of neglect.

Because of its defiance of the new Toryism, expressed in songs, strikes and the occasional riot, Liverpool in the 80s was a city that, once branded a treacherous fifth-columnist, embraced and relished this status with a typical blend of humour and menace. The Conservative Party's mistrust – loathing is perhaps nearer the mark – of the city persists. In May 2021, Conservative minister Robert Jenrick talked of an 'environment of intimidation' and a 'dysfunctional culture' at Liverpool City Council and took over some functions of the day-to-day running of the council. It was the first time Westminster had directly intervened in the workings of any city this big. Did the fact that Liverpool is one of the most solidly and visibly socialist cities in Britain have any influence on Mr Jenrick's decision? You must make your own mind up. Liverpool certainly thinks so.

In an editorial on 16 October 2004 the then editor of militantly right-wing periodical the *Spectator* said that an 'excessive predilection for welfarism has created a peculiar, and deeply unattractive, psyche among many Liverpudlians. They see themselves whenever possible as victims and resent their victim status; yet at the same time they wallow in it. Part of this flawed psychological state is that they cannot accept that they might have made any contribution to their misfortunes, but seek rather to blame someone else for it, thereby deepening their sense of shared tribal grievance against the rest of society.'

That writer was Boris Johnson.

Let's be clear, Liverpudlians do have a capacity for brazen self-mythologising and hubris every bit as great as their warring cousins down the East Lancs Road in Manchester. But Merseyside's comes with a little more leavening sentimentality, perhaps a trait from their Irish side, and wry good humour. It's useful to remember some of the things that have happened to, in or because of Liverpool and its people since Priestley's 1930s visit to get a sense of the character and image of the modern Liverpool: the Blitz, The Beatles, Shankly, *Boys From The Blackstuff*, *Brookside*, the Toxteth Riots, Heysel, Hillsborough, Cream and the Superclubs. Each has contributed to the mosaic of identity that is modern Liverpool. It's dynamic, creative, fervent, witty, bloody-minded, socialistic; either a crucible of drama, vitality and passion or a sink of self-pity, truculence and conceit, depending on your politics.

I arrive at Lime Street Station to be struck once again by the magnificence of the St George's Hall across the road. Rather like that famously belligerent 'This is Anfield' sign that greets the opposition as they emerge from the tunnel at Liverpool FC's home ground, St George's Hall was put just there to tell the world arriving by train that they were in Liverpool now, and one way or another they were in for quite a time of it. In the city centre, landmarks of varying beauty cluster around Lime Street. St John's, once Liverpool's premier 'mall', was built in 1969 and is showing its age, eclipsed in style and pizzazz by upscale neighbour Liverpool One across town. St John's is home to Greggs, Home Bargains and Fat Lolly Sam's rather than the top marque Apple, Nike and Disney stores of the newer complex. It's thronged with red-faced men in sportswear; girls in budget glamour; clusters of kids and mums with Maccy D's and party balloons, new trainers from Footlocker and tops from Primark.

There's the Liverpool Empire where I saw a succession of groups with differing trouser dimensions and hair lengths during my teenage years. Not far is the fabulous Walker Art Gallery and the Adelphi Hotel, a building for which the term 'faded grandeur' might have been invented. Jules Verne, here either on a mini break or to see Everton at home, compared the submarine interior in *Twenty Thousand Leagues Under the Sea* to the main lounge at the Adelphi. Staying at sea, Granada TV used it in their *Brideshead Revisited* TV adaptation for a luxury ocean liner setting. In the documentary *Don't Look Back*, Bob Dylan appears on the balcony of his room to wave regally down to his Scouse fans.

Well, Bob, I can only hope that you had a better stay than I did on my last visit, which was more 'Desolation Row' than 'Positively 4th Street'. A glance at Tripadvisor will tell you that opinions are 'mixed' about this venerable Liverpudlian fixture. Some guests admired the architecture and location, others were less keen about getting sworn at by the receptionist and the dank smell and mossy growths in the bathroom. A reporter from the *Liverpool Echo* who spent a night there reported of breakfast in Jenny's Bar that 'the mushrooms and the sausage on my plate looked like different sections of the Bristol stool scale.' I had all my just-purchased toiletries and expensive soap bag removed and binned and was told that I shouldn't have left them 'lying around' in the bathroom. I booked myself somewhere else this time.

Priestley said he'd never seen Liverpool in good weather. I arrive in blistering heat to find Liverpool slathering on the sun cream, the city so hot it made you fear for one of Liverpool's more undervalued pieces of public art: the fading jellybean mosaic of ITV stalwart and drag act turned dog enthusiast Paul O'Grady in a sweet shop window on the Albert Dock. I ate chips and ice cream (consecutively, not concurrently) from a fast-food van by the Billy Fury statue. Fury is an almost forgotten figure in British music, except perhaps by uber-fan Morrissey (which comes with its own baggage). A Liverpool tugboat hand originally called Ronald Wycherly and rechristened by Larry Parnes, he was the first to release an entirely self-penned album with his debut *Sound of Fury*. His only number one was in Singapore but his string of twenty-four hits of the 1960s were equalled by only one other pop act. They came from Liverpool too and they also have a statue on their pier head. Their name is rather better known, though. When the Voyager probe bearing their music reaches the Proxima Centauri system, they'll probably be big there as well.

We do not know what JBP thought of The Beatles. We do know, however, what 21-year-old Paul McCartney of Allerton, South Liverpool made of Priestley's 1963 stage adaptation of Iris Murdoch's novel *A Severed Head*: 'It was the crappiest thing I had ever seen,' he told chum and bandmate John Lennon. Here he was in tune with the audiences in the US where the play folded after just twenty-nine performances. But I reckon Priestley may well have liked The Fabs. For all his fusty public image, sometimes self-cultivated, he was no fuddy-duddy. He was a fan of Monty Python, science fiction and Morecambe and Wise. He loved the more interesting modern end of the classical repertoire from Debussy to Bartók. But he never gave us his views on The Beatles.

He would never have predicted that the economy of this great maritime city would depend not on liners and cargo but on the seeming flotsam of pop culture, on The Beatles, football and humour. These three things comprise a holy trinity that defines Liverpool to the world. Some people accuse Liverpool of overdoing The Beatles, but let's see this in context. This one band was arguably the most important cultural force of the late twentieth century. Without them, popular music might never have exploded and expanded into the force that it became, changing not just haircuts and hemlines but the borders of the world. When Communism crumbled, it was as much to do with the yearning of millions for the freedom, joy and energy The Beatles embodied as it was collapsing ideologies and the price of wheat. So, if Salzburg means Mozart and Stratford means Shakespeare, if Haworth can celebrate the Brontës and Tupelo Elvis, then we cannot begrudge Liverpool the greatest pop group there has ever been or will ever be. A 2016 report by John Moores University concluded that 'the catalytic effects of Beatles activity … [was] calculated to be £155m in turnover, providing jobs for 5,020 people.' That's a lot of happy families too.

In November 2021 Peter Jackson released his epic eight-hour film documentary *Get Back*, an astonishingly intimate account, based on over seventy hours of archive film, of The Beatles' last days, the recording of their final album and their last ever performance on the roof of the Apple building in London's Savile Row. And after nearly two years of misery and restraint, *Get Back* was a sudden vivid reminder not just of how wonderful The Beatles were, but how vibrant and dynamic England once was: a land where four working-class lads with no contacts, no old school ties, no friends in high places, could change the world with just their talent and energy.

Jackson's film was still some months off when I spent my long hot summer days in Liverpool, a brief sunburst in the clouds of a rolling lockdown. But The Beatles are present in Liverpool every day. Walk from Lime Street, where 'dirty Maggie Mae' plied her trade according to Lennon on the *Let It Be* album, down Whitechapel, and above the Barnardo's charity shop, you'll see a couple of crotchets still stuck on one of the dusty upper windows. This is all that remains of Rushworth and Dreaper where The Beatles bought guitars they couldn't really afford with money cadged from family. A little further along, there's a clothes shop called Forever 21, a US chain offering 'high fashion at low prices'. Sixty years ago, this was the NEMS record department of a furniture store, where a young man in a leather jacket walked in and asked manager Brian Epstein for a copy of 'My Bonnie' by local group The Beatles. His interest piqued, he went to see them play at the Cavern Club around the corner on Mathew Street and, yes, the rest really is history.

This whole area of town is now referred to as the Cavern Quarter and boasts several statues of wildly varying quality. There's 'Eleanor Rigby' by cockney entertainer Tommy Steele in which 'Eleanor' sits on a bench with a shopping bag, a milk bottle, the *Liverpool Echo*, a loaf of bread and a sparrow, none of which appear in the song. The plaque reads 'For all the Lonely People'. It's a classic naff example of what happens when the mystery and enigma of genius are 'explained' by inferior imaginations. See also John Lennon with the giant head way too big for his little body and, weirdest of all, the very creepy 'Four Lads That Shook The World' with three Beatle babies cradled in the arms of a ghoulish, faceless 'Mother Mary' draped in spiders' webs. The fourth representing Macca as a winged cherub playing the trumpet ('for obvious reasons' said the sculptor Arthur Dooley, bafflingly) was nicked in the 70s. More cheerily, there's also a statue of former Cavern cloakroom attendant Cilla Black. I stick my head in The Grapes pub for a reviving shandy, hoping that this was the table the Fab Four used to drink at.

The Liverpool waterfront, to which all Scouse strolls will eventually lead you, always feels far more like Manhattan than Lancashire. The United States' first ever foreign consulate was established here in 1790, a sign of the friendship and links between the city and America – many of course sadly forged through the slave trade. The Three Graces – that is to say, the Cunard Building, The Liver Building and the Royal Assurance – will always dominate here, but newer arrivals have staked their visual claim on the waterfront. One is the striking new Museum of Liverpool Life, celebrating Liverpool's history and communities. In a section on prehistoric Liverpool, some of the figures look suspiciously to me like they have been repurposed from effigies left over from The Beatles Story down on the Albert Dock. The iron age archer and roofer bear a striking resemblance to John and Paul circa *Rubber Soul*, if a little shaggier and less carefree.

The museum is not shy of embracing Liverpool's renegade, rebellious nature. Like the city, it relishes it, billing one section The People's Republic of Liverpool. Famous son and late newsreader Peter Sissons offers an explanation of such typically useful Scouse phrases as 'it's all kicking off'. Degsy Bruce of the era-defining 80s Scouse soap *Brookside* relates proudly how the city 'stood up to Thatcher.' There is a truly chilling section on the poverty endured by the nineteenth-century Irish community in the city. This, inevitably and uncomfortably, reminded me of the most problematic section in the whole of Priestley's *English Journey*. Confronted with this poverty, still rank and desperate in the 1930s of course, Priestley wrote: 'The Irishman in Ireland may, as we are so often assured he is, be the best fellow in the world, only waiting to say good-bye to the hateful empire so that, free and independent at last, he too can astonish the world. But the Irishman in England too often cuts a very miserable figure. He has lost his peasant virtues, whatever they are, and has acquired no others … If we do have an Irish Republic as our neighbour, and it is found possible to return her exiled citizens, what a grand clearance there will be in all the Western ports, from the Clyde to Cardiff, what a fine exit of ignorance and dirt and drunkenness and disease.'

It's hard to gloss this as anything other than bigotry. The only mitigation I can offer is that it may come from a misguided pride in England rather than genuine contempt of the Irish. But I am aware that that sounds very like a mealy-mouthed excuse. I hear it myself. Similarly, both the museum and *English Journey* reflect at length on Liverpool's Chinese community, the former more comfortably for modern readers. Visiting a local school, Priestley observes that 'all the faces of mankind were there, wonderfully mixed. Imagine an infant class of half-castes, quadroons, octaroons with all the latitudes and longtitudes [sic.] confused in them.' A well-meaning vicar points out a young lad. '"Now that boy looks English enough, doesn't he? But as a matter of fact, he's half Chinese. Yes, and he's all Chinese inside. He has dreams, that boy, and they're all Oriental dreams."' But there is real – if patronising – sympathy in Priestley's conclusions: 'There was something deeply impressive, almost moving, about the sight of these strange children, here in this slum corner of Lancashire. Although they had mostly been begotten, born and reared in the most pitifully sordid circumstances, nearly all of them were unusually attractive in appearance.'

The museum, as you'd expect, digs rather deeper into the real life of Europe's oldest Chinese community. Liverpool today is rightly proud of the rich history of family and working life on the boats and in the many Chinese laundries that thrived until the Second World War. Less comfortable is the following chapter. During the war, the British Merchant Navy began recruiting sailors from its allies across the world and Liverpool was turned into a reserve pool for these Chinese merchant sailors. Many gave their lives to ensure Britain's victory. But in 1946 more than 200 were forcibly removed during night raids, some tricked into voyages on ships that would never return, leaving behind abandoned wives and children who were never told the truth. The museum has heart-breaking testimonies that have been collected as 'Where has my father gone?'

Priestley concluded that Liverpool's Chinatown was declining, a result of the depression and its effects on the shipping business. He'd have been shocked, and delighted, to see Chinatown today, bustling, lively and relocated several streets inland (the old one having been bombed and then slum-cleared). I decide to head there to refuel, taking a circuitous route to see some more of the city. Wapping, when Priestley visited, was still a working dock. But only just. 'It was deep dusk ... Everything was shadowy now. The warehouses we passed seemed empty of everything but shadows. A few men – far too few – came straggling along, their day's work over. We arrived at the edge of the Mersey, and below us was a long mudbank. The water was a grey mystery ... We walked slowly along the water-front, from nothing, it seemed, into nothing; and darkness rose rather than fell; and with it came a twinkle of lights from Birkenhead that reached us not across the river but over a gulf that could not be measured. I have rarely seen anything more spectral and melancholy.'

Now the docks are luxury flats where, on this scorching late afternoon, glamorous women chat over coffee on sunlit balconies, their beautiful children playing at their feet. The giant warehouses of Wapping Quay, once alive with rice weevils that infested your clothes and hair if you got a student summer job here, are now vast, deserted hulks, surely awaiting their resurgence as arts spaces, 'digital hubs' or studio apartments. Past the Baltic Fleet pub and the Swedish Church and up through the Ropewalks quarter. Here, you won't be surprised to learn, they once made ropes on the long narrow streets. Now the area's main industry is pleasure, every doorway a bar or restaurant, or offering tattoos, sunbeds or the associated paraphernalia of self-actualisation. The big square, covered in tables, is already full at 5pm, a raucous, shifting mass of red faces, spray tans, cold lager and vape smoke. The evening is beginning to simmer in the streets. Heavy-set men in untucked floral shirts pass by in a sudden ozone whoosh of Aramis and Armani Code. Deep-tanned girls with astonishing eyebrows teeter by in clingfilm dresses laughing the laugh that comes with filthy jokes, shocking gossip and four 'pre-bar' Mojitos. Like every town and city in England through 2021, Liverpool was, like Macbeth, 'cabined, cribbed, confined' by the stasis of lockdown for months and so, as I arrive, is making the most of the new freedoms and the relaxation of rules. But Liverpool is not every other city, and you can sense the wild night that is already coming to the boil here, in what my Liverpudlian agent claims with Scouse bravura, is the 'most dangerous square in Europe.'

Once upon a time, when I was young and fearless and thought naught for the morrow, I would perhaps have relished a Saturday night here. But now I'm more drawn to the history of Chinatown, a look at the Chinese Gospel Church and the blue plaque outside the New Capital restaurant on Nelson Street that proclaims that the Blue Funnel Shipping Office was housed upstairs in this building between 1950 and 1969. There is a quote from the Victorian shipping magnate Alfred Holt ('Keep my funnels tall and blue, and look after my China men'), a belated acknowledgement of the debt Liverpool (and Britain) owes its Chinese sailors and the shame at their treatment.

Mei Mei restaurant is a Chinatown fixture. It's popular with tourists and locals alike, some who even have the reckless courage to order from the pages at the back of the menu where the tripe and chicken's feet lurk. I have visited once before. Late at night after giving a talk at the university, I came here as the guest of some notable academics. As there were eleven of us, I suggested that a 'banquet' type set-meal might be an elegant solution, and this was duly ordered. After a while, though, as plate after plate and bowl upon bowl of spare ribs, spring rolls, hot and sour soup, fried rice, sweet and sour chicken, chili beef, hoisin duck, egg foo yung and chow mein noodles arrived, covering every available inch of tablecloth, it dawned on me that we, or rather they, had ordered not the set meal for eleven but *eleven* set meals for eleven. It also occurred to me that the bill was going to push some way into four figures. By the time it arrived, I had made my excuses and was back at my hotel watching telly with a packet of Monster Munch.

Saturday teatime finds it full of shoppers and families and birthday parties. When Priestley visited hereabouts in 1933, he found rheumy old sailors, 'ochreous' babies and 'faces that had shone for a season in brothels in Victoria's time.' In short, what he harshly termed 'unwashed humanity'. He would be amazed at what had happened to the area. This is Liverpool's working people at their deserved play, chicly attired older folk with shopping bags, gorgeous young people whose racial mix would dizzy him and families like the one at the next table. He, fortyish in chinos and Fred Perry; she, blonde and smart and with two little versions of her between them, delightedly trying to use chopsticks and finger bowl. I fancy them living in an affluent suburb somewhere, West Derby maybe, with a Range Rover Velar on the drive and a pony in the top field.

And so, back to Lime Street Station where I once sat on the steps and drank and chatted with Barney from New Order dressed as Vegas-era Elvis (him not me) after recording the video for 'World in Motion' at Liverpool's training ground. It's early Saturday evening and I am headed to Manchester, next stop on Priestley's itinerary. Astonishingly, some treasonous Liverpudlians are doing the very same thing for a night out. In my carriage are a group of Scouse girls, dressed to whatever the nines are, applying 'lippy', drinking tins of M&S gin and slim and singing along to a Dua Lipa song blasting tinnily out from a phone. It's a lusty rendition but the arrangement could stand a bit of tightening. I pop my headphones in and dip into my Liverpool notes. Here's daughter of the city, Beryl Bainbridge, writing in the *Spectator* in 2007 on revisiting Priestley's *English Journey*: 'The very things that Mr Priestley deplored, and which in part have been swept away, are the things I lament, particularly in regard to Liverpool – the narrow streets, the old-fashioned houses, the flower ladies in Williamson Square.' Put simply, this is nonsense. Priestley may have liked many of these things. What he deplored was poverty, which is what those narrow streets and old-fashioned houses were steeped in. I doubt Bainbridge was writing in a cramped street or decrepit house when she concluded, as she did on the airwaves, 'If Priestley returned to Liverpool today, he would not know it. I think it's ghastly. It is full of glass buildings that simply do not do anything. Entering Liverpool is like entering a foreign land. It is all wrong.'

Try telling this to Molly and Suzanne with their G&Ts, implausible eyebrows and defiant glamour. Try telling that to the diners in Mei Mei accidentally drinking the finger bowl and massively over-ordering. Try telling that to the roaring thousands at Anfield and Goodison or the 5,000 kept in work by the genius of four lads from Allerton and Penny Lane and the Dingle. London's writer class making a commissioned anthropological visit to their hometowns and dashing off a few sneering words in first class back to Euston is an industry that is never in decline. Priestley even did a bit of it himself. But Bainbridge was right on one thing: JBP wouldn't know Liverpool today. He would not recognise this happy, busy, feisty city with its distinct absence of sepulchral gloom. On his trip back, as he cracked an M&S gin in the back seat of that fancy Daimler, he would drink to that.

2

If the Basques of Liverpool see themselves as a race apart, Manchester is then free to claim status as the capital of the North West, and with the same sense of hauteur that characterises Madrid. Paul Morley put it well: 'Manchester is becoming to the rest of the North what London and the rest of the south has traditionally been to the rest of the north; richer and more funded, its skyline rapidly changing, other northern cities and areas shrinking beneath its weight.' While those other towns and cities, the mile stations of the crumbling Red Wall, often fell under the spell of Brexit and the dissembling populism of Johnsonian Toryism, Manchester remains one of Britain's most left-wing cities, especially in its northern suburbs. In Andy Burnham, it has one of the most liked and respected socialist politicians in Britain. It has a young, left-leaning student population and at least one football team with a distinctly red take on things. It used to have a daily newspaper to match.

In *English Journey*, Priestley wrote that a Mancunian could read the best newspaper in the country in the morning and hear the best orchestra in the evening. The Hallé is still there and you can still read the *Guardian* on a Manchester morning. But it would no longer be your local paper. The Manchester prefix was dropped in 1959 to present a more national and international image and, five years later, the editorial department moved to London. Something of the *Guardian*'s liberal high-mindedness lives on in the city in the form of the Manchester International Festival, a biennial arts fest that is both brilliant and exasperating, and in full swing this Mancunian summer.

Because of this festival I've chatted with Laurie Anderson and Peter Mandelson in Albert Square, seen brilliant theatre pieces by Maxine Peake and Jane Horrocks about Peterloo and Lancashire textile workers, and watched extraordinary performances in the labyrinthine tunnels below Victoria Station with The XX. But as I spend time in Manchester for the most recent festival, I sometimes feel the dead weight of a certain cultural assumption and mindset. For instance, you can't miss an installation called 'Big Ben Lying Down with Political Books' in Piccadilly Gardens. Now, granted, anything in this awful public space that distracts from the overpowering smell of skunk and cider is welcome, so this installation is drawing quite a crowd. According to the blurb 'lying almost horizontal and covered in 20,000 copies of books that have shaped British politics, this 42-metre replica of Big Ben (is) the first major UK commission by Argentine artist Marta Minujín, who creates extraordinary large-scale artworks and participatory performances that put socially engaged art at the heart of everyday life.'

All good art should provoke questions. Here were some questions that leapt to my mind. Why Big Ben? Why was it lying down? Why was the choice of books so narrow and one-sided in perspective? This was a very partial, sponsored, consensual view, which might be close to mine, but has clearly had little sway or currency with many of the people of Lancashire for years. Take the *Communist Manifesto*, given pride of place here in the approved books. It shaped life for good and ill for over half of humanity, in Latvia and Lviv, yes, but not Lancashire's Red Wall. There was no room here for Hayek's *The Road*

To Serfdom, probably the most influential text on British politics in the last half century and the ideological basis of Thatcherism. None of the key writings of the New Labour project by Will Hutton or Jonathan Freedland were here either. There was a smug assumption, prevalent on the Left, that we all share the same set of beliefs and analyses. Priestley loathed Hayek, Thatcher and their views. But he'd be clearsighted and tough-minded enough to acknowledge their baleful influence rather than ignore it. Anyway, when they make me a consultant director of the festival, one of the first things I'll do is commission a new 'Twelfth Night' for the Palace Theatre with Peter Kay or Jason Manford as Malvolio and charge residents a fiver. It would trumpet that this really is a festival for the people of Manchester more powerfully than a thousand installations.

I follow the tram tracks from Piccadilly Gardens to St Peter's Square and almost into the foyer of the Midland Hotel. Modern Manchester leads the world in hipster boutique hotels, a sea of infinity pools, a forest of brushed copper and glass, where every room has a Nespresso machine and a minibar of white spirits distilled from the fronds of Finnish forests, each costing as much as a ticket to Helsinki. During his disastrous tenure at Manchester United, Jose Mourinho never bothered finding a flat, preferring the starkly sexy boudoirs and red leather minimalist chaises longues at the Lowry Hotel, Salford. In the midst of this upstart glam though, The Midland still fancies itself the original and the best, slightly brassy and blousy with the plumped bosom of its gilt and curlicues and balconies exuding a certain Bet Lynch cachet. It is soaked in history, sometimes of a bloody kind. It backs on to Peterloo Fields where, in 1819, the sabres of the Cheshire Yeomanry cut down innocent men, women and children protesting their lack of parliamentary representation. Rolls met Royce here in May 1904, and in 1976, in an upstairs room that was once the Lesser Free Trade Hall, the Sex Pistols played here to a tiny crowd of cognoscenti and lit the blue touchpaper of a musical revolution. Nowadays, my publisher has offices next door.

I'm staying at The Midland tonight for a couple of reasons. First, because Priestley did and I'm following in his footsteps, and second because, like him, 'I had other business of my own to attend to and was at the old difficult never-turning-out-quite-satisfactorily trick of trying to kill two birds with one stone.' He had a 'little comedy trying out' at The Palace. I have an engagement at The Midland itself which had appealed because of its sheer oddity.

Suffice to say that my humorous and informative talk about The North to a delegation of Danish processed meat salesmen does not quite set the Mancunian night aflame. My elegant and lapidary bons mots and observations are met with benign bemusement from a group of men who were, not unreasonably, seeking to get as drunk as possible while clinching that big streaky bacon deal with the buyer from Moto services. I console myself with the thought that Priestley himself might have gone down no better with a roomful of half-cut Friesian salami vendors, and also with the generosity of my lovely hosts from the Manchester wing of the processed meat fraternity, who have provided me with a suite overlooking St Peter's Square. It is a liquid, balmy night and as I stand at my balcony looking imperiously down on the straggling revellers below and the lighted midnight trams sailing away for Chorlton and Didsbury, I feel like Mussolini. But in a good way obviously, without the curtailment of human rights and suppression of democracy. Tomorrow I will take one of those trams out to the suburb of Withington to investigate a local lad made good – not just a terrific footballer, not just carrying the burden of being one of England's strikers in a major football tournament but, for one summer, the unofficial leader of the opposition.

Just before the Covid-delayed Euro 2020 football tournament, England manager Gareth Southgate published a well-crafted and fascinating open letter addressed to 'Dear England' (Later the basis for a lauded play by James Graham at the National Theatre). In it he stressed that he wanted the team to unite the country in a positive and progressive patriotism rather than the belligerent nationalism and ugly bigotry often associated with supporting England's football team. 'Our players are role models,' he wrote. 'It's their duty to continue to interact with the public on matters such as equality, inclusivity and racial injustice, while using the power of their voices to help put debates on the table, raise awareness and educate.' He stated bluntly: 'I have never believed that we should just stick to football.' It was a direct rebuke to many, including then home secretary Priti Patel, who had dismissed the England team's 'taking the knee' protests in support of the Black Lives Matter movement as 'gesture politics'. One Conservative MP, Lee Anderson, now party chairman, said he would boycott the games while they continued to make this 'gesture' but added, absurdly, that he would check the scores on his phone. Others on the Right were more considered. Ruth Davidson, the leader of the Scottish Conservatives tweeted: 'Really interesting – and impressive – to hear Southgate talking about the power of sport to influence national and cultural identity in these terms. He really is a class act, isn't he?'

Half of the 26-man squad could have chosen to play for another nation. The fact that they didn't shows a patriotism they might have been applauded for. But, as Andrew Rawnsley pointed out in the *Observer*, the England they were playing for was not the version beloved of Jacob Rees-Mogg or Nigel Farage: 'play up and play the game', class division and deference. 'I would not presume to guess which way individual members of the England squad vote,' wrote Rawnsley, 'but they do not present as natural Tories and their matches were not won on the playing fields of Eton. They have foregrounded life stories involving modest or challenging family circumstances when they were growing up. Several of the squad are effective social activists for progressive causes.'

Chief among them was Marcus Rashford of Withington, a dual-heritage Manc lad who by dint of talent, effort and the support of his single mum, was now a first choice for Manchester United and his country. In the year leading up the tournament, he had single-handedly forced Boris Johnson's government into a climbdown on continuing free school meals during the summer holidays, something he himself had needed as a child. Careful not to align himself with any party, he became a people's hero, not least in the Withington streets where he grew up. On one of them, a giant mural celebrating him was created. In his open letter, Southgate, a man who *Telegraph* parliamentary sketch writer Michael Deacon thought, only half-joking, could lead a new centrist party to government, said: 'It's clear to me that we are heading for a much more tolerant and understanding society, and I know our lads will be a big part of that.' Unfortunately, not everyone had got the memo. After a series of superb performances, England lost the final on penalties to Italy. In the shoot-out, three black players, among them Rashford, missed their spot kicks. Overnight, Rashford's mural was defaced with obscenities.

But this in turn provoked an extraordinary response. Within minutes of the attack, the mural became a place of pilgrimage for those who stood with Rashford, which turned out to be nearly everyone. Priestley loved football and hated bigots. He'd have taken in the Rashford mural on his *English Journey*. So, on a searingly hot Saturday morning, the kind that Priestley claimed never to have seen in Manchester, I leave a tram full of masked and perspiring passengers at Withington tram stop and made my way up the hill, past Hough End playing fields and the leisure centre where Rashford learned his skills as a kid, up wide leafy streets, past the big Bevan council houses, and eventually to the Coffee House café, where the mural is painted. An astonishing sight awaits.

The road has been closed by the police. It has had to be. Though it's been a week since the final, and the defacement, a crowd of about a hundred are gathered in front of the wall. An overflowing tide of flowers, cards, tributes, messages, and football shirts flows from the pavement into the road. It is almost too much to take in, but a few items stand out. There are flags from Thailand, Vietnam,

Brazil, Poland, several with legends like 'We Love You Marcus' or 'Rashford 4 Ever'. A chalk message reads: 'Thank you for our dinners from Reggie aged 6'.

I fall into conversation with a father and young teenage daughter from Huddersfield in the blue and white striped replica tops of their hometown team. 'We're only forty minutes away. We thought we'd come and show support. How could anybody do what they did?' he asks, shaking his head sadly. A well-spoken, well-dressed couple from London ask if I could take their picture, she in an orange cashmere shawl, he in Loake brogues and a mohair overcoat, tricked into believing it was always rainy in Manchester perhaps. A geeky lad from Taiwan over here on holiday is 'blogging' about it, he tells me, as he takes pictures on his iPad Pro and records his thoughts.

I imagine the Coffee House café hope things will continue like this. Unlike Lentils and Lather, a shop selling organic food, posh soaps and vegan ice cream (suggesting maybe Withington will go the way of neighbouring Chorlton), the Coffee House resists any hipsterfication, although they do have a salad bar. The more traditional chalkboard menu offers several artery-hardening and delicious treats. I plump, and I think this is the right word here, for the Spam and egg bap, a combo that was probably a greasy spoon staple long before lentils and vegan ice cream came to Withington. The café is clamorous with the banter of solidly proletarian regulars. A man in a wheelchair with an Aldi bag and a *Mirror* in his panier is grumbling loudly about the prices, I assume ironically since they are so cheap they would have jaws dropping in Bermondsey's greasiest spoon. With a concerted effort of will I forego the cornflake cake and custard (£2). The owner comes over and refills my milky coffee ('latte' feels so wrong here) bantering over his shoulder with the wheelchair critic. 'If you go and park yourself outside Marcus' image for half an hour, you might be able to stand up and walk. It might be the lord's will.' I ask about the vandalism as he fetches me the sugar bowl. 'We knew something would happen as soon as he missed that penalty. It's just the way of the world now, isn't it? It was a shame, yes, but it was probably just one kid that did it. Thousands have been here since. Still, it's sad that it might have been one of our own.'

The mural is still there and still drawing the crowds, part of a tourist trail that includes the Museum of Science and Industry on Liverpool Road in town. MOSI celebrates the workers of Lancashire and the generations of dynamic, industrious men and women either born, raised or working in the North West, that made it a crucible of industrial might and innovation; bright Cambridge boys like Alan Turing and Anthony H Wilson, and doughty entrepreneurs like Preston's Richard Arkwright or James Hargreaves of Oswaldtwistle. With its clattering looms and piercing lasers, flying shuttles and test tubes, it's not a very Bullingdon Club environment. But it was here, standing in front of Stephenson's Rocket, that Boris Johnson gave a speech that set the tone for another revolution of sorts.

'The centre of Manchester – like the centre of London – is a wonder of the world,' Johnson said. 'But just a few miles away from here the story is very different. Towns with famous names, proud histories, fine civic buildings where unfortunately the stereotypical story of the last few decades has been long term decline. Endemic health problems. Generational unemployment. Down-at-heel high streets. The story has been, for young people growing up there of hopelessness, or the hope that one day they'll get out and never come back.'

But it wasn't those young people who took the cue from Boris and, in a political switch that has been exercising commentators in the years since, took a pickaxe to the much-discussed Red Wall. It was their mums and dads, uncles and aunties, grannies and grand-dads who voted Conservative in 2020 in constituencies which had never returned anyone but Labour since their creation. The very names seemed inimical to Toryism: Bolsover, Blyth, Workington, Leigh. After the bustle of Liverpool and Manchester, Priestley headed into the hills and the towns in their damp hollows, where cotton was once king and the Labour Party his government. So did I. To Deepest Lancashire.

3

The Finns of Karelia have always been the purest in their national-ism, since the Russian bear is just a cloudy breath away in the neighbouring woods. And you'll find no more fiercely English people than in Carlisle, yet none nearer to Scotland. Lancaster may be the county town of Lancashire, but towns like Blackburn feel themselves to be Deep Lancashire. Radio Lancashire has its HQ here, broadcasting propaganda about Eccles cakes and football dominance, out east towards Burnley and the enemy realm of the White Rose, just a few contested miles distant.

Priestley had grown up in the wool trade, and so regarded the cotton industry as 'a mere upstart … it was nothing before the Industrial Revolution. But when it grew, it grew quickly … So colos-sal was the output that Blackburn was the greatest weaving town in the world.' But by the time he arrived in the 1930s, the mill chim-neys were 'innocent of smoke' and the streets and clubs full of the unemployed, 'good workless folk' as he calls them. He concludes: 'I do not know what will happen to the cotton industry. Possibly this is only the worst of its periodic collapses. I suspect, however, that not all the re-organisation and rationalisation and trade agreements and quotas and tariffs and embargoes in the world will bring back to Lancashire what Lancashire has lost.'

He was right. Entering East Lancashire in the early 2020s, you see that the chimneys are still there. They are the first thing the wide-eyed London broadsheet reporter notices as he or she arrives, notebook in hand. But they are still innocent of smoke and will be forever now. At the start of the 1980s, 45 per cent of the workforce of Burnley worked in manufacturing. A decade later, it was 36 per cent. By 2003, nearly 20 per cent of the town's working-age population were completely economically inactive. These statistics come from a book called *On Burnley Road: Class, Race and Politics in a Northern English Town* by Mike Makin-Waite. Analysing the collapse of the Labour vote in the Red Wall, he cites this industrial decline as crucial. But he also blames a kind of defeatism among the people, encouraged by the populist Right. 'In Post Office queues, hairdressers and over drinks at Burnley Miners' Club, people were encouraged in a beleaguered sense of lost entitlement … They were told that the party founded in their name, and which had run the town as long as anyone could remember, was favouring "certain others" over and above them. A new political identity was constructed, processing people's sullen sense of being badly done by, but also enabling them to feel assertive and proud.'

Makin-Waite is a Communist, which perhaps explains why he doesn't level much blame at the rabid unpopularity in these old mill towns of then Labour leader Jeremy Corbyn and his brand of internationalist anti-capitalism. But anyone who spends time here knows that was undoubtedly in the mix. In 2019 the Tories promised economic interventionism with cultural conservatism, a woolly but warming sense of feel-good Britishness and the complete absence of anything approaching a political ideology. It worked because, despite what the harder end of the Left think, the English are not and never have been a very ideological or radical people, or at least not since Cromwell. Tony Blair knew it. Gordon Brown knew it. Andy Burnham knows it. The smartest left-wing thinkers, like Orwell and Priestley, have always known it. Billy Bragg knew it once when he sang of 'sweet moderation, heart of this nation.' With the monomaniac ideologues of UKIP and its sister parties in retreat, having landed their single knockout punch, towns like Burnley and Blackburn turned to the more emollient version of right-wing populism offered by Johnsonian Conservatism. With Johnson gone and the Tories in disarray, it remains to be seen how smitten East Lancashire still is, if at all.

I arrive in Blackburn hoping for a better reception than Harry Houdini got in 1902. 'Back to this wretched town. Of all the hoodlum towns I ever worked, the gallery is certainly the worst.' Reading that reminds me that whenever New Order played the King George's Hall here, there would usually be trouble from an element of the football crew 'Blackburn Youth', who'd attached themselves to the band in a not entirely comfortable arrangement. I came here to watch them in 1985 when a mass brawl broke out during the final song. Inappropriately, it was 'The Perfect Kiss'. In 1884, well before the town gave Houdini a hard time, Blackburn's football team, the venerable Rovers, ended the football dominance of public school and establishment teams like Old Etonians, Corinthians, Royal Engineers and their ilk by winning the FA Cup. Dismayed, the *Pall Mall Gazette* reported in a jingoistic lather that the Blackburn fans were 'a northern horde of uncouth garb and strange oaths.' It is therefore entirely arguable that Blackburn invented the football hooligan.

But we might just as well talk of the town's more admirable sons and daughters, like film director Michael Winterbottom, actor Ian McShane, *The League of Gentlemen's* Steve Pemberton, contralto Kathleen Ferrier, fell-walking guru Alfred Wainwright and the town's former MP, the redoubtable Barbara Castle. There is a street named after her now, Barbara Castle Way, and I walk up it bound for what has been branded the Cathedral Quarter. In the twenty-first century English cities and towns have embraced this notion of quarters, districts, 'gaybourhoods', sestieres even, with gusto. Sometimes they have arisen organically from historic trades or associations like Birmingham's Jewellery Quarter or its Balti Triangle. Sometimes they've needed a little help from the PR department, as in Belfast's Titanic Quarter (perhaps the UK's only lively shopping, eating and leisure experience based around a maritime disaster claiming thousands of lives).

Blackburn's Cathedral Quarter is, let's be honest, just the grounds of the cathedral. But it is busy today. An event called Paint the Town is underway. An artist has set up her easel in a little designated square and is committing the cathedral to oils. I tell her I like it and she hands me her business card. 'Is Blackburn nice?' I ask Fawziyah. 'Er, yes,' she laughs, slightly bemused. 'But I've lived here all my life.' The cathedral itself is cordoned off and entered via a lane of crash barriers and tunnels of polythene. It takes a while for me to realise that it's been turned into a vaccination centre and Blackburnians – old ladies with tartan shopping trollies, children with teddies, students with pink hair, elderly men in turbans – are queueing to get into a converted church to be vaccinated against a lethal pandemic. How quickly and easily the tropes of sci-fi and disaster movies became the stuff of everyday life in 2021.

Behind the cathedral is a huge pub called The Postal Order. This was once Blackburn's grand Edwardian General Post Office, built in the early 1900s when it would have been the most important building in town. Today, the Post Office's reputation is in tatters – its systems and officials disgraced – and Blackburn's General Post Office is a Wetherspoon's. The other end of the street is a parade of takeaways offering the cuisine of every nation crammed into a few hundred yards. Smokers World are offering E-liquids and '6 Dram Pot Tub Vials', which sounds like something from an Elizabethan alchemist's manual.

I end up, unplanned, at the Bus Station, though there was nothing as prosaic as a sign saying 'bus station' to lead me to this conclusion. In fact, it bore the legend 'She held up the sky' for reasons I had to look up later.* In a moment of capricious madness, I board a bus to Accrington. I have my own personal reasons, which I shall come to soon. But for now, let's say that I'm in search of

---

* It turned out to be a quote from *A Poem From My Grandmother* by Jennifer Lee Tsai. Its relevance to public transport in East Lancashire remains unclear.

Hyndburn, another constituency that was a crumbled brick in the Red Wall. I know it's out this way somewhere though I'm having trouble finding it on a map or bus timetable.

As the 7A climbs up and out of the town, you realise what the textile entrepreneurs have always known: that Accrington, Blackburn and the other towns of East Lancashire sit in green, damp hollows cupped in rolling moorland hills with a soft rainy climate. This turns out to be perfect for both long, lonely Heathcliffian walks and for the spinning and weaving of cotton, whose delicate fibres are less likely to snap in damp climes. Ahead, the vistas open and the views become spacious. The afternoon heat and the gentle rhythm of the bus encourage reverie. In front of me, an elderly lady turns to her companion on the seat behind and says: 'Noreen, have you fallen asleep?' Noreen opens her eyes and laughs: 'Eee, I were miles away.' We drop down into Intack and Knuzden, names that sound more Martian than Lancastrian. I hope at no point today am I called upon to pronounce the latter.

As we enter Oswaldtwistle, or Ossie as the locals know it, we pass the Conservative Club. When I was growing up, the Labour Club and the Working Men's Club were the local social hubs, where everyone drank and congregated, watching drum and organ combos of varying skills backing up light tenors or girls belting out hits of the day while the old men shook their heads and blew froth off their mild. But some brave souls would occasionally enter the quieter, darkened portals of the 'Con Club' where the Queen's portrait and the Union Flag hung above the empty bar counter. You patronised the Con Club either because you were a rabid Royalist, a Freemason, or, more likely, because they had a less busy games room and better baize on the snooker table. It wasn't quite normal or acceptable behaviour though. But back then, neither was Blyth and Burnley voting Tory.

As the bus crests the top of a road called Mount St James, you are suddenly and thrillingly out under open sky and hills. This landscape may always be reductively noted for its 'dark satanic mills', but it's also a county of connoisseur's hills, high, bright birdsong and solemn, shy and lovely rivers. At Stanhill there are horses playing in fields and lemon stone cottages and a village green. The name of the local, The Stanhill Pub and Kitchen, tells you this is newly genteel Lancashire. Sweetly, unostentatiously prosperous, if Stanhill were a few miles nearer Salford's MediaCity then, like Marple and Didsbury, it too would have filled with BBC website editors and ITV drama producers and soon, there would be a cheesemonger here and a cycle shop. But if that were the case, ironically, it would probably have voted Labour in 2019, leaving at least one brick in the Red Wall still standing.

On arrival at Accrington bus station, I disembark with some trepidation. I am coming back like a prodigal. In 2008, I visited Accrington for a book called *Pies And Prejudice* and drew the ire of some, mainly for these few sentences: 'the main street is a crowded, unlovely hotchpotch of cheap shops, minicab offices and fast-food outlets that can fur your arteries just by looking at the logos, and a few desultory and cheerless pubs. In the doorway of one, a pallid, ginger youth is relating to an equally whey-faced companion an expletive-littered anecdote about a confrontation with the local kickboxer.'

If that seems harsh, that was how the town seemed that bleak day in 2008. It felt like a town in terminal decline, 'left behind' as we would soon learn to say. A minor kerfuffle ensued across local TV and radio and papers. The Chamber of Commerce and a few aldermanly types accused me of 'doing the town down' and pointed out that a branch of Costa had just opened. Interestingly, when the local early evening news 'vox-popped' people out and about, ordinary Accringtonians were largely in agreement with me. (Extraordinary Accringtonians include Jeanette Winterson and Harrison Birtwistle).

Today, it immediately feels different. Have I changed or has the town? Both clearly, I'm older and wiser and 'Accy' on first impressions is more vital, busier, smarter. But how high streets have changed. Not just in the rampant exoticism that would have stunned, and I hope delighted, Priestley – the Kurdish barber next to the Romanian grocers and the rest – but in what they are selling. What English high streets offer now is lifestyle. On sale is self-aggrandisement, the ephemera of a relentless pursuit of a good time and a statement of identity. But no butchers, tailors or hardware stores. These are for museums now, and period dramas.

Still here, though, is a properly great old-fashioned market hall, nearly as resplendent as when it was opened in May 1868 by one Mr Dugdale, with opera singers, pianists and a parade (and visited for a PR opportunity about 'levelling up' by newly installed PM Rishi Sunak in early 2023). Refurbished in 2010, upstairs are digital hubs and such, all very clean and new and admirable. Downstairs is where all those old high street shops are hiding, perhaps because of high rents or old habits. Here is where you'll still find Slack's the butchers, Maureen's Shoes and Bramwell's fish, a haberdashery, a fancy goods stall, the sweet shop pungent with the acetone tang of Pear Drops. There's an Accrington Stanley club shop with little replica kits for local kids too loyal for Chelsea and Man Utd. Fairbrother's bills itself as 'The Original Biscuit Stall' and sells pretty much nothing but. How can it stay in business, I think? But it does, and how! Every available inch of stall and shelf covered with jam rolls and Simnel cakes, lemon drizzle and hob nobs, ginger snaps and cinder toffee.

'Put your eyes away, you look like you've never had one before! What do you say? Thank you!' At Trickett's café and ice cream parlour, an embarrassed grandma is chastising her little blonde granddaughter for vacantly drooling as Mr Trickett pours lashings of lime and strawberry sauce over her cone. 'I do all the sauces you could want,' he explains, 'But I only do one flavour of ice cream. Vanilla. Kids can't make their mind up otherwise. It's Frederick's of Chorley too. Proper stuff. I don't serve that Mr Whippy rubbish. It's just milk and water whipped up.' I pull up a bar stool, like a gunslinger but with a 99 instead of three fingers of Red Eye, and we chat amiably. 'Every town in Lancashire had a market hall like this once. A grand building designed to show how prosperous we were, just how well we were doing. Hundreds of mills in every direction. And each of the towns were distinct and proud. Accrington, Ossie, Clayton, Rishton, Great Harwood. All proper with our own town councils. But then they put us under one umbrella. Hyndburn is a fiction, lad. No one would put that as their address.'

My original plan had been to visit Hyndburn town centre, till I realised there isn't one. Nor a school or a library or a market. Hyndburn is a borough and a parliamentary invention, created in 1983 and another Conservative win in 2019. I didn't ask Mr Trickett how he voted. As a matter of principle and courtesy I never do. But I do ask him why he thought the area went Tory under Johnson's inglorious reign. He doesn't know. Or perhaps he is that old fashioned kind of Englishman who feels religion, sex and politics are not fit subjects for polite discussion, at least not over a 99 with lime sauce and sprinkles in the company of sugar-dazed kids. He wanted to accentuate the positives, especially after a dark year. 'Normally it would be busier than this at quarter to three on a Saturday but it's getting busier. Might take a year, might be eighteen months, but we'll get through this, you'll see.' When you visit places like Trickett's and speak to people like its proprietor, you realise that the much-vaunted Blitz spirit is for many ordinary English people more than just a vacuous slogan. Dismissing these feelings as bluster or self-delusion has cost the Left dearly in these parts. People like Mr Trickett would have leaned towards the wireless on a Sunday night to hear Priestley's *Postscripts*. Moreover, because Priestley never mocked their simple patriotic good humour, he would also have listened to and heeded their calls later for a quiet revolution, the one that ushered in a new Britain in 1945.

Mr Trickett directs me to the railway station. I'm encouraged to take the train that goes through the Todmorden Curve, a line that sounds rather like crossing the Simplon to Lausanne on the Orient Express. Before I'm ready for that, I take a stroll around Accrington town square, the one that felt so bleak in 2008. Again, it feels brighter, livelier, less desperate, suggesting there's been some regeneration here. An enormous banner of the Accrington Pals hangs over the shopping parade, the regiment comprising a generation of the town's young men that was wiped out on the first day of the Somme. One of the shops below has been converted into the office of the town's Conservative MP, a young blonde woman. Sarah Britcliffe was born in Accrington in 1995, studied Modern Languages at the University of Manchester, was a councillor and ran a sandwich shop in Oswaldtwistle before standing as an MP. She was the youngest Tory to win a seat in 2019 and the first here since 1992. Her dad Peter failed twice before her, in 1997 and 2002. As Bob Dylan, who played Accrington Folk Club in 1962, might have put it, the times (and the North), they are a changing.

Two old boys with creased faces and stubble are smoking beneath a huge cross of St George in the doorway of the Nag's Head. Shaven-headed lads in football tops crowd the fruit machine. An elderly couple walk by with Lidl bags, he in long kurta, she in pale sari. Two young women leave the pub and I hear a snatch of their conversation: 'I thought it wasn't a good idea for us to be seen together as they've had a fight over me before. The only thing I could think of was to throw a hi vis jacket over my head and go out the loading bay.'

The train was late, naturally. But the Todmorden Curve was lovely.

4

Radcliffe is a small market town just south-west of Bury. It was not on Priestley's itinerary, but it became suddenly newsworthy as I travelled around Lancashire. Radcliffe is the heart of a constituency called Bury South, another one that fell to the Tories in 2019, albeit by only 403 votes. But then, just before a Prime Minister's Questions in which the nation awaited Boris Johnson's answers to yet more questions about Covid law-breaking and Downing Street parties during lockdown, Bury South's MP Christian Wakeford 'crossed the floor' – that is, defected to Labour. 'Crossing the floor' is rare and shocking enough. But Wakeford's stated reasons were more surprising yet. He claimed that he had been 'blackmailed' into voting a certain way in parliament, with former fireplace salesman turned education secretary Gavin Williamson threatening to withdraw funding for a school if he voted against the government on free school meals. Wakeford said: 'This is a town that's not had a high school for the best part of ten years and how would you feel holding back the regeneration of the town for a vote?'

The bits of Lancashire Priestley didn't like, which was most of them, were, he said, 'dreary regions infested by corporation trams.' Like the rest of Lancashire, I'm delighted we are infested with trams again. Cheap, sleek and efficient, they are both as modern as a Scandinavian parliament building and as nostalgic as carbolic soap and football pinks. You can enjoy free wifi as you pass through Abraham Moss and Besses o' th' Barn, fine names for clog dances or the scene of a Victorian murder.

On the tram, or Metrolink more formally, you come into Radcliffe over the dark, swirling Irwell and rows of terraced houses. It's a Saturday dusk, always an evocative time, redolent of the theme from *Sports Report* and *Doctor Who*. The cobbled ginnels fan away full of scattered wheelie bins and pizza boxes, and the little shops turn off their lights. A bridge overlooks the Irwell, the river that once made Radcliffe busy, if not rich. I stand in the chilly twilight watching the wide, sluggish water and noting the odd graffiti on the canalside walls and then mooch down to the Market Hall. A sign promises 'Great Food. Local Beer. Safe Space' and I'm not sure what safe space might mean in this context. Regularly disinfected? Free from wild animals? Or can they ensure you won't hear an opinion you disagree with? Unlike its homely, nostalgic Accrington counterpart, the 'market' vibe here is craft ales, Thai food and Yoga workshops. But the street food stalls are closing and the tattooed lads at the craft ale bar too loud, so I swing by the Bridge Tavern, looking in through the window at a thick throng inside and Jeff Stelling and Sky Sports on the big telly. A cheery doorway smoker, a stocky little man of about sixty in a work fleece, nods towards the lively interior. 'Looking for t'scores, lad? Go inside. You don't have to buy owt. They won't mind.'

They don't. No one in the jostling, familial pub, cosy to an almost uncomfortable degree, even notices me. I push gently to the bar corner and wait my turn, beneath a sign that says 'Friendship is like pissing your pants. Everyone can see it, but only you get the warm feeling that it brings.' I'm still trying to work this out when the woman behind the bar asks me what I'd like. I order a Talisker and turn to the big telly where Jeff Stelling is getting implausibly excited about something. Turning back, I try and pay but the landlady says 'it's taken care of' and gestures towards a man in glasses at the end of the bar who raises his San Miguel, nods and says, 'Your very good health, Mr Maconie.' Naturally I join him.

Brendan has a stall on the market repairing shoes and cutting keys ('why do we always do both? Don't ask me,' he laughs). From the pub window, we can see Christian Wakeford's constituency office. 'He's been MP for two years and I've seen him once,' says Brendan. I note the office is still painted a fetching shade of blue, but perhaps not for long. He only switched that week and he's the first Tory MP to do so for fifteen years, so Radcliffe has recently 'enjoyed' an unprecedented amount of London media attention. 'Oh, they've all been here this week, I've done the *Independent*. I've done Sky News. I told the *Daily Mail* to fuck off, obviously.' Despite this last, force-fully expressed before a pull of his lager, Brendan seems to have no strong political allegiance. 'I've spent three days a week here for thirty years. I talk to everybody on that square and that market. I think there's a bit of anger and bemusement about him defecting. But I don't know what motivates them. If you ask me why people voted Tory, all I could say is that I heard a lot of stuff about Brexit and immigration. But whether people know what they're talking about is another matter … Oh bollocks.'

Brendan has noticed the score in the Ipswich–Accrington game, a result his accumulator bet is riding on. He folds his slip wearily and puts it back in his wallet. It's my round, I say, but he's off: 'I want to get home for the City game. I'll get my tea from the market. Proper trendy now. The food's bang on. But the music's shit and it's freezing.' The more I roam on my English journey, the more actual conversations I have with strangers in small towns, rather than my bubble of Twitter peers, the more I hear not so much rage or passion, not even sweet moderation, but a kind of boredom or suspicion. 'There's a war on in Lancashire,' said Priestley in 1934, seeing the miseries of bad housing and poverty, casualties of the unequal struggle between labour and capital. But I didn't see any war, just a stalemate and a kind or weariness; a weariness with the lies and charlatanry, but a vague, grudging expectation that this is the way things are now.

As the lit tram rolls back through twilit Lancashire, I hope I am wrong.

9

TO THE TYNE

In which I take three steps to Hebburn via
a kickabout with the rabbis of tomorrow
and head out to Spanish City.

Perhaps he was homesick. Perhaps he was tired or ill or maybe just missing his Highgate home comforts. But whatever ailed him, by the time Priestley reached Newcastle, he was clearly in a very bad mood. He came via the fair cathedral city of Ripon, itself usually a delicious prospect, but it was raining heavily and he was in a grump. Some of Priestley's disconsolate mood as he passes through Ripon can be put down to the memories that returned to him via a reverie of sluicing windscreens and windows. He was last here as a young man in 1916 convalescing from the western front where a shell attack on his trench buried him alive for a while, leaving him with a lifelong claustrophobia so strong he would never use the Tube if he could avoid it. He hated the camp in Ripon ('there I was miserable, like everyone else I knew') but by the time he returned for *English Journey*, he had grown more philosophical. At one point, he even, as we might say these days, 'has a word with himself.'

'I said to myself: "Well, it's pouring with rain and you're a long way from home and you're going still further away from it and you've got a cold coming on and a worrying nagging, quite impossible sort of book on your hands, just when you had decided you needed a rest from books, but – by heck! – you're a prince, my lad, compared with what you were, seventeen years ago, when you were herded into the camp here like a diseased sheep." And that will do for Ripon.'

He might have been in better spirits had he come to Newcastle by train. No chauffeured Daimler, however plush the upholstery, can equal the vista afforded by the humble East Coast mainline as it enters the city. I find it hard to imagine anyone could approach Newcastle by rail without a stirring of the heart. From this superior vantage, this fine mobile communal belvedere, the city is breathtaking. The quaysides of Newcastle and Gateshead, renovated and developed with flair, teem with bars and restaurants and airy civic spaces to just hang out in. The riverscape is magnificent always; the grand bridges echoing each other like ripples from a stone skimmed down the glittering Tyne.

Back in 1969, Newcastle Arts Festival commissioned a suite about the (then) five bridges that spanned the Tyne from the late Keith Emerson and his band The Nice. To be honest, much as I love Emerson's playing, it's an unremarkable mélange of classical, jazz and rock, especially when compared to his brilliant later work with ELP. But as my train rides in high above the water on one of the now seven bridges, the King Edward VIII, it sounds suitably grand and majestic in my ears. I made a related playlist for the journey, downloaded it from the ether and am now listening to it on my phone as we pull into the station, a concept that would have seemed ludicrously 'sci-fi' in 1969 when it was composed, let alone in 1934. It's a playlist comprising entirely Newcastle artists and music of the

North East and includes Mike Hugg's gorgeous theme song from *Whatever Happened to the Likely Lads?*, that perfect evocation of male friendship, class and nostalgia in 70s Newcastle; Lindisfarne's 'Fog On The Tyne'; Prefab Sprout from Witton Gilbert; and Sam Fender, a new and passionate voice from the streets of North Shields, part of my Tyneside itinerary.

When you leave Newcastle Station, my advice is to turn around and glance at where you've come from. Newcastle Station is a beauty, a Grade I listed building that is one of only ten to get the full five stars in Simon Jenkins' *Britain's 100 Best Railway Stations*. Newcastle Station is, as far as I'm concerned, a far grander building than any you'll see in the Home Counties, far grander than Blenheim Palace and other private luxuries of the rich. Newcastle Station is more beautiful because it is a building of and for the people. Every day they move through it, use it, occupy it, engage with it. One fine day, when we see sense, they might even own it again.

I pass the Station Hotel which is where Beryl Bainbridge stayed when she was retracing some of Priestley's itinerary for BBC TV in the early 80s. 'I have been to Newcastle once before many years ago,' she said on arrival, somewhat haughtily, as if this were Newcastle's fault rather than hers. 'It's not short of people in the streets that's for sure and that's probably because most of the people are unemployed.' Apart from marvelling at how a Scouse girl from Formby got such a brittle, dowager accent, I was flabbergasted at how this crass, inaccurate generalisation was allowed to stay in the script. It wasn't true when she said it, and it certainly isn't now. As she checks in with a few peremptory remarks to the receptionist, she acknowledges the pleasantness of the hotel but whinges, 'All the same I'm beginning to get a little tired of all this travelling and I think I'm starting a cold.' Quite what those unemployed millions of 80s Newcastle, who after all were paying for Beryl's nice room at the Station Hotel, were supposed to say to this, their Findus Crispy Pancakes balanced on chilly knees in unheated hovels, I hesitate to think.

Unlike La Bainbridge I've been here many times before and have never not had a good time. My love of and familiarity with 'the toon' actually poses something of a problem. I have written about this great city at least twice before and so I must find new angles, perhaps suggested by a close reading of Priestley's original. Unfortunately, a close reading of his Tyne chapter is not always a comfortable experience. For a Bradfordian and a Scouser, both Priestley and Bainbridge seemed to me very 'nesh' about their footling little colds and the business of checking in at their nice hotels. Neither seems to arrive in a very 'good place', attitude-wise. In the case of our man JB, here he is, almost immediately laying into the local accent: 'I can find nothing pleasant to say about it. To my ears it still sounds a most barbarous, monotonous and irritating twang … The constant "Ay-ee, mon," … of the men's talk and the never-ending "hinnying" of the women seem to me equally objectionable.'

Leaving aside the fact that 'hinny' is a lovely word, a term of fondness and endearment for either sex that derives from the sweetness of 'honey', let's be fair to sniffly old Priestley in acknowledging that he was not the first outsider to have difficulties with the accent of the North East. Benedictine monk and early fourteenth-century travel writer Ranulf Higden said that 'the language of the Northumbrians is so sharp, rasping, piercing and unformed that we southerners can rarely understand it.' I discovered this remark in Dan Jackson's excellent and bestselling *The Northumbrians*, in which he also states that 'any Northumbrian can instantly tell by the way a person pronounces, say, the word "beetroot" whether they come from north or south of a line that runs from Whitburn north of Washington in between Birtley and Chester Le Street.' He also quotes the stock joke about the Ashington man who goes into the hairdressers and asks for a perm. 'Certainly sir, "Ah wandered lurrnly as a cloud …"'

It is also notoriously difficult to get right if you're an outsider. Actor Alan Rickman said 'I think every English actor is nervous of a

Newcastle accent.' Rodney Bewes didn't even bother in 'The Likely Lads', merely peppering his soft native Yorkshire tones with the odd 'pet'. Perhaps in part because of this wonderful show, feelings towards the Geordie accent have seemingly changed since Higden and Priestley. In rather the same way that the fells and crags of the North's hills, once thought too savage and terrifying to be viewed directly by the faint-hearted, are now rightly regarded as beautiful and dramatic, so the speech of the North East has become one of England's best-loved, as heard by Ant and Dec, Cheryl Tweedy and Lauren Laverne. In a 2021 survey by language learning site Babbel, the Geordie accent was chosen as 'the most desired and fun-sounding' regional UK dialect.

Pace old JBP, the Geordie accent is clearly neither ugly nor unmusical. But to outsiders, especially the southern variety, it is sometimes incomprehensible until you 'get your ear in' and immerse yourself, rather like the twelve-tone serialist music of Schoenberg, Webern and the second Viennese school. In June 2021, fans of the TV show *Love Island* begged for the words of one hunky Geordie labourer to be subtitled. 'Brad is gonna have to curb his lingo and accent. No one who's not from the North East gonna have a clue what he's on about,' tweeted one while another fulminated: 'Jesus lord, what is this man saying? I need google translate!' All of which confirmed my suspicions about people who voluntarily watch *Love Island*.*

I have no such qualms about the people of the North East. In *The Northumbrians*, Dan Jackson quotes back at me a line of mine about them from *Pies and Prejudice*, in which I offered that they were 'kindly, funny, roguish, tough but not nasty, bluff but warm.' That's a touch reductive, I admit. But I stand by it. In a long, absorbing piece for UnHerd, Ed West wrote of how George R R Martin visited

---

* I just prefer 'The Likely Lads', OK? Also, I am very proud of this short paragraph, perhaps the first one in the history of English literature to reference both the dodecaphonic music of Arnold Schoenberg and *Love Island*.

Northumbria and Hadrian's Wall territory in the 1980s and how that clearly influenced his depiction of the lands north of Westeros and the people who live there ('stark unforgiving masculine and wild') in *Game of Thrones*. Comedian Stewart Lee once opined: 'In places like Newcastle, audiences have a tradition of being amusingly combative. But they're not trying to ruin the act, they're trying to give you a challenge. It's like a cat playing with a mouse – the cat doesn't want the mouse to die, it wants to keep it alive for its own amusement and to be entertained by its struggle.' There is some wry generosity here. A lot more than Priestley could muster when he traversed the old waterfront, anyway. 'We began by running along the old Quay Side as far as we could go. There I noticed nothing but a lot of miserable fellows hanging about, probably looking for the chance of a job … These were all mean little streets. Slatternly women stood at the doors of wretched little houses, gossiping with other slatterns or screeching for their small children, who were playing among the filth from the roadside.'

This is tough stuff to stomach; not far away from the kind of bigoted tripe that Rod Liddle might trot out in the *Spectator*. The difference is, I think, that Priestley cannot surely be coming from that same putrid place of gratuitous hack nastiness. But it is still one of a handful of moments in *English Journey* when I put the book down and wished I could have had it out with him over a late whisky in the hotel bar.

Maybe his hotel room stank of moss. Mine does. Moss overtones with a detectable bottom note of industrial-strength disinfectant. It is tired, shabby and clearly something quite bad has happened here not very long ago. I just hope it was nothing worse than a flood. But all the Newcastle hotels I like were fully booked and this one's position on the Quayside does at least offer a view across the broad Tyne to newly fashionable Ouseburn as well as stained mattresses in the car park and a burned-out warehouse. Downtown Newcastle is a handsome city and its riverscape is truly sensational. But I seem to have found its ugly side. My room also has one of the weirdest quirks I have ever encountered, so odd that I hesitate to relate it in case you think I'm mad. Every time I zip up my coat, the TV switches on. I offer this in the vain hope that someone out there will read this and think 'ah, the old Ferric Zipper Wavelength Cathode effect,' and fill me in. But as of now I remain baffled.

Fortunately, I don't intend on spending much time in my room. Priestley had taken himself (or been taken) to Gateshead, Hebburn and the Shieldses North and South, and so will I tomorrow. But at least part of the evening still stretches before me so I walk down to the Tyne. Things have certainly changed here since Priestley passed along it, but there was some tremendous life here then; an online film from the North East Film Archive from about that time shows a quayside teeming with life and people, flower sellers, trolleybuses, horses and carts. But outside these few busy frames, decline and waste were creeping along the river, literally and metaphorically. The Tyne Bridge, opened in 1927, is a magnificent structure straight out of Gotham. But its effect was to bypass the Quayside area for the more handsome city centre. Businesses closed and few people wanted to visit an unattractive stretch of river which stank of the sewage that went untreated directly into it – 35 million gallons in 1958 alone. It was a river devoid of life in every sense.

Now it boasts boutique hotels and high-end retail, skateboarders and street food vans, markets and microbreweries. After an initial failure to turn Newcastle into 'the Brasilia of the North' (a weird mission statement and an initiative involving infamous council planner T Dan Smith in the 60s and 70s, whose progress became mired in recession and corruption)* the 80s saw a largely public and council-driven regeneration. Even as late as 1967, Graham Turner could write morosely in his seminal text *The North Country*,

---

* Events fictionalised in Peter Flannery's epic tale of the city *Our Friends In The North*.

'Newcastle is a black and brooding city. It looks as though it is either in mourning for some last splendour or else in the monumental sulk.' Just a few decades later, enthusiasm, drive and vision have transformed it into the best-looking city in England, a place for southerners to weep in envy over when they visit from costly, cramped and dirty London. This opinion reinforces itself each time I walk along the riverside, as tonight in the chilly autumn air, over the new Millennium Bridge and up to Ouseburn.

Ouseburn was once a dense mix of industrial buildings and a crucible for the city's glass and pottery trades. But following the Second World War, it declined into dereliction. Its journey from cradle of industry to post-industrial creative hub is a happy success story, albeit tinged with regret that an entire manufacturing tradition had to die to make room for it. Being named 'one of the coolest places to live in the world right now' by *Time Out* is some consolation. You can still visit the Victoria Tunnel where the coal wagons once rumbled underground, but Ouseburn's main landmarks now are less likely to get your hands dirty. Take the kiddies to the Seven Stories National Centre for Children's Literature or see a 'happening' indie band at The Cluny before hopping into your voluminous queen size bed at the Hotel du Vin. There is still a Kiln and an Old Coal Yard in Ouseburn. But the former is a vegan restaurant and the latter a craft micro-brewery. Of course.

Albaik or The Bake, a Lebanese restaurant that feels like a Beirut tearoom, has been a staple of Ouseburn eating for many years, beloved haunt of local families, students and travel book writers. It has no license, a fact I had noted but then forgotten until the shawarma and a gorgeous glistening salad the size of Mount Lebanon had been placed before me. There was a Morrisons across the road, its yellow lights promising shelves of reasonably priced reds, but I was too cosy by then so I opted for the mango lassi. I was the only customer for a while until a middle-aged woman and a studenty lad, maybe mum and son, came in, took their seats and were immediately, visibly stunned to find there was no alcohol for sale. 'What country do they come from?,' he asked in an appalled stage whisper, suggesting that he was neither a student of geography nor comparative religion.

On a 'school night' as grown-ups will insist on saying (teachers excused of course) Ouseburn was dark and somnolent. Its patchwork of alleys, ginnels and steps are disorienting for an out of towner who's walked 35,000 paces, even with nothing stronger in him than a mango lassi. Then I have a pint of Wylam in The Cluny and the fatigue hits me like a sandbag, so I head back to the river. The most beautifully situated Pitcher and Piano in England glows out across it. At weekends, it must be rammed but tonight its huge, illuminated window reveals a lit interior empty but for a couple of lone drinkers, a Tyneside version of Hopper's Nighthawks.

On the other hand, the Millennium Bridge, my route back to my bed, is crowded with young people huddled against the deepening night, laughing, cuddling, having maybe neither the funds, culture or inclination to seek out pubs or clubs. They look cold but cheery, shining eyes reflecting the lights in their river, city dwellers enjoying this grand bit of their city, a happy connected band of Nighthawks. I take this sweet image back to my room above the soiled mattresses and the charred warehouse, to the now familiar reek as dank and fusty as the bottom of the Tyne.

2

Priestley spent little more than a 'raw gloomy evening' in Gateshead. But the few pages he wrote about the town are now dragged out, quoted and pored over in every piece on Newcastle's grittier neighbour across the Tyne. Most recently, Sebastian Payne began his book *Broken Heartlands: A Journey Through Labour's Lost England* with one of Priestley's many withering sentences about his hometown: 'No true civilisation could have produced such a town, which is nothing better than a huge dingy dormitory.'

Payne himself opens more generously: 'There is a sense of pride to growing up in Gateshead. It is not the prettiest town in the north-east of England, nor the most economically buoyant. The continual deprivation and poor education in some areas are a national disgrace. Yet we are still filled with an affection for our hometown, especially its high-spirited people.' According to Payne, the main reason Gateshead turned its back on the Labour Party in 2019 was Jeremy Corbyn. What JBP would have made of Corbyn is impossible to know. It might be guessed at, though. He was as intolerant of the ideological Left as he was of the smug, uncaring Right. Less ambiguous is his verdict on Gateshead: 'the whole town appeared to have been carefully planned by an enemy of the human race in its more exuberant aspects. Insects can do better than this: their habitations are equally monotonous but far more efficiently constructed … The town was built to work in and to sleep in. You can still sleep in it, I suppose … If anybody ever made money in Gateshead, they must have taken great care not to have spent any of it in the town.'

You might feel this to be unworthy trash talk. But you'd be as wrong as those aldermen and chamber of commerce stalwarts in my hometown who thought Orwell was an aloof, judgemental old Etonian who should have spent more time talking about Wigan's delightful Haigh Hall and the excellent rail connections. Neither Priestley or Orwell painted their bleak pictures for fun or clickbait, for sport or mockery, but out of a cold, quiet anger that English people were living like this in a self-congratulatory land of baronets and ermine and plump businessmen. Priestley, like Orwell in the dingy hovels of 1930s Wigan, came neither to praise Gateshead nor to bury it, simply to record it clearly and vividly so that readers in well-lit studies in Bloomsbury could glimpse the lives of others.

These days, the tourist board presents Newcastle and Gateshead as a single, throbbingly virile, identity: twin cities like Minneapolis and

St Paul or Buda and Pest, a whole nexus of fun in eighteen compacted lower-case letters. 'Why Aye! You're welcome in newcastlegateshead! United by seven iconic bridges across a bustling quayside Newcastle and Gateshead form a single, diverse and extremely vibrant visitor destination in the North East of England.' It's a nice concept, but it doesn't get much traction from folk on the actual banks of the Tyne. On message boards, locals assert time and time again that the twain shall never really meet, that Newcastle is a city and Gateshead a town with its own council, no mayor (it didn't want one) and its own attitudes.

Escaping the primordial murk of my hotel room, I slog up the unglamorous curve of asphalt that climbs up behind the graces of this Quayside – the Sage concert hall and the Baltic Centre for Contemporary Art – into Gateshead itself. Priestley, feeling very sorry for himself, managed to get lost on his expedition, concluding: 'I had to explore a large part of Gateshead, and there was nothing in this exploration to raise my spirits.' But some new additions to Gateshead's townscape might have given him food for thought as he meandered. Gateshead College is festooned with slogans that seem profound and empowering until you pause to think about them: 'Women are not Pigs'; 'You are now entering a Judgement Free Zone'; 'We are all Human'. Each has that combination of assertiveness and vapidity, bullish yet vacant, that characterises our age. Sourpuss that I am, my spirits are low as I push on up the hill into Old Gateshead. The afternoon has clouded over and become gusty and dark and the sharp wind has rain and chip papers in it. The college and its neighbour, a huge arts complex called Northern Design, looks posh, and doubtless good stuff is going on in there. But as you leave the glitter of Newcastle far behind and climb into the hinterland of Gateshead, the buzzy modernism fades away to reveal that random tawdry mix of old and new, civic and retail that's so common in the working-class northern town.

Trinity Square has colonised the centre of Gateshead with a squat, uncompromising retail space, a giant superstore parked like an invading space cruiser. What would JBP have made of a Tesco Extra, a shop the size of a cathedral, which in many ways it is of course: a temple to consumerism. I'm not being snooty here. We have always bought things from the shop at the bottom of the road. But at the bottom of this road is a shop where you can buy a ride-on lawnmower and an enormous television rather than, say, pop in for two ounces of boiled ham. On the walls of the Tesco Extra are a gallery of images reflecting Gateshead's history, my favourite being Owen Luder's long-gone but never to be forgotten Brutalist car park from whose upper tiers Michael Caine brusquely despatched Bryan Mosley (playing Cliff Brumby), also known as *Coronation Street*'s Alf Roberts. If you recall he was, as Caine put it, 'a big man but he was out of shape', and he certainly was by the time he reached the pavement of Trinity Square. I pop into the store itself and buy a bottle of scotch and a can of Febreze, the latter to mask the corked wine and seaweed smell of my room, the former to help me not care about it.

'Attractions' compete for my attention at each corner of the next crossroads. There is the Park Lane, a nightclub destined never to be confused with its London namesake and the 4Play Sex Shop, shrivellingly anaphrodisiac in its setting of grime-streaked concrete and fag packets. Opposite, Curley's is hosting a comedy drag night, a contradiction in terms for me, but then I seem to be unique in modern Britain in finding drag bleakly unentertaining. One day I hope we shall see it for what it is, a kind of blackface offering crass stereotypes of women by men. On another corner is the Metropole pub; 'card bingo 4 till 6 then Northern Soul.' The older, tough-looking crowd look settled in for a Monday night of 'eyes down … legs eleven' and backflips.

I forego all these delights and continue up Bensham Road, past the Bensham Jockey pub, another defunct boozer eyeless and shuttered, headed for, yes, Bensham. Bedraggled and nursing his cold,

Priestley came here to see a couple of examples of pioneering social action. Bensham Grove was home to the first nursery in the North East, a godsend for the local kiddies, although the sample menu of 'mutton stew, minced liver and eggs' would meet with some scepticism from the modern toddler. Close by is the Bentham Grove settlement, a large house given over to a theatre and arts facilities with the intention of providing unemployed men with new skills. JB seems to have liked Bob, the communistic organiser, but was grudging about the 'grim concert party' and some of the young men present; 'undisciplined and carefree, the dingy butterflies of the backstreets. They had no sense whatever of waste and tragedy in themselves. They were not at odds with their peculiar environment, which by this time had moulded their characters and shaped their way of living. They had little or no money, but never having had any, they did not miss it.'

The Bentham Grove settlement is still active, receiving a quarter of a million pounds in 2013 to carry on the good work. But the lady I get chatting to at the bus stop is unaware of it. At least I think she is, but her accent is so strong that I am completely unable to decipher her kindly smiling chat, feeling every inch the 'Midlander' my Gateshead mate Stod used to accuse me of being. I give up trying to get my head around the bus timetable, and decide to walk back to the river. On the way down I come across a miraculous sight: a gang of young Jewish lads in white shirts and kippahs playing a lively twenty-a-side football match in the street outside the Borough Arms. Lively but not rowdy. There is no swearing or violence, just a great collective youthful release of steam after a hard day at the Talmud.

Later, back in my hotel room, I learn that this converted old pub in Gateshead now houses part of the Gateshead Talmudical College. This is the Oxford and Cambridge of the Jewish faith, the largest yeshiva or rabbinical school in Europe, and the largest outside New York. Not far away is the Gateshead Jewish Academy for Girls. Both these draw students from around the world, reflecting the sizeable

Haredi Jewish community in Gateshead. This was established by Zachariah Bernstone in the 1890s, a hard man who, finding the Newcastle brethren too lax and lenient, crossed the water to make a community here which still thrives. During the festival of Purim, the streets are thronged with revellers intending to observe the ancient rituals and traditions and, according to community leaders, 'to let their hair down and have a few drinks.' I watched some footage on YouTube and it looks fantastic, with streets full of people dressed as pirates, tigers, admirals etc. According to a brilliant last line in the *Newcastle Chronicle* report, 'The footage ends with a few lads ordered down from a caravan by Northumbria Police.'

I raise a glass of my scotch to them, give the room another gaseous floral salvo of Febreze and retire to my mossy bed, ready for my big day out on the Metro.

3

Gateshead Interchange confronts you on entry with a huge mosaic of a range of high, cloud-strewn peaks which I'm fairly sure aren't in Gateshead.* Nice, though. The whole station is something of a treat for fans of public art, with a giant peacock, an installation of car park interiors, and a general design scheme of red and white blocky tiles which make the traveller feel like they've been dropped into a giant game of Tetris. Annoyingly, it is not 'Three stops to Hebburn' but five. But as the Metro clanks along I still have some fun inventing other songs that could commemorate my destination. Hebburn Is A Place On Earth. Knocking On Hebburn's Door. Stairway To Hebburn. And so on.

---

* Nocturnal Landscape (Keith Grant, 1983) 'a shimmering mosaic which transports passengers to a magical Norwegian coastline, reflecting the historic connections between the North East and Scandinavia.'

Priestley was no more taken with Hebburn than he was with Gateshead. 'You felt that there was nothing in the whole place worth a five-pound note'. He would have been amazed, then, that one day Hebburn would get its own eponymous TV series. You may have seen it. It's an angry Marxist analysis of the exploitative nature of capitalism told through avant-garde animation and Japanese Kabuki theatre. Only joking, it's a heart-warming tale of working-class Geordie life, of course, starring Vic Reeves and Gina McKee, the latter one of the brilliant ensemble cast of Peter Flannery's *Our Friends in the North*, another great north-eastern contribution to modern TV culture, and a slightly grittier one.

Hebburn reminded me very much of its neighbour Jarrow, which I know a little. There was a Palmer's shipyard in both and Hebburn's fared better than Jarrow's. When the company collapsed in 1933, the Jarrow works closed and three years later the 200 men marched to London, to great public sympathy but little avail. But the Hebburn works were purchased by Vickers-Armstrongs and then Swan Hunter in the early 1970s, and after a few dalliances with the receivers and Cammell Laird, they are now in the hands of the A&P group, still repairing ships on five acres of the Tyne. From the doorway of the Mambo 2 Italian restaurant, where I pause for a moment, I can see the swinging cranes. There were big ships down there, too. I look them up on my phone. *Ulisse*, it says, is a cable-laying barge getting a new mezzanine deck and some lifeboat platforms. But it is getting chilly, the restaurant won't open for another hour and the rich fug of garlic is making my head swim. Hebburn knows I'm miserable now, I think. So, I head into town, hands stuffed in pockets and collar up against a stiffening breeze. My route takes me past the Orange Hall of the Hebburn Protestant Conservative Club, which is every bit as ugly as you'd imagine, large Union Jack fluttering limply on its dirty grey blue artex walls. On the next block stands the Iona Club, this one done out with shamrocks and green livery. It was a scene more like Belfast than Tyneside, reflecting South Tyneside's Irish diaspora.

After London, Liverpool and Glasgow, the North East had Britain's largest influx of Irish immigrants – mainly to work the shipyards. But Hebburn had hundreds of Scottish immigrants too, to the extent that it was once known as Little Aberdeen. They say that the Sporting Arms in Denton had UVF flags as well as Union Jacks behind the bar. Happily, though, there's been little of the sometimes poisonous sectarianism on Tyneside that you might find on the banks of the Clyde or the Mersey, perhaps because there are no football allegiances for it to fester within. Newcastle has one football club, and everyone goes to St James' Park.

Back in town proper, I pass a cheerless hour in the grimly utilitarian Mountbatten Centre, a shopping precinct named after the IRA-assassinated great uncle of Prince Charles for the tangential reason that he commanded a destroyer built in Hebburn's shipyards. In a crowded little café I am offered squirty cream on my latte, a delightful first this, and eat a stottie, which is what we Lancastrians would call an 'oven bottom muffin'. For the particularly ravenous, there's a 'Gutbuster' variety on the menu, but I resist. I read the Hebburn section of *English Journey* again, cream tickling my nose, and in particular the paragraph where Priestley ruminates on the lavish funerals he saw in Hebburn and across working-class England. Back on Station Road, I note that three adjacent shops offer some form of self-beautification: Nails and Beauty, MHA Nails and Sorento Tan and Vibro. These are the modern corollaries of those funerals. Here is where looking good and celebrating oneself matters, in the nightclub or the funeral parlour, a defiant glamour in the face of tough circumstance. And at the end, maybe, a floral tribute wreath that reads 'Hebburn must be missing an angel.'

4

Readers of a certain vintage may remember the old Yellow Pages*
advert which stated that it was 'not just there for the nasty things in
life.' I feel the same about social media. It can sometimes feel like
merely a toxic cesspit of bile stirred by the massive paddle that is
Piers Morgan. But it can be fun, informative and genuinely social. I
have made good and true friends through it. Bluff TV food baldie
Gregg Wallace even married someone that he met on Twitter. It's not
all bullying, body shaming and hot takes, is it Gregg?

Throughout my research for this book, I 'reached out' often on
Twitter and I was always heartened by the wit and generosity of the
replies. When I mentioned I was headed to Tyneside, advice flowed
in regarding chip shops in Tynemouth and the curry houses on
Ocean Road, South Shields. Many correspondents told me to look
out for the ferryman between North and South Shields who is,
apparently, the spitting image of homegrown superstar Sting. Bri
Hodgson tweeted 'Great to see you're up this way Stuart. I look
forward to reading the results. I thoroughly recommend the Old
Low Light Tavern, North Shields'. In a similar vein, Dan Jackson,
whose book was proving invaluable, offered good advice: 'Try some
of the toffee-coloured taverns of North Shields. But remember kids,
unless you're a 10th Dan in karate I would advise against drinking
anywhere west of Howard Street *taps nose*.' We do, however,
arrange to meet for a pint next day up in his neck of the woods in
Monkseaton when my travels are done. And so, to the Metro again.

Jarrow, Bede, Simonside, Tyne Dock, Chichester (home of
Catherine Cookson, proudly pronouncing the first syllable 'Chai' as
if to distance itself from the pretty cathedral cloisters of the Sussex

---

* A thick book-sized listing of businesses in your area, now as archaic a notion
as a spinning jenny or a ducking stool.

one) and eventually to South Shields. After the tight, narrow streets of Hebburn and Jarrow, South Shields immediately feels airy, light and open. Perhaps because the clouds have drifted off towards Norway and the sun's out on Tyneside. I step down from the train with a spring in my step, bound for the ferry. Even in places where to elect a Tory would have been once unthinkable, like Blyth Valley, Redcar, Bishop Auckland, Hartlepool, Sedgefield, they did in 2019. But the Red Wall holds in South Shields, once the constituency of David Miliband (the Prince Across the Water of the Labour Party), and now represented by Emma Lewell-Buck, the daughter of shipyard workers. She once came to a show I did in the old Customs House by the Tyne and so is clearly a person of rare gifts and discernment. On that trip, I'd stayed in a brilliantly quirky hotel in Little Haven, where north-easterners once took holidays in the days before Magaluf was as accessible as Morpeth.

The art deco frontage of the prom faces a glittering expanse of blue where the Tyne meets the North Sea, two great piers arching their arms into the briny to welcome the little fishing boats home. The water buzzes from morning till night; tugs, smacks, ferries and the occasional giant car transporter the size of a destroyer. Maybe it was a destroyer. I wander down to Colman's Seafood Temple, once a ruined bandstand and public toilet, now transformed into a paradisiacal version of a fish and chip shop where you can have elderflower gin, scallops and mushy pea fritters and watch the sun go down over the water. No time for that today, though. Before my rendezvous with Dan in Monkseaton, my itinerary needs to take in North Shields, Tynemouth and Whitley Bay heading north along the coast. To get there will involve a trip on one of the region's best loved excursions.

People have been crossing the Tyne by boat for millennia, since an intrepid, inquisitive Iron Age resident of South or North Tyneside wondered what was going on over there. There's actually been a commercial ferry service across the Tyne for nearly 700 years, but only one route survives: the 'Shields Ferry' connecting those two subtly different Geordie neighbours. People once spoke of 'the sunny side and the money side' though there is no consensus as to which was which. These days South feels a little more affluent but the North funkier. Each has a football club, the Robins and the Mariners, but the rivalry is nothing like as intense as that between Newcastle and Sunderland. Circa 800 years of co-dependence have seen to that.

Headed through South Shields for the ferry I fall into step with a 'Swedish granny' (her description) who has cycled from Stockholm bound for the Cop 28 environmental summit in Glasgow. Down at the terminal, she becomes an instant celebrity, the focus of some warm and encouraging interest, even if she clearly understood not one syllable of the accent. As *The Pride of the Tyne* pulls in, there's an almost childish level excitement from at least one passenger. It isn't the Sting lookalike at the helm today, sadly, but you can't have everything. Getting my sea legs, I wander the deck catching stray fragments of conversation. Two nurses are talking about their daily struggles and tribulations in the beleaguered NHS. One man says to no one in particular: 'Just think what all this was like when the ship-yards were open'. An older woman is sharing nostalgia with her friends: 'We had a twin tub. You could never get anything clean.'

The journey takes seven chilly minutes across the shimmering water and then we come ashore in North Shields. I like it immedi-ately. Dan Jackson rightly characterises this tough, vivacious little town as 'Tyneside profonde' with streets packed with 'tremendous historical depth and emotional power ... the authenticity of the place is still striking.' The Fish Quay and the adjoining Bell Street are fantastically characterful, the pubs, cafés and tapas bars all packed on a weekday mid-afternoon. The apartments for sale promise 'incredible panoramic views of the River Tyne.' The feel is not at all gentrified but quirky and individual with a genuine salt tang of the sea. North Shields is full to the brim with bars and pubs (reminding me of the local joke 'North Shields is a drinking town with a fishing problem'). But there's no doubt which is the most currently famous. The Low Lights Tavern is the oldest pub in the area and an alehouse for 400 years. It styles itself 'a traditional pub with a real community of friends, many of them Real Ale lovers, who have joined a long list of fishermen, career sailors, travellers, merchants and ne'er do wells who have populated the cosy, low ceiling bar of the Grade II-Listed tavern in its history.' It's also the only one to recently get a photo shoot in the arts section of the *New York Times*.

Great pub though it is, the *New York Times* didn't come to the Low Lights for the IPA but because of its most famous regular. As of 2022 they are calling Sam Fender the British Bruce Springsteen. That's the kind of thing 'they' say all the time, but there's some truth here. Young Fender is declaredly a fan of the Boss and his music has the same raw energy as early Springsteen, sharing its rooted sense of place in working-class communities. But there's not much of the florid romanticism of 'Born To Run' here. There are no 'highways jammed with broken heroes on last chance power drives' in Fender's music, but Poundshop Kardashians: 'Newcastle on a Saturday night … all muscles and V-necks and fake tan.' In 'Howden Aldi Death Queue', he views the pandemic through a crazed and hilarious punk analysis of Covid measures in his local discount supermarket. His anthem is 'Seventeen Going Under', a song which presents teenage life in North Shields not, as in Springsteen's New Jersey, as a cinematic dream of neon and boardwalks and barefoot girls on car bonnets in soft summer rain, but of rucks on the cold September beaches, porn videos and 'the boy who kicked Tom's head in.' This is the anonymous but haunting bully to whom the song's most viscerally memorable line refers: 'I was far too scared to hit him/But I would hit him in a heartbeat now.'

The video for 'Seventeen Going Under' feels compelled to add, in 'edgy' fashion shoot way, a distorting MTV gloss. There are a few shots of authentically pallid white teens looking authentically fucked off in the North Shields sand dunes. But far fewer than those of a bevy of beautiful, ethnically diverse models with fabulously shaved, dyed and sculpted hair writhing in an imagined nightclub presumably far, far from North Shields. The subtext is clear, if maybe unintentional. You can celebrate or mourn these towns and these kids in a song about them as Fender does brilliantly. But you couldn't possibly put them in the video. Starchy as potatoes and just as unhealthy, they just aren't photogenic enough. Fender himself, handsome as Brando but pale and surly in a short-sleeved shirt with an electric company logo, is the only one in the video you might conceivably find at the bar in the Low Lights or the Gunner or the Prince of Wales. Or the Mariners, the Northumberland Arms or the John Gilpin, legendarily terrifying pubs of which, when they closed, locals commented that 'they weren't as rough as people said', proving that they absolutely were.

These were not pubs you would pop into for a glass of pinot, a half of organic microbrewed craft ale, or even worse a soft drink, which is just what I do in the Low Lights. None of the daytime drinkers bats an eyelid and a few even ask me what I'm writing. ('He was horrible to Gateshead, was he? Well, he seems a very perceptive bloke, like.') A man in a fleece with a battered sci-fi paperback, suggests I walk up the coast to Tynemouth and then hop on the Metro. Slightly sheepish from my elderflower pressé, I push on along Fish Quay, still busy with working fisheries and shacks offering whiting, cod and various unspeakable looking denizens of the cold rocky shelves and bays here. The motto on the crest of Tynemouth borough is the beautiful 'Messis Ab Altis' ('Our Harvest is from the Deep'), reflecting the fact that this region is built on two demanding and dangerous industries: sea fishing and coal mining. Here stands a touching and grave statue of a fisherman looking out to sea for friends lost in the deep. It is called Fiddler's Green after the mariner's heaven, a place of perpetual mirth, endless food and drink, a fiddle flying forever for dancers who never tire. I rest a while on a nearby bench and cast my eyes out to sea too, deep in thought and making the occasional note. I must have presented a forlorn figure since a passing lady of about eighty comes over and sits by me, enquiring with a gentle lean of the head: 'Now pet, I hope that's not your last will and testament you're writing, is it?'

Still chuckling, I carry on with my bracing, gusty, salty stroll along the harbour wall, a saunter that could tempt even the suicidal to stay on this earth a little longer. The path passes the Knotts flats, which are surely the most beautifully situated social housing in England, a fortress-like structure that gazes commandingly out over the North Sea. Everything about this great building speaks of a time when England had different priorities. Modelled in a proto-Brutalist/art deco style on the famed Karl-Marx-Hof in Vienna, the flats were given to the people by Sir James Knott, a local benefactor who lost two sons at Ypres and the Somme and devoted himself to the public good, liberally spraying cash around the region.

When Priestley came to the North East, the flats were being constructed, to be completed in 1938 and opened the next year. The idea was to provide homes for seafaring families all living in the North Shields district, relocated from slums in the area and with rents kept affordably low. Each of the 135 households' windows would face the sea to help families watch for their loved ones' return. They boasted a basement boxing club and recreation facilities. But they were also the first accommodation anywhere built with an eye to the coming war, with fire resistant materials throughout and huge cellars designed as air raid shelters. They never needed to be used thankfully. The biggest clock in the North East, 12.5 feet across, stands high on the centre wall and kept good time until relatively recently. Now it stands forever at twenty-five past three, and I hope there's stotties and pease pudding still for tea.

A little further, past the monument and up over the headland, is Tynemouth, a 'ta da' moment of wind-torn cliffs and gothic ruins. Below you are King Edwards Bay and Longsands where, sometimes, hardy Geordie surfers brave the icy breakers of the North Sea. This cold, grey churning expanse of water, stretching implacably all the way to Bergen was, up until the Great War, known as the German Ocean, but then, like our own royal family, underwent a name change to avoid those unacceptable Teutonic associations. Front and centre is the photogenically crumbling Tynemouth Priory. Here lies Malcolm III, slayer of the bloody tyrant Macbeth. As someone who once played Macbeth,* I've never had much time for the goody two-shoes who bested the troubled Thane of Cawdor. Macbeth is clearly and substantially cooler than the earnest milksop Malcolm.

Aimlessly walking about has a rich intellectual and aesthetic pedigree. Baudelaire invented the concept of the flâneur, the idle if thoughtful wanderer of the city streets. The Situationist Guy Debord gave us the 'derive', a revolutionary idea that meant basically an unplanned ramble giving rise to random invigorating encounters. But long before either of these gallic notions, northerners have set great store by the virtues of 'mooching about'. Recreational mooching is likely to involve a pub, some light shopping and a chippie.

Tynemouth is a fabulous spot for mooching, especially on a Saturday where the whole railway station becomes a sprawling vintage bazaar, the kind of place where, under its wrought iron lattice canopy, you can get hot fresh Swiss tartiflette, a vintage Ebbets Field Flannels Atlanta Chiefs 1967 baseball cap and a copy of series two of *Sapphire and Steel* on Betamax. It's a huge hipster car boot sale. Then stroll down Front Street and check out the chi-chi independent shops (I bought a cool shirt) and fetch up for a moment's reflection, and possibly a battered sausage, at Marshall's fish and chip shop. Tynemouth has two blue plaques; one on Huntingdon Place commemorating Garibaldi's 1854 visit, the other

---

* In a radical and thought-provoking production, updating Shakespeare's tragedy to the Liverpool of Militant, with Macbeth as Derek Hatton. Still spoken about in awe in Skelmersdale.

at Marshall's stating that 'Jimi Hendrix, legendary rock guitarist, ate fish and chips from this shop on a bench overlooking the sea after playing at the Club A Go Go Nightclub, Percy Street, Newcastle, Fri March 10th 1967.' Now, as Hendrix (whose middle name coincidentally was Marshall) was managed by local muso Chas Chandler of The Animals, who were resident at the club, this could well be true. But something was nagging at me. He had chips here after he'd played a nightclub? Would even the most liberal and groovy of chippies fry that late in 1967? I checked and was pleased with the results. Hendrix played two shows; the first (for under-18s) at 8pm, the second at 2am. So it's entirely possible, even likely, that he dined at Marshall's in between. In the audience for that first teenybopper show was one Gordon Sumner, later Sting, tantric sex adept, smackable lutenist, doppelgänger of the man who pilots the Shields ferry and peroxided front man of unfeasibly popular blond cod-reggae act The Police. It sounds a good night, though I would love to have seen him a few nights before at Kirklevington Country Club in Yarm.

I could happily have spend longer in Tynemouth. I could happily move there. But I must away to Whitley Bay, or rather Monkseaton, the latter being essentially an inland suburb of the former. It's getting dark when I hop off the Metro, but I still take a stroll along the darkening esplanade. No one with blood in their veins can resist an esplanade, redolent of neon and candy floss and dodgems whirling and throbbing to KC and The Sunshine Band. Whitley Bay was once the Blackpool of the North East, a vibrant, slightly roguish place, as cheap and cheerful as a toffee apple or a kiss-me-quick hat. During its 90s stag and hen do 'heyday', Dan Jackson vividly recalls seeing a naked man being cling-filmed to the promenade clock at 3.30 in the afternoon.

Many of the guest houses and B&Bs here proclaim themselves 'boutique'. I've been highly sceptical of this descriptor since the night I spent in Morecambe's 'premier boutique hotel', a grim dosshouse which stank of chip fat and had all the chicly welcoming ambience of Greenland's Arctic tundra. In similar vein, the North Sea looks terrifyingly cold and choppy on what has become a freezing Monday evening. I walk past Hinnies restaurant and whatever the collective noun for fish and chip shops is (a shoal? A catch?) In the dusk, one hardy soul in bucket hat and chest waders, always a strong look, is fishing from the beach. He cuts a melancholic Canute-like figure, surf crashing at his knees as he struggles with his cast to reap his own 'harvest from the deep.'

By gritting my teeth and steeling every sinew, I am not going to use the term 'iconic' as we now come to Spanish City, although here it would have been justified. Built in 1910 as a smaller Geordie version of Blackpool's brash Pleasure Beach, it was once a fun palace: concert hall, restaurant, roof garden, tearoom, ballroom and funfair. This was where generations of Northumbrian kids were weaned on rock and roll and the menace and thrill of an evening of lights and loud music. One of these was Mark Knopfler of Dire Straits, raised in nearby Blyth and exposed to his first primitive blasts of rock music here in the early 60s. Later, he namechecked Spanish City in his song 'Tunnel of Love'. It was played every morning until the complex closed and fell into disrepair at the turn of the twenty-first century. Newly restored, Spanish City has opened again on a smaller scale with a summer funfair and an 'iconic' wedding venue, of course. I just make it to Valerie's Tearoom before it closes to scoff a slice of cake and a coffee and charge my phone as the young staff very pleasantly bustle and clear up around me. Then it's off up through the backstreets of town, past the shisha bars and the Turkish restaurants and more boarded, shuttered shops and a rendezvous at the Left Luggage of Monkseaton Station.

For once in my absent-minded life, I am not aiming to recover my wallet or charger. Monkseaton station's Left Luggage is a bar, and a bloody good one too. I get the first round in and, settled with beers, Dan Jackson (for it is he) talks me through my itinerary, beginning with Priestley's visit to Gateshead. 'Those remarks of his get quoted and dredged up every time anyone writes an earnest thinkpiece about Gateshead, or by extension the North East, or even the North. It's really just a strange quirk of history that it's not a suburb of Newcastle but a town in its own right.' I tell Dan and his dad, who's joined us for one, that after the constrained feel of Gateshead and Hebburn, I warmed to South Shields, found it airy and even buzzing. 'Once upon a time it would have been much more so. I worked for the council there for ten years and I saw a slow decline. It was the third town of the North East once. That's how the 80s marketing brochure sold it. That main shopping street used to have all the High Street big guns, Marks and Spencer, BHS, Burtons. All gone. It's on a peninsula, so no one passes through. It was always a shipyard and coal mining town. Now it has neither of those things and it hasn't really been able to reinvent itself like North Shields has done. But it has real history. It has the oldest Muslim population in Britain; the lascars, as they were called. It was said that because of their background they could tolerate the incredible heat in the hold of the steam ships where they were shovelling coal. They came from what was then Aden, now the Yemen. According to the old tales when they first arrived, the Aden migrants turned left and went into South Shields while the West Africans settled in North Shields. Now, North Shields is a drinking town …', 'With a fishing problem?' I offer. 'Ah, so you've heard that one already. Well, there's some truth in it. It's always been very lively. A town full of pubs and the pubs full of songs and music. Sam Fender worked and sang in one and in another there was a Slovakian pianist who'd break out the Chopin at closing time. Neil Tennant was born here. It's always had a bit of a rough edge but it's always fun. It's seen tough times. Biggest civilian loss of life in the Second World War when the Germans bombed an air raid shelter. Did you notice that great grass escarpment behind the Fish Quay? That was a notorious "rookery" or slum called Bankside between the High and Low town where people's houses would cling in these stacked rows at forty-five degrees to the hillside. Cheryl Tweedy's family were from there.'

Looking up at the wall of grass and scrubby vegetation now, one struggles to believe that hundreds of families lived there in precarious squalor, in houses so tightly packed that people could barely pass two abreast in filthy ginnels. But in 1912, two-thirds of Tynemouth Council had substantial property interests as private landlords and therefore little interest in providing affordable council accommodation. Publicly, they declared, that the poor working folk of North Shields were to blame for their own squalid circumstance. 'Put some of these people into Alnwick Castle and by the time they have been there one month it will be a slum,' said one, the delightful Alderman Coulson, a Tory councillor (and builder). There was fear mixed in with snobbery; communism was strong in the bankside slum, but sadly not strong enough. In his *Municipal Dreams* blog, John Boughton sketches the nature of life here: '48 residents occupied 17 rooms in Union Stairs, sharing a single water tap. Liddle Street's 405 residents enjoyed (if that's the word) one earth privy for every 11 people. Only two homes had piped water; none had baths.' When the slums were demolished and the residents deposited in the new estates like The Ridges, later cosmetically renamed Meadow Well, strong bonds, connections and familial skeins were broken. When Britain periodically rioted and its sink estates self-immolated in the late 80s and early 90s, it was perhaps not surprising that Meadow Well was among them. But things are quieter now.

'North Shields has always been rougher than Tynemouth', says Dan, 'and they're separated by the *cordon sanitaire* of Northumberland Park. Tynemouth has always felt more liberal and suburban. Whitley Bay was where everyone went for their holidays. It was crazy during the Glasgow factory workers fortnight. It took a bit of a battering over the years and there's still some run-down bits. But it's on its way back. Then once you're past Whitley Bay you're into the coalfield and there is a discernible difference. It sounds harsh, but things get tattier in that overlooked corner. But that is where all the people were in Northumberland. Blyth, Ashington, Newhart, the new towns like Killington, Newton Aycliffe, Cramlington, where according to local lad Ross Noble "there was a paracetamol factory at one end and a razor blade factory at the other.' But there's a very interesting dynamic at work here these days, culturally and politically. Tynemouth was a solidly Tory seat till '97. Now they've flipped to Labour while so many constituencies around here have gone the other way. Take Blyth Valley up the road. Always Labour when I was a kid. It had an ex-coal miner for an MP. Now it's Conservative. Unthinkable once.'"

If community is strong here, so too is a kind of tribalism, although Dan thinks it's been both overplayed and played up to. 'It's like the Gateshead/Newcastle division. It only really gets brought up when you get into these tedious debates about who qualifies to be called a Geordie.' According to one variety of local folklore, only those born within the sound of the Vickers-Armstrongs shipyard hooter can lay claim to being a real Geordie. This is guff, though, as linguists cite the first usage in the late 1700s and some romantics even as far back as the Venerable Bede. Until relatively recently it was applied to both Tynesiders and Wearsiders with no complaint from either.

'Until not that long ago, everyone from the old Northumberland and Durham coalfield were Geordies, even people from Sunderland. It's essentially grown out of the football rivalry, and even that's a fairly recent tribal division.' Dan's dad recalls that members of the same family would follow different teams and even watch both depending on who was at home and who was doing well. That said, it should be noted that crowd trouble forced a match between Newcastle and Sunderland to be abandoned. In 1901.

What's not in doubt is that football is in the very DNA of the North East, and vice versa. Football was once as dominated by Northumbrians as table tennis is by the Chinese or volleyball the Brazilians. Sunderland and Newcastle were giants of the game for the first two thirds of the last century, before both those giants began to snooze. The first £1,000 footballer, Wearsider Alf Common, was transferred between Middlesbrough and Sunderland. Two Durham pit men have managed Barcelona (Bobby Robson and Jack Greenwell) and the region has produced more top-flight footballers and managers than most: Brian Clough, Bob Paisley, Howard Kendall, the aforementioned Robson, the Charlton Brothers, Paul Gascoigne, Chris Waddle, Jordan Henderson, with the list still being added to.

But in the week that I come north, the talk across Tyneside was of a sleeping giant set to awake after an invigorating shot of strong, black gold from the middle east. The perennially underachieving (well, since the 1950s) Newcastle United had just been purchased by a consortium, of which the state of Saudi Arabia were the major players. That's totalitarian, homophobic, torturing, journalist-murdering, human rights abusing Saudi Arabia. Liberally minded football fans were appalled. At the next game Crystal Palace fans unveiled a banner of an executioner wielding a sword dripping blood. All of which made you wonder why half of Manchester weren't so exercised by Manchester's City's 2009 sale to Sheikh Mansour of the UAE, another totalitarian state with a murky human rights record. The Newcastle takeover seemed to be too much for some, possibly because it wasn't their team. A few supporters of both Newcastle United and Chelsea (in the wake of Abramovich being forced to sell Chelsea after Ukrainian war sanctions) complained that we were all being 'too PC' about all this, as if we were talking about insisting on 'Ms' on official forms rather than objecting to public beheadings and amputations.

Dan and his dad drop me back at the ferry terminal and soon I'm watching the lights of North Shields recede as I head back south on the last boat. I think about how much has changed since Priestley came, doped up on cold remedy, snotty (in every sense) and having the thoroughgoing bad time that would cast a long shadow over all the writing about the North East to come. In 1933, as he gloomily stalked the banks of the Tyne, Saudi Arabia was at war with Yemen. It still is. Yemeni refugees are still fleeing to South Shields to join their kinfolk. But this time the man bombing their African homes, Mohammed bin Salman, also owns their local beloved football team and has been welcomed with open arms by many a Geordie, the ones who are not too 'PC' anyway.

To the man with a hammer, everything looks like a nail. To the mooching/journeying travel and culture writer, every fact can seem blazingly significant. But this one does have a dark irony. Priestley would have been astonished to learn that a foreign government, and a brutal dictatorship at that, now owned the mighty Newcastle United as a trinket. It would have put him in an even worse mood. As it was, he was barely more sympathetic to the region and its people than Alderman Coulson. 'If T S Eliot ever wants to write a poem about a real wasteland he should come here,' he concluded, managing a swipe at both Tyneside and his elitist modernist poet peer. But like Orwell in Wigan, he had never come here to encourage tourists or provide good copy for the marketing brochures. He was here to illuminate by fire, and there was warmth in that fire too. 'England would not be the England we know if the Tyneside were not the Tyneside we know,' judged Priestley and that is still the case, I think. But I'm not sure Mohammed bin Salman either knows or cares about that.

10

TO EAST DURHAM AND THE TEES

In which I learn what makes a Mackem, hunt for sea
glass among the slag of a Prison Planet, talk
Priestley and poppadums in a town 'as weird as a
cart-horse with scales and fins' and join the
'passegiata' of the hidden Tees.

One of the posters in my 'work room' (I call it my 'work room'
because, if I called it a 'study', I may as well go the whole hog and get
a top hat and a manservant) is part of a series commissioned by the
London, Midland & Scottish Railway in 1924. It's a depiction of the
Durham coalfield by Royal Academy member George Clausen. The
image is a haunting one; silent, shadowed miners emerge on the
penumbral hillside heading homeward after their shift. Behind them
loom the moors and the mine workings, desolate but gravely beautiful. In the distance, dark and remote figures are in unknowable
conversation. The mood is one of twilit strangeness and melancholy.

Nine years after Clausen came to paint the hidden lives and landscape of the Durham coalfield, Priestley came for *English Journey* and

found a world and a culture just as secret, mysterious and opaque to the rest of England. An England that was nonetheless sitting by fires, riding on trains, working in factories all lit and powered by the labour of the miners of the Durham coalfield, harvesting 'black gold' in subterranean darkness. 'Unless we happen to be connected in some way with a colliery, we do not know these districts. They are usually unpleasant and rather remote and so we leave them alone. Of the millions in London, how many have spent half an hour in a mining village? … If there had been several working collieries in London itself, modern English history would have been quite different.' It really would. England's mines were far from the Palace of Westminster, in far-off lands of which politicians knew nothing. Like Tyrannosaurus Rex and the Soviet Union, King Coal was a mighty colossus that vanished overnight. But when Priestley came to East Durham and the Tees, the communities of the Durham coalfield may have been isolated and hermitic, but they were as rooted and deep as the mineshafts and as fiery as furnaces, and the collapse of the coal industry would have been unthinkable.

Not long after Priestley was on Tyneside, George Orwell came north to my hometown of Wigan, to live among and write about the life and work of coal miners. Motivated, perhaps, by the snobbery of an Old Etonian towards a wool man from Bradford, Orwell mistrusted and feared Priestley. He put him (entirely wrongly) on the tawdry lickspittle 'red list' of suspected Communist sympathisers he put together for the Foreign Office, along with Charlie Chaplin, Michael Redgrave and Hugh MacDiarmid. But the miners of Wigan brought out his better side. True, he found their houses, meals, children and wives disgusting – he was a snob, as we have said – but he respected them profoundly. 'You and I and the editor of the *Times* Lit. Supp., and the Nancy poets and the Archbishop of Canterbury and Comrade X, author of *Marxism for Infants* – all of us really owe the comparative decency of our lives to poor drudges underground, blackened to the eyes, with their throats full of coal dust, driving their shovels forward with arms and belly muscles of steel.' Orwell thought that coal was the basis of modern civilisation.

Nearly a century later, as I make my way south from Newcastle, I read about the latest bump in the rickety fairground ride of controversy surrounding another Old Etonian. Boasting to reporters of his eco-credentials on a visit to a Scottish wind farm Boris Johnson had 'joked', 'Look at what we've done already. We've transitioned away from coal in my lifetime. Thanks to Margaret Thatcher, who closed so many coalmines across the country, we had a big early start and we're now moving rapidly away from coal all together.'

I wonder what Orwell and Priestley would have made of Johnson's joke – and Johnson the man – as I cross that Durham coalfield. This is a place where coal dust still hangs heavy in the air, if only metaphorically, pervading the atmosphere of these towns and villages, the shape of the landscape, the names of pubs and schools, the memories of granddads, dads and uncles, of tragedies and grand days like the Durham Miners' Gala, perhaps Britain's most enduring and beloved celebration of working-class culture and industry.

Enduring, yes. Durham still has a miners' gala. It just doesn't have any miners.

2

The Metro from Newcastle to Sunderland pushes across scattered grey industrial suburbs, through scrubby fields where rangy horses graze and canter, alongside regimented council estates, through Fellgate and East Boldon and Seaburn onward across the seams of carbon towards the breaking waves of sea, bound for the coal-dirty coast. Two neighbouring bridges cross the Wear into Sunderland at Monkwearmouth. Priestley and I both come this way, he by Daimler, me by Metro, over Keir Hardie Way, past the Stadium of Light, where the colliery once stood and where the perennially embattled

Black Cats of Sunderland AFC now put the faithful through fort-nightly agonies. And so into Sunderland itself. From his upholstered seat, Priestley observed: 'Though there is, I believe, considerable unemployment and distress in the town, it looked fairly prosperous, clean and bright that morning.'

It is clear and bright on this fresh morning, too. I could even believe a 2018 survey by the One Family finance group that claimed Sunderland was England's best city to live in, with residents 'happy with almost all aspects of the city.' I don't know enough about the city today to make claims about its prosperity or otherwise. I do know that between 1975 and 1989, with the dying of the coal and shipbuilding industries, the city lost a quarter of its jobs, though much of these were replaced thanks to international business invest-ment such as the high-profile arrival of Nissan in 1986. But according to the Sunderland Economic Masterplan, a vaguely Maoist sounding initiative, the city 'suffers from serious deprivation as well as average wages that are lower than the rest of the UK.'

As the biggest shipbuilding town in the world in the 1950s, Sunderland made the ships that went to Newcastle to be fitted. This arrangement has given the townsfolk their nickname, 'Mackem'; in Sunderland, they 'mak'em' and the world takes 'em. But there's some dispute about how longstanding and deep these tribal nomen-clatures and affiliations run. The OED cites the first mention of 'mackem' in print as coming as recently as 1988. Veteran BBC presenter Jeff Brown has said that when he left Sunderland in the early 70s to go to university, he was a Geordie, but came home to discover that he had become a Mackem. On the Sunderland message boards I found 'Mackems' galore who backed this up. One stated that he was '50 years old. Sunderland born, always consid-ered myself a Geordie up until mid-80s when I first heard us called Mackems.' The comically monikered Paddy O'Dors (geddit?) said: 'Anyone from the North East was called a Geordie up until the 1980s (especially to anyone from outside the area). When

Sunderland won the cup in '73 they were often referred to as being "Geordies". A lot of this "Mackem' and Geordies being born within sight of the Bigg Market or whatever the criteria is just recent nonsense.' Some speculate that after Newcastle Council's corruption scandals of the 70es, Sunderlanders were keen to distance themselves from their Tyneside neighbours and develop an identity all their own.

Maybe something of that individual spirit was behind Sunderland's decision to leave the European Union in 2016. Theirs was one of the first and most emphatic declarations of 'taking back control', with over 60 per cent voting for Brexit. This seismic decision caused the *New York Times* to head for Wearside, Hollywood 'mean girl' (and unlikely Europhile) Lindsay Lohan to rage 'Where's Sunderland?', and local comic Ross Noble to declare he was stockpiling Mr Kipling French Fancies. But looking back at a Channel 4 news report from a few days later (one of many shocked despatches from a horrified metropolitan media), what becomes apparent is that the large Brexit vote was not so much anti-EU as anti-Westminster, with Mackem after Mackem repeating the charge that London politicians of every stripe were cossetted, out of touch and self-serving but barely mentioning the European Union. With Durham's own Dominic Cummings being the intellectual architect of the Leave vote, it's tempting to conclude that Wearside was the crucible and spiritual home of Brexit.*

These were questions one could spend a long time mulling in the bars of Castletown or the cafés of Roker, but, like Priestley, I was merely passing through. On the road from Sunderland to his next destination, Priestley saw something which stirred him to a more sympathetic cast of mind towards the North East than he ever felt in Gateshead or North Shields. He watched men on bicycles holding

---

* Other than Newcastle, every single region of the North East voted for Brexit.

bags of dusty and broken coal they had scavenged from the shoreline and steep cliffs nearby. They were taking these bags to sell for a pittance in Sunderland. His response was caustic. 'Those people who still believe the working folk of this country live in an enervating atmosphere of free bread and circuses might like to try this coal-picking enterprise for a day or two, just to discover if it is their idea of fun. To some of us it hints at desperation.'

Those men had come from the place that I was headed to. It sounded as fanciful as Narnia the way Priestley introduced it. 'Seaham Harbour itself is like no other town I have ever seen. It is a colliery town on the coast. It looks as weird as a cart-horse with scales and fins.' That's putting it a little strong, but he has a point. When we think of pit villages, if at all, we picture cottages huddled under Welsh mountains, or in the shadow of dark Lancashire slag heaps, or dotted across the scarred and smoky Lawrentian Midlands. Seaham Harbour is nothing like that. It is a seaside town, except with nothing of the gaiety that implies. Seaham is built not on candy floss or saucy postcards but the scheming of a rapacious nouveaux riche coal baron straight from central casting, Lord Charles Stewart, the 3rd Marquess of Londonderry.

Already a pretty pungent order of stinking rich, Lord Charles Stewart, 41-year-old widower of the Irish gentry, took as his second wife a teenage County Durham coal heiress named Lady Frances Anne Vane-Tempest. Stewart was an army chum of the Duke of Wellington, himself a brutal landlord in Ireland during the Great Famine, who insisted on his right to employ child labour. Stewart knew as much about coal mining as Boris Johnson, but he did know that having to pay wages to the 'keel men' who lugged the coal on carts from his new wife's pits at Rainton and Penshaw to the river Wear (and thus the world) was eating into his profits. To further annoy him, the whole ungrateful coalfield went on strike in 1844 for idle fripperies like a decent wage and safe working conditions. Londonderry, as he now was, reacted by evicting the strikers, bringing in Irish and Welsh blacklegs (strike-breakers)* and by intimidating all local traders into denying strikers credit or succour lest they be evicted and bankrupted themselves. He raged that he would ruin the town if he did not get his way, and after four hungry months he did. The strike was broken and to prevent any further similar inconvenience to his operation, he built a harbour and turned this quiet coastal village into a port with a private railway to his pits. Seaham Harbour was born, and Seaham became a boom town of sorts, albeit one built on the queasiest of foundations. Londonderry refused to allow health or safety regulations or inspections in his mines. Some 160 people were killed in a single explosion at Seaham Colliery in 1881.

Essentially, then, the 3rd Marquess of Londonderry was a complete arsehole. Back in Monkseaton, Dan Jackson had cursed that there was a statue to the marquess in Durham market square 'sneering on his prancing horse,' rather than someone like Tommy Hepburn, 'one of the greatest figures the North East has ever produced, who led a victorious strike against Londonderry or Lahdandry, three syllables, as the Lord himself would have said it, in that way they speak, their mouths frozen like stage ventriloquists.'

Here's the thing. Now that we are tearing down statues of slave traders and imperialists, with good reason, how about we start taking a pickaxe to those ruthless exploiters of England's workers that still insultingly have pride of place in towns and cities across the land. Paul Simpson, local historian, writes in his blog that 'Londonderry was brutal even by the standards of his time. On the Tory benches in

---

* According to local historian Tony Whitehead, they too had it hard. They were not told they were strike-breakers till they arrived but then had no funds to return and no option but to work. Once the strike was broken, Londonderry could take his pick of the workers and the blacklegs were no longer needed. At Seaton Delavel, the Welsh blacklegs were beaten by the locals and all but one driven out. He remained completely ostracised by the community for twenty years until eventually, he got the message and left.

the House of Lords, he led the opposition to the Mines Act 1842, which among other things, prevented boys under the age of ten from working underground … The often-heard claim that we cannot condemn historical figures because "people didn't know any better at the time" simply does not apply.' To my mind, Londonderry belongs in the Wear in the same way that Colston belonged in Bristol Harbour. Or in museums alongside some relevant discussion of their 'legacy'.

They seem a tough bunch to love, the Londonderrys. Even Lady Frances, when entertaining other gentry in the finest building around, Seaham Hall, would claim that until they arrived in Seaham it was a uncivilised wasteland without even a proper road. But whether because of them or in spite of them, by the 1841 census, Seaham was booming, not just with the trades of the sea such as pilots, seamen, ropemakers, chandlers and sailmakers but cotton weavers, dressmakers, tailors, drapers, shoemakers, potters, hairdressers, paper makers, straw hat makers and bookbinders. There was also a thriving middle class of teachers, clerks and lawyers. For a while it prospered and soon got its own colliery, as well as a jail, a cemetery, several churches and a score of pubs. In the 20s, though, the bottle works and engine works closed, the shipping trade ceased, even the once-productive mines were hit by the depression of the early 30s.

Priestley arrived after Seaham Colliery had been inactive for two years: 'You saw at a glance that there was very little money about.' But the history of Seaham offered by the council website paints a different picture of the town at the time. 'Many Seaham folk remember the 30s as hopeful, happy, romantic and sporting. The town's three recreation grounds provided football, cricket, tennis and bowls. The cinemas were popular. Social evenings and dances were enjoyed in church and chapel halls; brass bands were to be heard practising in Miners Halls and playing in the parks.'

Of course, it's possible that so much bowling, dancing and euphonium practice was going on because no one had a job. The economic

crisis of 1931 had split the ruling Labour Party, leading to the forma-
tion of a 'National Government' led by the infamous Ramsay
MacDonald. MacDonald is still regarded as a traitor by many on the
Left, who know a thing or two about bearing a grudge. He also
happened to be Seaham's MP, even though he had been expelled
from the Labour Party and the local branch had asked him to resign.
At the 1935 election, MacDonald, emblem of weakness and compro-
mise, was soundly beaten in Seaham by the official Labour candidate,
the pugnacious Emmanuel 'Manny' Shinwell. So, this was the
Seaham JBP came to; fractured, depressed, ugly, a town that had
never become the magnificent architectural achievement, a
mini-Newcastle on the rugged Durham shore, that Londonderry
wanted. Priestley found it 'almost entirely composed of miners'
cottages, laid in dreary monotonous rows. They were all so small that
they made the whole town look diminutive, as if it were only playing
in a miserable fashion at being a town.'

I step down from the train into a fresh morning full of seagull cries
and crisp sunshine and, for better or worse, not a speck of coal dust.
The Miners' Strike of 1984–85 was the longest and bitterest of all the
coal disputes woven into East Durham's history and it proved final
and climactic, sealing the fate of British mining. In October 1992
British Coal, as part of their euthanising national strategy, announced
the closure of the four remaining pits in the old County of Durham.
Seaham's remaining site was razed; you can still see the great open
wound in the land. In 1992, c. 150 years of mining in Seaham, with
all the human stories that implies, was laid to rest under the tyres of
bulldozers. Coal slag still littered the beaches and bays of Seaham and
the coast was ravaged, dirty and desolate. All of which made it perfect
as Fiorina 161, the sinister, bleak foundry-cum-maximum-
security-prison-planet in *Alien 3*, filmed on Blast Beach, Seaham and
released in 1992, the same year that mining ended here.

Thirty years on from that terrible movie (don't @ me) and nearly a
century after *English Journey*, twenty-first century Seaham is, if not

quite transformed, then changed for the better. A £10 million cleaning bill later (funded in part by the National Lottery and partly by the European Union), the black, despoiled beaches are nature reserves and recreational spaces for walkers, cyclist and foragers. Seaham Hall is a luxury hotel so while you probably still get dislikeable rich people hanging around, at least they can't kick you out of your cottage. Lord Byron got married here, and so can you, later decompressing in the Serenity Spa, recently voted the best in western Europe and Scandinavia for its 'inspiring wellness retreat that draws influence from Far Eastern healing rituals.' Perhaps this narrowly failed to make the cut in *Coast* magazine's recent feature '8 Reasons Why You Should Move To Seaham.' This was an admirable boost for an area that's had it tough, even if two of the reasons were that 'Newcastle, with its airport and high-speed rail link to London (King's Cross in under 3 hours), is just 18 miles away' and that the final scene of *Get Carter* was filmed near here. If you recall, this features Michael Caine wandering along a forlorn stretch of polluted shoreline before being shot in the head by a sniper and dumped in a massive coal scuttle. I mean, it's a famously grim dénouement but as a tourist boost, it's hardly *Roman Holiday*.

I'm as keen as the next man on the wellness that comes only from the influence of Far Eastern healing rituals, but my budget doesn't run to several hundred quid a night for a suite at Seaham Hall. My wellness would have to come from a cosy room at No 16, (just off the 'front', the former house of the colliery's first manager), a curry and a couple of pints. According to local historian Tony Woodhead: 'Like all ports, Seaham Harbour would have been a den of vice, drinking, gambling and prostitution. The pimps and ladies of the night would have disguised their presence in the census by declaring to the enumerator that their profession was something very different, a dressmaker perhaps, or a labourer. Until the coming of gas lighting in the next decade Seaham Harbour may well have been a very dark, threatening and frightening place when the sun went down. Some people would say it still is.'

I steel myself for that as dusk creeps over the North Sea. All the advice I'd had mentioned the Tommy statue and Downey's chippy, and as it was nearly lunchtime this seemed an urgent and pressing first port of call. Battered sausage and chips in hand, I settle down to twenty minutes of good, solid eavesdropping. Two older guys seated at a window table with salt-and-pepper crew cuts and Patagonia fleeces are having a chat about the environment. An organisation called Insulate Britain are in the news this morning for causing havoc by blocking roads to demand the government lags everybody's boilers (a gross over-simplification, I know). I'm conflicted about groups such as this and their compatriots Extinction Rebellion. It's a hugely pressing issue but I don't think preventing cleaners in Canning Town getting the Tube is the best way of winning hearts and minds. 'Bloody treehuggers' says one of the men, spearing a chip forcefully with a wooden fork. 'This is one of the top five chippies in the world,' announces a lady in the queue to a small boy with a plastic helicopter, lightening the mood.

The Tommy statue is a First World War commemoration made by Ray Lonsdale, who also sculpted Fiddler's Green in North Shields. The day is growing chill and the sea steel grey as I walk up the North Road past the lifeboat hut, the Masonic centre and the Beachcomber hotel and eventually down to the long and sandy beach that runs beneath the mildly savage cliffs. Here I meet a scene more Bruegel than *Geordie Shore*, except for the dark backdrop of the cranes of Sunderland docks. As far as the eye can see, dotted all along the beach, are scores, maybe hundreds, of people stooping and bending, scavenging and foraging, sifting in the silt and seaweed and shingle. Not for coal, as Priestley found them. But for glass.

During the Victorian and Edwardian eras, Seaham was home to a great many bottle works and glass-making factories. In fact, it 'boasted' the largest one in Britain in the Londonderry Bottleworks (yes, that guy again). The Seaham Bottle Works crafted 20,000 hand-blown bottles every day: perfume bottles, black glass bottles, 'sock darners', 'doorstop turtles', 'friggers' and 'whimsical canes' (search me). As a by-product, every day large amounts of colourful waste glass were dumped straight into the North Sea. A century or so of 'surf tumbling' in endless churning tides mean that Seaham Beach is one of the world's finest sea glass beaches, a place where beautiful, multi-coloured detritus washes up constantly, smoothed and glazed by sea action into tiny objets d'art. People come from far and wide to hunt for them.

Some of our beachcombers are obviously here for fun and an afternoon's diversion; retirees in quality Norwegian outerwear, teenagers in baseball caps, family groups laughing and splashing, picking up bits of flotsam and tossing it back into the waves. But there's another species of Seaham sea glass hunter too. They come prepared, armed with little rakes and special satchels and blankets and buckets. By the harbour wall a lady in her mid-70s, wearing a knitted poncho and raggedy woollen hat, sits squatly on a gym mat. All around her are buckets and rakes with which she sifts and sorts the wrack and shingle. It's an image from Dickens, a minor character in *Our Mutual Friend*, mudlarking the liminal water's edge. She catches my gaze and returns it, defiantly. Rightly too; this is her world not mine, her patch. I lower my eyes and walk on, making the odd desultory stoop here and there and finding it to be a ring pull or a semi-consumed Starburst. The whole mise-en-scène is somehow melancholic; tiny figures at work among the giant black rocks that look like huge, piled coal cobs, the cold fury of the waves at their backs. Bleak and alien.

If you're in the market for a humorous sign about the benefits of drinking gin, or fancy learning to paddleboard or just want a massive cake, County Durham's only marina, the former Seaham Harbour, is the part of town for you. Built by the villainous Londonderry to undermine the power of the keelmen, and once a place of blood and coal dust, it has been gentrified into a tourist attraction with no less than three ice cream parlours and a fitness centre to work off the ensuing calories. A little crocodile of toddlers in sou'westers ambles adorably down to the outdoor play centre, huddled in the shadow of the loading cranes.

Further along the coast road though, the knickerbocker glories and rhubarb botanicals recede into a gathering gloom and a grimmer Seaham. In the now chilly twilight, there are men at work in heavy canvas overalls and rubber boots on the deck of the *Ultramar*. One guns and revs his forklift back and forth among piles of shale and coal dust. The Stygian seaside scene is lit by the occasional flash of oxy-acetylene and the stench of ash and burning rubber drifts across the deck and the quayside, over the twisted piles of scrap metal turning gold in the last of the sun over Blast Beach and the gunmetal of the North Sea.

You can still see the sea and the last bar of sunlight on its horizon from my table in the Ashoka curry house. It's a view best appreciated with a big glass of red and a prawn puri, I think, rather than downwind of the ash pile on the late shift on the *Ultramar*. It's heaving at seven o' clock, but they squeeze me in on a corner table between a young couple and a big family where the kids are being introduced to the glories of Indian food via kormas and dahls and peshwari naans, the waiters in benign, indulgent good humour. I have *English Journey* propped up on my wine bottle and am reading about Priestley's time in Seaham but become happily distracted by the conversation of the neighbouring young couple. It becomes apparent that they are English teachers, chatting about their set texts and their students' enthusiasm (or lack of it) for various giants of world literature. The students are finding *Animal Farm* 'depressing' (fair enough, I suppose, it is low on zingers) but think *Macbeth* is 'thrilling' and are quite getting into Milton ('weirdly'), which is more than I ever did.

But then, and here you will just have to believe me and trust that I've not invented the conversation, they start to talk about Priestley, and specifically *An Inspector Calls*. I wait for a good moment between poppadoms and pounce, explaining as quickly as possible my Priestley-related reasons for being in their town. They don't know *English Journey* and so are surprised that he came to Seaham. 'Did he like it?' they ask suspiciously. I choose my words carefully. 'More than Gateshead,' I answer truthfully and point out that he came here after two years of inactivity at the mine, in the middle of a depression and before it got a curry house. Finding eight reasons to move to Seaham then might have been 'a big ask'.

Their students love *An Inspector Calls*, which was written in a single week during the last winter of the Second World War. No British theatre was available to stage it and so it received its premieres in Leningrad and Moscow, Priestley being popular in the Soviet Union. A huge hit initially, it fell out of favour for several decades when it was lazily regarded as a cosy piece of drawing room theatre. That was until Stephen Daldry's brilliant 90s expressionist revival, still one of the most visceral experiences I've ever had in the theatre. The plot is so well-known and simple as to be quickly summarised. A prosperous and comfortable Midlands family are made to realise that they are all implicated in a young girl's tragic suicide. But at its moral core is Priestley's socialistic conviction that, in any decent society, we are all responsible for the welfare of each other, especially those more vulnerable than ourselves. *An Inspector Calls* is the utter antithesis of 'there's no such thing as society'.

That plot, that message, is well known to most young people in Britain, since for many years now the play has been a fixture of the GCSE syllabus. There's some interesting divides by gender in Seaham: 'The girls completely understand the play's message that we are all part of society and that we must look after each other. But the boys are more willing to take the side of the Birling family. They understand why some of the men act as they do to protect the family. But they all love it. We must tread carefully, of course, because we can't be seen to be imparting any political views.' But that is exactly what Priestley was doing. *An Inspector Calls* is not a whodunnit; it's a morality play.

Both give a wry smile and crunch the last of the poppadoms. It's a long time since I stood in front of a class, then a whey-faced Smiths fan teaching people of my own age and older in a Brutalist block in a Scouse new town. It would have been an interesting challenge to leave the politics out of *An Inspector Calls*, or to deliver a contrarian hot take, to argue it's an unfair 'woke' criticism of a 'hard-working family' just trying to get on in the world. You know, like O'Brien was 'just doing his job' down there in Room 101.

It has been a good conversation over good food and wine and, buoyed by it, I decide to stay out for a while. I check online for some bar recommendations and decide to try down the other end of town. My joie de vivre begins to evaporate almost immediately. Seaham's night-time streets are largely deserted. It's a cheerless trudge between the hinterland of silent houses and the cold North Sea up to the pub, which is down a street where a gang of young lads in hoodies are trying to do BMX tricks and swearing performatively, a hopeless little tableau in every sense.

But a few minutes in the pub and I begin to think hanging out with the guys on the bikes would have been a more fun evening. Maybe it's me having the temerity to a) be a stranger and b) quite blatantly walk in off the street expecting to have a drink. The young barman was polite enough, granted, but the clientele made the regulars in *An American Werewolf in London*'s Slaughtered Lamb seem warm and hospitable. A gang of locals are crowded around a big central table. They have clearly been here some time, and will be staying for some time, possibly for ever. I swiftly drink a pint of bitter, closely watched by the now entirely silent table, an unlovely mixture of sexes and ages. An awkward icy impasse. Obviously, I can't leave immediately; the bar room code of the Samurai meaning I would have to commit ritual seppuku with one of the picks and shovels behind the bar. Determined not to let this sour my night in

Seaham, I leave slowly and with as much brooding machismo as I can in suede loafers and determine to find somewhere more convivial. There is nowhere. Every bar in town is deserted. At Dempsey's the young woman is taking the chalkboard in and wiping the outside tables, while in the deserted bar, on some weird satellite channel, a Dutch Eredivisie relegation battle plays out to no one.

Eventually, I fetch up at the Big Asda, passing as I do four kids on the sea wall playing some nasty thumping plasticky Euro House on a tiny, rattling speaker whose coloured flashing lights are so pathetic, it's kind of heartbreaking. But then I remember my own youth in the ginnels of bleak estates and I feel a sudden kinship with this little huddled group, above a coal dust beach with just the distant lights of Sunderland to ignite your teenage dreams.

The doors of the Big Asda are firmly guarded at 9pm. They open up for me warily, explaining that they have closed because of an 'earlier incident'. I buy a bottle of Malbec, some Ferrero Rocher and the *Sunderland Echo*. They must have thought that I was on my way to very odd kind of date. I glance at the headlines. 'Black Cats cautious welcome for Hugin return'. 'Ryhope woman loses parking battle.' For a brief, mad moment, I think about buying those forlorn kids a few bottles of WKD Blue.

3

'If there is a queerer village in all England than this, I have never seen it.' That was Priestley's verdict on Shotton Colliery, County Durham in the autumn of 1933. You might agree if your opinion of the place were gleaned only from YouTube. The first of two 'hits', and there are very few, is an ambient music piece for 'Guided Meditation' called, inexplicably, Shotton Colliery; the second is footage of a march there by the far-right English Defence League in 2013, angrily objecting to a proposed Muslim education centre.

Playing the two together was a strange juxtaposition, the dreamy and the ethereal sound of panpipes soundtracking the contorted, boiled-potato faces of several generations of ugly, bald men in highly flammable sportswear. Anyway, Shotton Colliery seems a place whose sense of purpose disappeared along with the winding gear and the dark smudges of the pitheads. Priestley called it 'a symbol of greedy, careless, cynical, barbaric industrialism.' Now even that has left town.

Shotton Colliery, like the Durham Miners' Gala, is named for something that no longer exists. The village (technically, it is one) was born solely to serve the pit sunk here by the Haswell Coal Company in 1833. The agricultural land became a scarred warren of tunnels and shafts and the local farm hands became pit men. Life was never predictable and always precarious. After several decades of plenty, the mine closed in 1878 for twenty-three years. Houses were boarded up, streets abandoned. Shotton Colliery became a place of ghosts. Then, at the turn of the new century, came new owners, new shafts and several more decades of feast and famine.

By the time Priestley arrived by car, with a young miner as his guide, Shotton Colliery was still struggling with the global depression and the long legacy of the General Strike, when people would collect dust from the slag heap and ball it with water to make a cheap, almost useless coal for their fires and ovens. That slag heap dominates Priestley's description of his visit. He was horrified by it. 'This volcano was the notorious Shotton "tip", literally a man-made smoking hill ... It had a few satellite pyramids, mere dwarfs compared with this giant; and down one of them a very dirty little boy was tobogganing. The "tip" itself towered to the sky and its vast dark, bulk steaming and smoking at various levels, blotted out all the landscape at the back of the village. Its lowest slope was only a few yards from the miserable cluster of houses ... The atmosphere was thickened with ashes and sulphuric fumes; like that of Pompeii, as we are told, on the eve of its destruction.' These last words bring a chill now, knowing of the horror at Aberfan, Wales in 1966 when a school was engulfed by a slag heap, killing 116 children and 28 adults. But Shotton became a different kind of Pompeii.

Searching for old images of Shotton Colliery online brings forth a striking picture from 1948. Two women in headscarves, arms folded, faces turned from us, stare out of a brick door frame at the glowering hulk of the slag heap. It is an image both doom-laden and defiant. Of this 'Gibraltar made of coal dust and slag,' Priestley concluded with heavy sarcasm. 'I hope it will always be there, not as a smoking "tip", but as a monument to remind happier and healthier men of England's old industrial greatness and the brave days of Queen Victoria.' But, like England's industry and Queen Victoria, Shotton's volcano, its hellish smoking hill, is now completely gone, magicked away with a swish of a conjuror's cloth that Priestley would barely believe. Today, the pit site is as flat as a pancake, flat enough to be an airfield, and indeed it is home to the Sky-High Skydiving company. Above the quiet, stolid redbrick streets of the town, you can see the tiny figures drift and circle, like midges in summer heat. Tempted as I am, like the mine, the slagheaps and Priestley himself, it was time for me to head south, reflecting as I went on his valedictory words in 1933: 'I stared at the monster, my head tilted back, and thought of all the fine things that had been conjured out of it in its time, the country houses and town houses, the drawing-rooms and dining rooms, the carriages and pairs, the trips to Paris, the silks and the jewels, the peaches and iced puddings, the cigars and old brandies; I thought I saw them all tumbling and streaming out, hurrying away from Shotton – oh, a long way from Shotton – as fast as they could go.'

4

Is there a train from Darlington to Stockton, I wonder later that day over my books and maps in a railway tearoom? Fortunately, I wonder this to myself and not to any of the other customers or staff. They might have forcefully and pityingly pointed out that, yes, you can get there on the very first and most famous line of railway in England. The Stockton and Darlington Railway was the world's first public railway, officially opened on 27 September 1825, and the start of a new era for England, Britain and the world. At the station in 2022, there was a small picket and a large banner of a pugnacious looking man in a Khrushchev hat barking into a loudhailer. It was the General Secretary of the National Union of Rail, Maritime and Transport Workers Union, the RMT. Once upon a time, union leaders were like pop stars, famed, powerful, glamorous even, spoofed and impersonated on comedy shows. As a kid – OK, quite an odd kid – I could have named them and their unions all on sight; Spanish Civil War veteran Jack Jones of the TGWU, thick-lensed communist Mick McGahey of the NUM, blonde anti-matter Thatcher Brenda Dean of Sogat 82, Vic Feather, Len Murray and the rest. After quite some time and thought, I recalled that the man here was Mick Lynch, whose name and hat and loudhailer were all classics of the genre. The poster and the picket seemed to belong to the Golden Age of strikes, which I guess was roughly equidistant from both Priestley and myself, namely the 1970s. Perhaps, like flares and cassettes, they were about to enjoy one of their periodic revivals.*

Anyway, the first run from Stockton to Darlington took three-and-a-half hours thanks to several breakdowns and the fact that over

---

* Indeed they were; when Mick and the RMT called more industrial action and defended it in the face of inane TV reporters and the usual press hysteria, he became something of an alternative national treasure to some of us.

400 passengers were clinging to every conceivable surface of the train. Some unfortunate man's foot was run over and crushed and, at journey's end, coal was distributed to the poor. Now it takes a mere twenty-two minutes and is much less eventful, passing quietly through what sound like made up villages in a golden age crime novel; Dinsdale, Allens West, Eaglescliffe and finally Stockton. For a station so steeped in significance, it's rather an unprepossessing little halt now. There's a pretty curved row of houses by the station, but after that it's as utilitarian as all station approaches are.

The town is gearing up for the long Platinum Jubilee weekend, with notices of road closures and bunting strung across all the pubs. I remembered how I spent the Silver Jubilee of 1977 with the gang of other mid-teens and some older scenesters that comprised Wigan's small but passionate and self-supporting punk 'family'. We spent much of the day away from the trestle tables and street parties, downstairs in the basement of the Bier Keller Wigan, listening to the Sex Pistols' 'God Save the Queen' on the hour every hour. I read this morning that it has been re-issued for this jubilee, forty-five years on, and is in a 'chart race' with tenor Alfie Boe's stentorian reading of our dreary national anthem. Last time, as is widely acknowledged, the chart was rigged to prevent the embarrassment of the Pistols reaching number one. I imagined the same would happen again today, whatever the sales. But that may be the teenage punk in me, not quite dormant yet.

Priestley's snap judgement on Stockton was that it was 'better-looking than Middlesbrough, but not so cheerful and prosperous as its other neighbour, Darlington.' In the first, he was surely right. Middlesbrough has its transporter bridge, an engineering marvel, and the glittering nightscape of its chemical works lit the imagination of local lad Ridley Scott, inspiring the kinetic LA skyline of *Blade Runner*.* Stockton, though, has its high street,

---

* The dystopian cybernetic space colonising future of *Blade Runner* is set in 2019.

justly famed wherever very wide high streets are celebrated. It is said to be the broadest in England, and I see no reason to doubt that. But on a weekend afternoon, it is deserted. Priestley came on market day and found it filled with 'stalls and women shoppers and brick-faced lads from the country. The hotels along the street were loud with farmers roaring for beer.' But after the carts and farmers had trundled off into the soft dusk, he 'saw that there was something wrong with this town of 67,000 persons, that somehow it was not living up, in these days, to that enormously wide main street. There were people about, chiefly men with caps and mufflers; but the atmosphere was not that of a prosperous town at the end of a day's work … The hotel, the whole town, the very night air, all were too quiet and subdued.'

The mild afternoon air of Stockton spring 2022 is subdued too. Two Turkish barbers are smoking in their salon doorway, scrolling through their phones, glancing around for trade that will not come, I think. A troubled-looking woman in her thirties asks me quietly and nervously for money. No one else comes or goes. The shops are silent, the mood somnolent. The long slow death of the high street has been much dissected and mourned for the last decade or so. What has happened in Stockton has happened all across England, exacerbated by Covid. But where the high street is so grand, the decline seems crueller. The wider they come, the harder they fall. Sad remains of extinct giants lurk miserably everywhere, Marks and Spencer, Debenhams, New Look. Alongside these fossils are those harbingers of a retail mass extinction; charity shops, Poundland, B&M Bargains. But here, on the corner, the trend is being reversed. The Globe Theatre, barricaded and derelict since even its bingo hall days ended in 1997, is reborn in gorgeous 30s art deco curves and neon. It looks stunning. Handsome friezes outside tell the story of past glories. The Rolling Stones played here in October 1965 and Mick Jagger was cut above the eye by a coin thrown by some berk in the crowd. Jagger carried on with a blood-soaked handkerchief pressed to his head after a nurse applied stitches in the wings. (Somewhat unsympathetically, the *Northern Echo* reported all this next day with the headline 'Blood from a Stone'). The Beatles had already played here in 1963, with news of JFK's assassination reaching them and the crowd between sets. Less seismically, perhaps, but doubtless fun, highlights of the last few months have included An Evening with The Waterboys, former Radio 1 DJ Judge Jules and A Night of Laughter with Rob Brydon. Tonight, one of the many competing variations of Brummagem's feuding family reggae-lite troop UB40 is playing here, though Lord knows which one.

I'd even 'gigged' myself in Stockton once before. I did the show, signed some books, left in a torrential downpour and dried off in a Chinese restaurant. I should say Stockton-on-Tees, of course. But any visitor could be forgiven for giving it that shorter, more prosaic name. The 70s civic fathers of Stockton seem to have been committed to not letting you know that Stockton is in fact 'on Tees'. I wouldn't go as far as saying that the Tees has been Stockton's dirty little secret (though it was a blackened, dirty watercourse for decades) but short-sightedness and bad decisions managed to consign the Tees, one of England's great rivers and swelling to its pomp here, to the margins of town, an afterthought, a shabby reminder of busier days. Let us name at least one of the guilty men.

The architect John Garlick Llewellyn Poulson was jailed for his role in the corruption scandal that wormed through the councils and planning departments of the North of England in the 1960s and 70s. There's no evidence that there was anything untoward in his dealings with Stockton Council. But there are many people here who think he should have done time just for what he did do to their town. In what one local blogger called 'the biggest act of vandalism since Oliver Cromwell demolished Stockton Castle during the Civil War,' the quaint Victorian terraces that once tiered down from the grand high street to the river were razed and replaced by Poulson's blocky, functional Castlegate Centre. Stockton-on-Tees seems to have been doing its damnedest to hide its best side from us.

All this is going to change. That's the plan anyway, proclaimed on billboards all over town, each emblazoned with hyper-real computer visualised images of a new Stockton. The Council intends to demolish the Castlegate and the whole ugly eastern wall of the High Street. Instead, there'll be a riverside park three times the size of Trafalgar Square with sweeping vistas and easy, attractive access to the river via a cascade of steps forming an amphitheatre. The Market Square will flow naturally into a park fringed with cafés and bars, and perhaps a new library. Some devotees of Brutalism are already mourning the loss of Castlegate's striking modernist features, like the Piet Mondrian and Bridget Riley echoes of its dazzling geometric food court ceiling, described by local aficionado Jonathan Thompson as 'like a modernist cathedral'. But mainly, the town seems happy to see it go. I wasn't used to meeting townsfolk genuinely caught up in enthusiasm for a large-scale civic redevelopment. 'It's going to be great' says Boomer, handing me a pint of a deliciously appley golden IPA. 'Get rid of that dated old Castlegate monstrosity, put some life back in Stockton. It gets a bit of a bad name, this town. I mean it's not the most well-off area, that's probably obvious. But I have no problem with it. The people who come in here are lovely. And did you see the plans? To open up the town to the river? All decent towns and cities make something of their river, and we never have till now. It's going to be great.'

Boomer is the young barman of The Golden Smog, a craft ale bar tucked away down Hambletonian Yard just off the High Street. His dad owns the place, and the name reflects both one of his dad's favourite bands, a country act from Minneapolis that I'm ashamed to say I've never heard of, and that Smoggies is a wry nickname for people from Teesside. It's short for 'smog monster', these strange folk who live beneath the dense, lurid clouds of Middlesbrough's petrochemical industry. I'm chatting with him and a regular named John, a local railway worker, over a pint of Northern Downpour 4.5% Mosaic IPA. Refreshingly, like the beer, John is just as supportive of the Council. 'They're trying. They're trying a lot harder than some places. You've got to give credit where it's due. All high streets are dying in terms of shops. I'm not happy about that, but that's the way it is. So, let's try something else.' 'Yes' agrees Boomer, 'Have you seen Newcastle these days? All those bars and little shops down on the river. Maybe Stockton could be like that.'

I take a turn along the High Street. There is no smog or acrid chemical taint to the air here anymore, though maybe you can still taste it in Middlesbrough. It's a fine, clear, crystalline evening now, the sort that twanging 60s popsters (and North East lads) The Shadows must have had in mind when they wrote 'Stars Fell On Stockton'.*

Outside the pub adjacent the Globe, punters who have come to see what we might call the breakaway provisional UB40 are enjoying a beer, or maybe a red, red wine. I nip into Tesco and find the staff eye-rolling and moaning genially about the grubby mess around the self-service tills left by a regular customer they call 'Cider'. 'Why doesn't he just come to us straight away. He knows we have to validate booze. Anyway, he's gone off down to the river.' I'm headed the same way myself as there's enough of the sunlit evening left to take in the Tees properly with a riverside stroll. Down the steps from the Tesco, across the A-road, and there is the Tees, blue in the evening sun, broad and majestic, bending its great back to let Stockton sit on its shoulder. The Tees is why the Anglo-Saxons came to Stockton 1,000 years ago and why it grew rich on shipbuilding. So away with the Castlegate Centre, however notable its high geometric ceilings. This is the jewel in Stockton's crown.

---

* B-side of 'Wonderful Land'. Not as good of course, but some jaunty whistling. Proud North Eastern lads, they also had a track called 'Alice in Sunderland'.

The evening 'passegiata' along the Tees proves rich and fascinating. I pass an Eastern European family enjoying a McDonald's picnic, Ukrainian I guess from the blue and yellow badges on their fleeces. I essay a low key 'Slava Ukraini' as I pass them, and the little boy, suddenly serious, gives a salute with an onion ring. Next a very glamorous middle-aged lady wobbles past me a little unsteadily eating a drooping slice of Hawaiian from a huge takeaway pizza box and occasionally chucking a morsel of ham to the small toy dog in her wake. 'Evening,' she greets me brightly and is about to say something else, I feel sure, when her pooch drags her forward slapstick style. A little further on, by one of the many bridges, I note a man lying on a duvet drinking Strongbow from a can and muttering, seemingly alternately amusing and enraging himself. This, I feel sure, is 'Cider'. I also note with a wince that he has stripped down for the evening to a pair of upsettingly brief shorts. I move briskly on. As I do, I note that a boat called the *Teesside Princess* glides by with a hoot of her horn which Cider, comically, acknowledges with a wave of his can as if he were a rear admiral inspecting the fleet at Spithead. Two boys are trying to impress a bored-looking blonde lass of about seventeen by tiptoeing along the narrow breakwater wall. I stand and watch hopefully that at least one will fall in, not through any ill-will or animosity, just the natural human desire to watch other human beings fall into water.

If they had, they'd have been OK. Twenty years ago, the Tees at Stockton was a sewer, filthy and lifeless. The water was the colour of dirty ink and was officially declared dead in stretches, poisoned by the iron and steel works at Middlesbrough and the petrochemical works at nearby Billingham. That's gone now, and the heavy industries of Middlesbrough have contracted and slowed. It was hard on the people and their pockets for many years. But good for the trout and the bream, the swans and the seals. Yes, if you're lucky you can see seals now down by the new barrage and up as far as the sleek new Infinity Bridge. Perhaps when you're doing a spot of white-water rafting. Who'd have thought you'd see swans and white water on the mucky, sluggish Tees. Tonight, it looks magnificent, as grand as the Tiber from the Ponte Sant'Angelo. I want to come back here when they have swept away the Castlegate and I can see Stockton's passegiata elegantly process along its banks, bantering and wobbling perhaps, to the little trattoria and bars for caffe corretto with a slug of Vecchia Romagna. Part of me even hopes they keep a little perch beneath the bridge for Cider. But I hope he puts some clothes on.

11

TO LINCOLN AND NORFOLK

In which I go the long way, via Hull docks and
a steep hill called Steep Hill to the fattest,
most murderous, most Eurosceptic yet most
Eastern European town in England and
eventually, Aha!, to Tombland.

There was a spring in Priestley's step, or at least a bit of poke in his
Daimler, as he moved east. The weather and his mood improved
considerably, even treacherously. 'Next morning it seemed as if I
awoke in another England. The northern desolation had been
banished.' Sons of that northern desolation both of us, I found this
a bit rich. But then, the North East he left in 1933, bound for
Lincoln, was a polluted, failing, benighted place – a monochrome
newsreel of grimy streets, gaunt faces and hunger marches. I left a
North East that was modern, fresh and coursed by fine, clear rivers,
a place of hi-tech car plants and arts centres and city breaks.

As Priestley glides across North Yorkshire, he nods to Beverley
Minster and imagines himself living a bookish idyll by the pond in

Bishop Burton, before finally coming again to Hull. My journey is a little more problematic. At Stockton, all trains east are 'meeting with delays and cancellation' due to a perfect storm of staff shortages and industrial action. A whiff of sedition is in the air. Strikes are back, donkey jackets, loudhailers and all. RMT leader Mick Lynch greets me again from a banner at Stockton Station. Even his name is straight out of a gritty docudrama about the three-day week.

Once regarded as a natural and normal part of industrial relations in a democracy, half a century in which working people's rights have been steadily eroded has left us clutching our pearls and reaching for the smelling salts whenever a strike is mentioned. Little has changed in the language of the news since those good old/bad old days of braziers, picket lines and comb overs. Bosses, smooth and conciliatory, still make 'offers' while unions bark 'demands'. Mild disruption to people's daily lives is still 'chaos'. It's all quite nostalgic really.

For this and other practical reasons I almost gave Hull a miss. Plenty of people do. Its splendid isolation was what appealed to Hull's most famous adopted son. Philip Larkin called the city his 'lonely northern daughter' and loved that there was 'less crap' around than in London. In one of his few published interviews, he told Miriam Gros: 'I like it … because it's so far away from everywhere else. It's in the middle of this lonely country, and beyond the lonely country there's only the sea. I like that … I love all the Americans getting on the train at King's Cross and thinking they're going to come and bother me, and then looking at the connections and deciding they'll go to Newcastle and bother Basil Bunting instead. Makes it harder for people to get at you. I think it's very sensible not to let people know what you're like.'

Hull doesn't have quite that dour (and mischievous) insularity, but it does have an assertive individuality, a uniqueness even. On the gable ends of some of the 50s council houses on Shelby Street, near enough to see from your train window, different coloured bricks have been used to make some big mosaics. One is a huge trawler, the other a prop forward handing off an incoming tackle. Rugby League and deep sea fishing are two things Hull – or Kingston upon Hull to give it its proper name – excels at. You notice at the station that the trains are 'Hull Trains'. You spot outside on the street that the phone boxes are cream not red, because Hull has never been part of BT and has its own comms network called KCOM. Hull isn't the North East. It isn't Yorkshire. It isn't the East Riding. It's Hull.

It's more Riga than Redcar. Priestley noticed this in 1933; 'Unless you should happen to be going to one of the Baltic countries, Hull is out of your way,' he advised. 'It is not really in Yorkshire, but by itself, somewhere in the remote east where England is nearly turning into Holland or Denmark … Something of the outward character of the Scandinavian and Baltic countries with which it trades has crept into the appearance of Hull.' Hull was the first city in England to have a Danish Church. It still stands there on Ferensway as you exit the station, just opposite the fabulous mid-century cinema called, weirdly, Cecil. That's now a bingo hall and Den Danske Sømandskirke is living precariously these days. Its full-time pastor has gone and the internet is a quicker, easier way of staying connected to communities at home in Aarhus and Odense.

The Scandinavian church was established in Victoria's reign when many Danish ships docked in Hull with holds laden with cattle, bacon, butter and corn. By the time Victoria died, Hull was the second biggest port in England and the hub of trade lines that spanned the world. Priestley writing in 1933 could confidently state, 'it was founded by Edward the First, and it has been growing steadily ever since. It is still growing.' Such confidence was short-lived, regarding the shipping trade at least. Hull's fleet has been declining for decades. The six deep-water trawlers still working from Hull at the start of the millennium have been bought by an Icelandic/Dutch operator. Without salting old sores or exposing my ignorance, I'm always slightly baffled by those seaports, always facing other lands, which voted in 2016 to sever ties with the continent. Hull was one, enthusiastically voting for Brexit. It remains to be seen whether it will prove a glorious new dawn for the port.

Hull Docks has success stories though. I'm bound for one. To get there, I pass along Porter Street, a riotous motley of several generations of social housing. Other blitzes are better known but Hull was the most devastatingly damaged of all British towns and cities during the Second World War. A vital, prosperous seaport and ripe target for German bombs, 95 per cent of its houses were damaged. Over half the city was made homeless. A massive rebuilding programme began right here, with what the locals call the Australia Houses. The pub on the corner may have closed, and the theatre group based there may have moved on, but if the Australia Houses – circular balconied art deco tenements overlooking a central communal garden accessed by a pretty arch – were in Shoreditch or Hackney, it would cost you a million and the view from your bedroom window would be a fried chicken shop, not the seabirds and tides of the Humber estuary.

Hull's docks, still the briny, beating heart of the city when Priestley came, have had fortunes you might call mixed. Albert and William Wright docks closed in the early 1970s but were revived by the relocation of the fish dock in 1975. Both survive as docks, berths and training centres. At about the same time Iceland declared a 200 mile 'exclusion zone' for ships during the Third Cod War in November 1975, St Andrew's Dock was a major casualty. The proud, busy home of Hull's fishing fleet, the largest deep-water fleet in the world for nearly a century, it is now a sad relic, silted and vandalised, owned piecemeal by several parties, including a local vet, and full of ghosts and graffiti.

For a happier story, stroll to Humber Dock. By the time you read this, it may actually be a stroll too. But in the summer of 2022, enormous excavations and demolitions, phalanxes of diggers and battalions of hardhats, made it about as congenial and navigable as the Cretan labyrinth, your narrator a desperate, disoriented Theseus seeking the Minotaur of the docks. Huge colourful boards and hoardings had been placed everywhere to cover yawning, chasmic holes in the road. On them, interesting facts were displayed such as that people from Hull are referred to as Hullensians and that pioneering aviatrix Amy Johnson was one of them. These titbits are intended, one assumes, to distract from the fact that it is getting dark and starting to rain, you haven't eaten in hours and you are weeping silently with your fingers hooked in a chain link fence looking at the clonking masts of the Humber Dock, so tantalisingly near yet seemingly unreachable.

Okay, it wasn't that bad, and it was worth the trip. Humber Dock closed in 1968 and later re-opened as a marina. There are hundreds of craft here, and here is where I should talk of skeffs and ketches, bowriders and sloops. But they were just a lot of quite pretty boats to me, the lubbiest of landlubbers. One looked a bit like a pirate ship if that helps set the scene. By the quayside, there was a chandlery, which means a place where they sell 'boat stuff' and I tried on a couple of jaunty caps before the suspicious assistant asked if there was anything specific I was looking for. I was tempted to make up something plausible: 'Do you have a Newfoundland Skeffers Gob Hat in turquoise, me heartie?' But instead I strode towards the estuary, eyes narrowed, as if scanning for ketches on the bobbing horizon.

A statue here on the Bullnose commemorates the 2.2 million people from Northern Europe who passed through Hull bound for new lives in America. There's an identical companion on the Liverpool waterfront, from where the trip must have been a lot easier as you were facing in the right direction. But again, I'm no Jack Tar. Today I have the quayside to myself but for two couples glamorously dressed in leopard prints and blingy shades, filming themselves throwing music video shapes to what sounds like Ghanaian highlife. Behind them the North Sea rolls and rocks. It's kind of funny and sweet. There's a small queue for The Deep, a gargantuan new aquarium. I take the perfect opportunity to look windswept and thoughtful over the harbour wall out across what Larkin called 'the widening river's slow presence, the piled gold clouds, the shining gull-marked mud.'

Left lies the ferry terminal, from where you can go only to Rotterdam, a feisty, sport mad, beery sister port in Holland which has always been a closer cousin to Hull than London is. Right, along the Hessle foreshore, after six miles of fine if dullish walking, is the span of the Humber Bridge. The longest suspension bridge in the world when it was opened in 1972 after a century of campaigning, it is still the longest in the UK and the longest anywhere that you can walk across. A couple of years back I did just that from Ferriby to Barton-upon-Humber, a charming market town steeped in history that for centuries was a very separate and unique place with its own character and dialect, linked to its big city neighbour only by infrequent small boat ferry. The bridge has brought it nearer but it's still quirky and idiosyncratic, and the mile-long narrow Ropery Hall (where they once made the ropes, obviously) is the longest listed building in England. It's an arts and craft centre now and an excellent one. The ropes have gone but carrot cake, handmade amber brooches and stand-up comedy keep the place buzzing.

I retrace my steps into the Fruit Market, a little piece of Humberside that aspires to the condition of San Francisco. They were trading here for four centuries, firstly in fish and then, as the name suggests, mainly in fruit and veg. In the nineteenth century the bustling community here could support a circus, a theatre and a chapel and at its peak was selling 20,000 lettuces a week, fact fans. But the Luftwaffe and market forces conspired to end these boom years and the market itself was moved out of town in 2009. For a while, it looked like the Fruit Market might go the way of St Andrew's Dock, a melancholic decline into dereliction until the bulldozers came. But, as in post-industrial spaces from New York's Meatpacking District to the weavers' cottages of Hebden Bridge, these derelict spaces became colonised by bohemians and creatives on the hunt for basic studios and cheap, funky places to live. Now the Fruit Market is the trendiest place in Hull. The 'fishy-smelling pastoral' of the streets, as Larkin called it, now includes a community café, a distillery, a gallery, a tapas bar, an artisanal gelateria, a ceramics workshop, a high-end Indian restaurant, a jeweller and a clutch of bars and pubs. In a nice touch, the council have left the 'ghost' signage of the market's previous life just visible above these chic modern outlets, names that echo a disappeared Hull: Humber Fruit Brokers; Gibson Bishop & Co; Connolly Shaw Ltd; J. Bradnum & Co, Fruit Merchant (now a posh chocolatier). A bloke about my age passes by with his young son and points at an upstairs window: 'That was my dad's office when it was a fruit importers. I used to go and pinch all his stationery.'

The Minerva pub overlooks the estuary. Reputed to have the smallest rooms of any British pub, it's no surprise that they're all full. So I take my pint outside and watch a small boat, possibly a cutter or a yaw, plough the smudgy blue waters of the Humber. Hull was the second UK City of Culture I've been to on my trip and it reminds me a little of Coventry; blitzed almost into dereliction, resurgence then recession, now embracing the move into a post-industrial phase, confident, creative, full of students and artists yet still with the character of a proper city, not a 'pop up' hub. When Northern and Midland industrial conurbations become cities of culture, they are the softest of targets for snobs further south, setting up rote cracks about whippet racing and clog dancing. But in both cities, the impact has been considerable.

An excitable crowd on the quayside turns out to be a wedding party. The bride is posing with her gartered leg up on a capstan for the photos; the groom's laughing, handing her a prosecco as the bulbs flash. Obviously, I'm reminded of one of adopted Hullensian Larkin's many masterpieces *The Whitsun Wedding*, his elegiac, wistful account of newlyweds boarding a train full of hope and anxiety. I checked the date. Whit Saturday was last week, but it was nearly the 'frail travelling coincidence' he wrote of in that verse. I finished my beer and headed for the station, even later getting away than Larkin was, wondering as always about that 'arrow shower, somewhere becoming rain.'

2

Evening was drawing in over fen and field when Priestley came to Lincoln in a crepuscular fog, imagining himself a Victorian solicitor coming to read the will in a Wilkie Collins romance. No such gloom or murk attends my arrival in the city. A sudden thunderstorm has moved across the vast, flat fields of Lincolnshire as I approach, piled dark thunderheads flashing and sluicing over Saxby and Market Rasen. By the time I arrive, though, it has swept out over The Wash as quickly as it came, swishing its dark cape of rain, and I arrive in a Lincoln showered and glistening in the sun. It is half term, and the streets are thronged with locals and tourists. Once upon a time – twice and three times, actually, maybe during the Roman, Norman and Medieval period – Lincoln was a city to rival London in wealth and importance. That may no longer be true, but on a late spring morning after a reviving rainstorm, as citizen and tourist pass and mingle beneath the arch from the Strait to Bailgate, Oxford Street and the Square Mile were no comparison to Lincoln.

Except perhaps some of the prices. My hotel is a smartish gaff on the Brayford Waterfront where the room service menu offers a fish finger roll for £13 plus £5 tray charge. In other words, £18 for a fish finger sandwich. Baffled once again by the elevation of this 'dish' from the penurious student's meagre lunch to gastro pub delicacy, I decide to eat out. There is a nice symmetry in that my English journey, like Priestley's of course, is beginning and ending on ancient, prosperous waterfronts, in Southampton and Lincoln, in places where our island nation has traded and explored, made friends and gone to war, set sail for new shores and sought to protect its own. Brayford was the first known settlement in Lincoln and was once Lindon, 'Lin' meaning pool and 'don' meaning 'foot of the hill'. Later the Romans called it Lindon Colonia, and by contraction, Lincoln. After a century of decline as the barge trade dwindled with the coming of road and rail freight, Brayford Pool, the oldest natural harbour in England, is now reborn as an upmarket marina where masts and highball glasses clink and chime all day and night. The last of the old wharfside buildings was demolished in 1993 and the Royal William IV pub is the only pre-1945 building that remains. I notice on the chalkboard outside that tonight is quiz night and mentally file this choice nugget of intel for my evening plans. Before then, I have a date with history. Headed downtown, I pass the Drill Hall where I'd played my one-man show before lockdown.

We were once a nation of drill halls. Every town had one, and when Priestley came it would have rung and clattered to army volunteers marching and presenting arms and standing at ease. Even as late as 2015, Historic England estimated there were about 1,500 still around, now turned into flats or gyms or, as in Lincoln's case, an arts centre. When I'd played here, it was threatened with closure and I filmed a heartrendingly powerful yet elegantly witty appeal for them in which I encouraged people to sponsor a brick for a quid. I'd like to think that it was this urgent bulletin that saved the day, but I acknowledge that being taken over by some energetic and skilled people at the college probably helped.

In Lincoln, all roads eventually lead to The Strait and a steep hill called, with admirable clarity, Steep Hill. I stop off briefly at the Back To Mono record shop to nose around the weird stuff. A middle-aged man enters in search of Pet Shop Boys collectibles and a studenty girl buys the new Arcade Fire on vinyl. William Goldman was speaking of the film business when he said 'nobody knows anything' but he could have been describing the music industry. Decca records told Brian Epstein that 'groups of guitars are on the way out', the major labels told us that 'home taping was killing music' and that we should sell our beloved vinyl records and buy 8-track tapes, DATs and Minidiscs and a host of other forgotten 'innovations' now cluttering the attics of the world's audiophiles. Sweetly, in utter defiance of the industry's predictions, I have found a vinyl record shop in every town and city I have visited on this journey, often combined with some other quirky retail function; a coffee shop or patisserie, clothes shop, haberdashers, abbatoir, fishing tackle shop etc. As I stroll up town in the newly-rinsed air I pass a sax and trumpet duo comprising a young lad and his dad in a wheelchair giving a spirited, if not entirely note perfect, lounge jazz version of 'Somewhere Over The Rainbow', a daring piece of recontextualis-ation à la John Coltrane's reading of 'My Favourite Things'. Worth a few quid of anyone's loose change.

Steep Hill is, according to the council bumph, the fourth steepest cobbled street in England. When I mention on Twitter that I find it hard to believe there are steeper, a volley of texts informs me of terri-fying gradients in Clovelly, Devon and Shaftesbury, Dorset, the hill from the Hovis ad where 'it were like tekkin bread to't top ot world'. But let's not get bogged down here. Steep Hill is steep. That's for certain. Chris Florance tells me that 'as a sixteen-year-old YTS lad I worked in the bookshop at the top of Steep Hill in the mid 80s. It was not unusual for customers to come in and need medical treat-ment from the hard walk up the hill.' Ironically, Steep Hill is a great leveller. Just as I am wondering if I can give my aching calves and tight lungs a breather by pretending to take in some architectural features, a young and athletic looking woman overtakes me on the rise then, just as I'm feeling ancient and decrepit, turns and says to me: 'This is insane'. We both park ourselves on the convenient-ly-sited benches outside St Michael's parish church, the Mayor's Chair, 'traditionally a place to rest on Steep Hill'. Once upon a time,

Steep Hill was the city's busiest food market, and would have echoed to the cries of fishmongers at the top, butchers at the bottom and poulterers in the middle.

When Priestley came there was apparently a distinction between 'uphill' and 'downhill' Lincoln, an upstairs/downstairs style division. 'It appears that there is great local snobbery about this hill. To be anybody in Lincoln you must live "uphill" … In short, a successful social life in Lincoln is essentially uphill work. You labour down below, in the clanging twentieth century, and spend your leisure by the side of the Cathedral, in the twelfth century.' A lady in an ice cream shop, Lincoln born and bred, tells me this distinction no longer applies, though anyone lucky enough to live in Cathedral Close is 'winning at life'. Next door is a shop selling all kinds of vintage militaria and ephemera, including a box of second-hand parachutes and bungee cords – something I would be decidedly keen on having in factory-fresh working order.

The oldest building on the hill, indeed one of the oldest residential buildings in England, is The Jew's House, originally owned by a wealthy Jewish trader, Bellaset of Wallingford. Lincoln's Jewish community were rich and powerful but, as always, regarded with suspicion by some, stoked by a confected libel surrounding a child supposedly kidnapped and killed by a nationwide Jewish conspiracy. In 1290, Edward I expelled all Jews from England and the house was seized. Over the intervening centuries it has been many things, and since 1973 a restaurant where now chef Gavin Aitkenhead can rustle you up some beef fillet carpaccio and roast squab pigeon if the climb gets too much.

But after a little exertion, and a restorative pause at the Mayor's Chair with an ice cream, you're at the top and keeping that date with history. Look right and here's the cathedral, once the tallest building in Europe and one of the finest Gothic structures in the world. Commissioned by William the Conqueror soon after he'd come to power – still a sore point with some of us – you can easily imagine it giving an eleventh-century peasant a surge of the devo-tional willies. Here was God's eternal and limitless power rendered in stone and glass and flying buttresses. A constant and permanent scaffolding orbits its enormous walls, one circuit taking approxi-mately forty years. No single architect has ever been in post for a full restoration circuit.

Around the same time that he commissioned the cathedral and as part of his ongoing brutal suppression of the rebellious North, William the Conqueror built its neighbour, Lincoln Castle. Over the next couple of hundred years, this fine building was a favourite stopping off point for various bigwigs. King John enjoyed a mini-break here in Lincoln in September 1216, shortly before losing all his jewels, valuables and luggage in the murky tides of The Wash. Within two weeks, he was dead, perhaps beset by feelings of intense melancholy similar to those one feels when realising upon arrival in Marbella that all your underwear is in a suitcase bound for Anchorage. A recent archaeological dig in the castle's old rubbish pit found bones and scraps of plover, lapwing, swan, conger eel, oyster and venison thought to be the remains of a feast for King Henry II. A couple of centuries later, another Henry, brought his young Queen Catherine Howard here for the Tudor version of Netflix and chill en route to York. The honeymoon period not only didn't last, it ended about as badly as can be imagined. Within a year, he'd cut her head off.

Henry VIII, it seems to me, spent his royal tenure doing pretty much as he pleased, some of it quite harmless like tossing partly eaten chicken legs over his shoulder, other stuff less trivial like decap-itating innocent women and destroying some beautiful old monasteries. I mention this just to prove that kings were still getting away with murder centuries after a meeting by the Thames at Runnymede in the summer of 1215 was supposed to rein them in a bit. The extraordinary evidence of that meeting is here, kept behind shatterproof glass in the low-lit, air conditioned, temperature-controlled vaults of Lincoln Castle. It is the reason that the out-of-condition history buff, the camera festooned Japanese and American tourist and the unruly school parties haul themselves up Steep Hill every day of the year (except Christmas Day, Boxing Day and New Year's Day). It is one of the most important documents in the history of the world. I mean it. You can't really oversell the Magna Carta.

The Great Charter, as its resonant name prosaically translates to, influenced the course of history. On 15 June 1215, King John reluctantly assented to his barons' demands at Runnymede and agreed a charter of liberties that enshrined the principle that the king was not above the law. The Magna bit, by the way, was to distinguish it from the smaller Charter of the Forest. Those of us who love the outdoors think this every bit as important since it guaranteed free men access to much of the countryside. Today they sit side by side in the Castle, the only place in the world you can see these documents together. Only four original copies of the 1215 Magna Carta survive: two in the British Library, one in Salisbury Cathedral and one here. Seventeen others were made in 1297 and one of these much later copies still fetched over $21 million at public auction at Sotheby's in New York in 2008, then the most expensive piece of text ever. Hence the bulletproof glass, chilly ambience, sepulchral lighting and quiet whispered injunctions of 'no photography please'.

Just above this vault in a 360-degree viewing suite, a film detailing the history and import of Magna Carta plays continuously. It's tremendous. I urge you to get up that hill and see it. People come and go and some younger kids are naturally a bit fidgety, keen to get out up on to the castle walls or the gift shop. But I notice that on the front row, hugging his dad excitedly, one little lad looks enthralled, especially at the coronation of the nine-year-old Henry III. I'd like to think a lifetime's love affair with history is beginning right here, and perhaps an acquaintance with the notion of civil liberties and rights. Magna Carta, of course, only applied to barons and wealthy men, not the peasantry of England like you and me. But something had been set free that summer morning by the Thames. It was an idea, the principle that the law applied to everyone whatever their status. Earlier, eating my ice cream on Steep Hill, I read in this morning's papers that questions are being asked as to why the Metropolitan Police did not investigate more of Boris Johnson's attendance at the seemingly constant round of illegal Downing Street lockdown parties. Later, as the paperback of this book was being prepared, the country was convulsed in anger at how the Post Office could blithely and maliciously misuse their power to ruin the lives of hundreds of innocent sub post masters and mistresses they accused of theft. Maybe some of the Met's top brass should come to Lincoln and refresh their memory of Magna Carta, and the notion that no one is so rich, privileged or powerful that they are above the law.

Stunning though a close-up date with Magna Carta is, there's something else in the castle just as gripping and considerably creepier. In 1788, a gaol was constructed here for debtors, those awaiting trial on remand and those who had been convicted and sentenced to either transportation or death. By transportation, of course, we mean to Australia. Interesting that such transportation was seen as a fate nearly as bad as death. By the time Priestley was writing and even to the present day, many poms, tired of economic woes and terrible weather at home, would dream of a life of barbies, sun cream and regular work down under.

In the Victorian era, though, the old gaol was demolished and a radical, not to say deeply weird new penal experiment was tried. A new prison was built in 1847 operating on the 'separate system' of prison discipline. It was believed by some that crime and criminality were, in effect, infectious. Thus, prisoners were to be kept apart as much as possible to negate the individuals' sense of self and eradicate the criminal subcultures that proliferated in densely-populated prisons. In Lincoln Castle jail, this extended even to the chapel. It's still here, just as it was in the 1840s and is one of the freakiest places I've ever set foot. The congregation were kept in tiny, locked stalls with partitions reaching almost to eye level, so all could see the minister but not each other. This is eerie enough if you just take your place in one of the stalls. But hop up into the pulpit and take the Vicar's eye view. Then you'll notice that the castle have thoughtfully occupied some of the stalls with dead-eyed and forlorn mannequins staring balefully at you from their tiny pens. Do visit the castle and try it. What's a couple of nights sleep for such a striking experience?*

After all this I am keen for some fresh air so embark on a breezy circuit of the castle walls. From this vantage point, I survey the green below. Kids mill about, men in tabards build stages and hang bunting, all preparations for the Queen's Jubilee. Perhaps somewhere, plover and conger eel were roasting. These were scenes that might have taken place here a millennium ago, which is either wonderful or depressing depending on your point of view. This was certainly the best viewpoint for the adjoining cathedral which, even if Europe has built higher and wider in those intervening thousand years, is still an extraordinary, imposing sight. It would be even more glorious but for the events of four days in May 1644. On 6 May, with the English Civil War raging and Lincoln on one of its most fractious fault-lines, Parliamentarians, after taking the lower town, stormed the besieged castle where the Royalists had retreated and dug in. Casualties were few, but the triumphant Parliamentarians pillaged and ransacked the upper town above Steep Hill, stampeding and vandalising the castle, smashing its statues and stained glass Taliban-style. Though I know it's hardly a pressing matter anymore, I find myself very conflicted with regard to Civil War allegiances. By nature, I am a Republican (because I'm a grown up) but I have no affection for Cromwell's brutish, dour fundamentalism. Essentially, I feel the same way about the English Civil War that I do about

---

* As well as being creepy, the separate system was a failure. As the guide told me, it tended to 'send them loopy'.

derby matches between elite London football clubs, i.e. that these are contests in which ideally both sides would lose.

No questions about the Civil War were to come up at the quiz. On my way down to the pub, I bump into two old friends of mine from the London music radio business, Kieron and Kerry, who I hadn't seen since long before the pandemic lockdown. This has been so often the case. They left London initially for Huntingdon but found that too much of a shock to the system. 'I went out on the first Friday night,' said Kieron 'and there was literally no one about in the high street. After London, I felt like I had the bends.' So they moved to Lincoln, which they loved. 'It's beautiful and steeped in history, but it's lively. There's gigs and young people and students and tourists.' With admirable modesty, they mention that the 'people they had staying with them' loved it too. This turned out to be a Ukrainian refugee family that they had taken in, an act of generosity that suddenly shamed me. I ask somewhat hopefully if they all fancy forming a quiz team but they are headed for some comedy down at the Theatre Royal 'otherwise they'd have loved to'. I believe them.

3

How long does it take to get to Boston? Well, I wouldn't start from here, as the old joke has it. It works pretty much wherever you tell it, because of the remoteness of the region from the big population centres and the desperate, piecemeal nature of the English transport system. Unless you're lucky (or unlucky) enough to be coming from London, it will take you about four hours to get to Boston wherever you set off from, even Lincoln. Even in 1933, Priestley noted: 'From Lincoln to Boston is no great distance, but the train makes a leisurely journey of it, lounging along by the side of the river, the Witham, like an angler.' It's probably a little worse now, so it's as well to adopt Priestley's for once relaxed state of mind, sit back and enjoy the trip.

Sadly, my journey turns out to be about as relaxing as appearing at the High Court or on *Mastermind* (only one of which I have done). My train is packed with a bizarre, absorbing mobile tableau of modern England on the move; Jesuits in flowing black, doting grandparents helping adorable kids 'colour in', icily hip Japanese teens, squaddies, podgy young guys with ponytails and massive fantasy paperbacks called things like 'Dragonlaird of Witchbastard. Pt 6 of The Barrington Levy Chronicles of Eaglebreath'. The train is headed for its terminal destination of Skegness, Lincolnshire's bracing final frontier of frivolity by the chill North Sea. Thus, it is also full of people going on holiday with a kind of grim, recalcitrant desperation that suggests they've been ordered to go by the Gestapo. The carriage rings with the cries of bored and hungry kids, and then, as if on a silent pre-arranged signal, everyone opens bags of Quavers, Nik Naks etc. as big as their suitcases and began to eat robotically as the drear cabbage fields and drainage sluices flash by.

A tiny, lunatic part of me is tempted to follow them to the sea and renew my acquaintance with 'Skeggie'. My little family in the 70s, mum, dad and me, would often holiday in Butlin's, those bastions of affordable holiday fun. Even as Priestley travelled this coastal stretch of Lincolnshire in the early 30s, South African-born entrepreneur Billy Butlin was building a pleasure compound at Ingoldsmell near Skegness on a piece of land leased from the Earl of Scarborough. He had already made a little amusement park here with a tower slide, haunted house, hoopla stalls and Britain's first dodgems. Now, Butlin's Skegness became the first of, at their peak, ten camps, including one in the Bahamas. We never went to that particular one – my mother once had a funny turn on a replica coracle crossing the River Dee at Chester, let alone a transatlantic flight – but we went to many another of Billy's affordable Xanadus for the proletariat.

Thus have I been to Minehead, Ayr, Pwllheli, Clacton and Skegness without ever seeing a single thing of those doubtless fine towns beyond the search lights and chain link fence. I adored Butlin's.

We never left the confines of the site as to do so would have been sheer madness given the various (and paid for) delights of the camp: ping pong, donkey derby, pitch and putt, glamorous grannie, monorail. Butlin's is obviously still with us, but now in fewer and classier incarnations with lakeside lodges and the like. I should imagine all the above vulgar activities have gone to be replaced by Hopi ear candling therapy, reiki massage and sourdough baking classes.

As the train heads east towards the silty flatlands of The Wash, we pass through a land utterly alien to me, of massive empty skies and fields to match, of distant spires and lost horizons. Heckington looked nice, or at least the hanging baskets on the station platform did. Grantham I went to once and didn't like, very possibly because of the associations with its most famous daughter. The plaque commemorating Margaret Thatcher's birthplace is on her dad's old grocer's shop, where she inculcated her grim ideology at his elbow as he sliced the bacon thin and refused credit. It's about eighteen feet up on the wall, presumably to deter vandals.* Sleaford means to me the Mods of the same name, a band whose caustically gritty, corrosive tales of modern English urban life belie the fact that it's a pleasant market town and, according to the local Mumsnet, really quite a nice place to live.

Not so Boston apparently. Even the mums were stirred to use words like 'hell', 'dreadful', 'godforsaken misery' and even 'shithole', which my mum would never have said unless she'd had one too many whiskies. One testimony was almost lyrical in its disparagement; 'The "countryside" around is just plain flat fields that go on for miles and smell like cabbages, no hills, no scenery, nothing fun to explore unless you like angry farmers.' I couldn't spot the latter from my seat, nor smell the cabbages. But I could see that landscape.

---

* While revising this chapter, a statue of Mrs Thatcher was unveiled in her hometown. At the unveiling, protesters pelted it with eggs. Not Guilty, Your Honour.

The flatness became mesmerising, like the music of Morton Feldman or the paintings of Rothko or Malevich, an unbroken geometric of dull fields stretching to the horizon, where the occasional town poked the occasional church or tree line into a sky the colour of a dying laptop screen.

When Priestley came, he described it as 'Dutch England', emphasising its traditional, geological, cultural and trade links with the Low Countries. None of the current literature about Boston I'd read mentioned the Netherlands. They all mentioned Bulgaria, Romania, Lithuania, Poland and Latvia, though. Boston is the most Eastern European city in England. One in ten of its population originates from the region, attracted, at least initially, by the free movement encouraged by Tony Blair's government and the promise of agricultural work in the fields of East Anglia and Lincolnshire. For not entirely unconnected reasons I surmise, more than 75 per cent of Boston voted to leave the EU, that being the highest 'leave' vote in the country. Two-thirds of its residents are clinically obese and in 2016 it had the highest murder rate in the UK. Welcome to Boston, then, the fattest, most murderous, most Eurosceptic yet European town in England, recently voted by its own townsfolk the forty-second worst place to live in the UK. It doesn't say this on the road sign, naturally.

Nothing about Boston's tight little terraces beyond the station reminds me much of Groningen or Utrecht. It feels more like Chorley or Rochdale. There's even a pub, closed of course, called the Great Northern. Another difference between Priestley's days and mine. Back then pubs were grimy dens of vice best avoided by the gentler kind, places where workers would drink their meagre wages. In the twenty-first century, they have become threatened emblems of cosy, traditional Englishness. From an open window further down Station Street came the mournful, exotic sound of gypsy accordion music, Romanian I thought, and it was my first palpable hint of the strangeness of what's been called 'England's most divided town'.

Every voice and face, every shop and sign up the main drag of West Street is seemingly Eastern European. The Municipal Buildings are flying the Ukrainian flag as a gesture of solidarity, but the more everyday signage told its own story about a changed town, one shop advertising (deep breath) Turkish, Kurdish, Polish, Portuguese, Latvian, Lithuanian, Russian and Bulgarian food. In the 1630s, a group of Lincolnshire Puritans, escaping religious persecution, left Boston for America. So Boston gave its name to Boston, Massachusetts and this West Street gave its name to the one in that New England city. But resemblances are few. Massachusetts' West Street is in the National Register of Historic Places, a grand, venerable place of Renaissance revival architecture, music publishers, candy stores and boutique hotels. My hotel was in West Street too, a doorway among the shisha bars, shawarma cafés and the huge Polish supermarket. Ashton's Discount Carpets has been here half a century, but Mrs Ashton did not seem hugely enthused when she told the local paper 'West Street has had it. People won't come down here.'

West Street may have changed out of all recognition in the half century since the Ashtons first started flogging cheap Axminster. But the view from the High Street must not have changed much in a few hundred years. Tan Express won't have been there then, or Mediterranean Kebabs or the Moon Under Water. But the rather handsome White Hart Inn would have been, looking out across the town since the days when Boston was a thriving seaport. So too the old Town Bridge across the sluggish Witham, and in the background, St Botolph's Church, 'The Stump', which is the most remarkable thing in a remarkable town – a tower nearly 300 feet high, its head almost in the clouds. Priestley climbed it, so I'll have to. But it can wait for a bright morning and a good breakfast.

For now, I take a walk around the Market Place. Priestley came on market day when the whole wide curved piazza was full of 'either broad-faced beefy farmers and their men or enormous bullocks'. With the brilliant timing that has become my stock-in-trade, I have dropped a bullock by not coming on market day. But maybe that is no bad thing. Cleared of that pzazz and paraphernalia, I can see Boston going quietly about its day, older women with their shopping trolleys, mums with recalcitrant toddlers and, everywhere, groups of Eastern European men, aged twenty to sixty, laughing and arguing loudly, with seemingly nowhere to be.

Boston is very pretty in parts. Wormgate for instance, though it doesn't sound it. It's a narrow, cobbled street with a few cafés and a cosy-looking pub. But Boston somehow contrives to wear that prettiness shiftily, almost grudgingly, hiding it among the rags and the defunct Polish shops and fly-tipped garbage. Wormgate soon opens, if that's the word, into shabbier, cramped little streets with silent pubs and empty shops. But puzzle your way through and there's relief when the sun suddenly rounds The Stump and you turn onto the Wide Bargate, an important thoroughfare when the town was a thriving medieval port. It has a Next and a Waterstones, those bellwethers of middle-class retail, and a sense of life and vivacity, especially when the grammar school gates open, and the street is flooded with black-clad kids gossiping and flirting their way around the lovely war memorial.

Some 600 years ago, all of Boston would have felt like this, bustling, lively and noisy. In medieval times, Boston was the most important port in England outside London, with trade connections throughout northern Europe. In 1377 Boston was the tenth largest town in the country, grown rich on wool, wax, dried fish, oil, furs and goatskins. Central to all this prosperity was access to the sea via the River Witham, Lincolnshire's great watercourse, a conduit for Hanseatic trade with Germany and the Low Countries. Rising in Grantham and becoming the tidal Haven at Boston, the Witham flows out into Frampton Marsh, now an RSPB reserve, and thence into the North Sea.

The Grand Sluice is a remarkable piece of Georgian engineering separating the Witham from the Haven, saving Boston from regular flooding and reclaiming much agricultural land. Inasmuch as anything with the word 'sluice' in its name can be considered a tourist attraction, Lincolnshire tourism do their best to market it as a fun, family day out. There is a cluster of folk here taking pictures and I want to engage them in some light investigative chat, but am thrown by the attentions of an ancient, bloodied and scarred man, who may have been Bulgarian but whose accent is so guttural and English so limited that I have really no idea what he wants of me. I make a guess and push a quid into his gnarled hand. If you were trying to share some observations about how the sluice was substantially enlarged and improved in 1881, sir, I can only apologise for jumping to conclusions.

There's still a little fishing fleet here, boats bobbing and clanking beside me as I stroll. When Priestley sauntered along here, the shops along the riverside and marketplace were full of 'vast jars of piccalilli', which seems odd. He thought so too and wondered was it because it was something portable and warming when you were out at sea. I found none of the tangy bright yellow pickle. Captain Cod sells more longstanding English 'street food' fare: Vimto, battered sausages, jars of pickled eggs, that most ubiquitous and yet rarely purchased of chip shop fare. I hear the clank of dumbbells in the Boston weight training club (established 1951) and outside Pescod Hall, once the grand home of a merchant family but now a Mediterranean restaurant, two men who look like primary school teachers are quietly and thoughtfully discussing the career prospects of cage fighting.

On a whim, I decide to get a haircut, having noticed in the shaving mirror that morning that I looked quite a lot like Rod Stewart circa 1972. I dip into a tiny barber's shop in a little side street by the new bridge where the beaming owner greets me warmly. His little shop is full of potions and oils and sprays and gels, all arranged in neat pyramids. While he snips and shaves and we chat, his wife dozes full-length on the bench where, at busier times, customers would wait, her head on a little black pillow. Farhad, as we'll call him, is originally from

Iran but, after seventeen years in Peterborough, has spent the last four in Boston. 'People come from all over world, you hear every language in the market square, it is like a souk!' 'Do you like it here? Is it nice?' I ask. He smiles noncommittally 'It's OK, you know.'

The young English lad on my hotel reception desk is not even that positive. 'Boston's dying. It used to be a lovely place, a lovely market town. Lots of shops and lots of life. But now …' He indicates West Street outside where a group of young men in hoodies pass by. This Englishman is not some florid-faced tankard-owning Farageist, the stuff of St John's Wood and Brighton's most lurid nightmares. He strikes me as calm, articulate, thoughtful and in his own mind has no doubt where Boston's modern decline began.

'Firstly, they came for the work. That's absolutely right. Hard work too, cheap labour for the farms and then the few factories we have. But not now. Those lads out there aren't working. They come for the benefits. Romanian and Bulgarian men. Ten to a house made for four. They hang out by the statue in The Stump because you can pick up the free wifi from the bank there. Our crime rate has rocketed and it's mainly violence and sexual offences. It's statistically shown. It's not just prejudice. I can't think of a positive element too. I don't like being here after a certain time. You can sense the intimidation after dark. I advise the guests to be very careful, especially the women. After six, there are parts of Boston that are no-go areas. We're the murder capital of Britain, after all.' He laughs, mirthlessly, and this all seems deeply depressing for many reasons, not least that I was just about to head down one of those no-go areas for a curry. 'Oh, you'll be fine. It's still light, and maybe I'm laying it on a bit thick. But watch your step.'

Between 2004 and 2014, Boston's migrant population grew by 460 per cent, and the proportion of residents from new EU countries such as Lithuania, Poland and Latvia, stands at around 12 per cent now. One of them is the young Polish woman serving in the curry house. She's been here four years and is clearly known and liked by the regulars tucking in. In the Stump and Candle pub or Goodbarns Yard, you will hear all kinds of opinions, some not as downbeat and judgemental as the young receptionist's, but many even more so. You will hear that most famous tenet of cognitive dissonance, that immigrants are both stealing 'our' jobs and 'sponging' on benefits, and, not for the first time, I think that anyone who claims to know the truth about all this is either a liar, has an axe to grind for their own reasons, or is a fool, and very possibly all three.

Less contentiously, we can be pretty sure that Boston takes its name from St Botolph, a young Saxon noble who became a monk and gave his name to the grand church and its tower that dominate the Boston skyline. Priestley thought that 'The Stump' had the quality of the Empire State Building but said that this was all context, since Boston's little houses and Lincolnshire's billiard table of damp fields and marshes stretched out in every direction to the horizon. That accepted, The Stump is far, far taller than its daft nickname implies. Standing below it, it's genuinely painful to arch one's neck back far enough to take it all in. But I'm not letting JB score a trans-Pennine point for Yorkshire over Lancashire, so climb it I must.

On the way next morning, I stopped off for petit-déjeuner at the Café de Paris, as French was about the only European language I had not encountered in Boston. An elegantly dressed Frenchman in navy sweater and yellow tie guides me suavely to my seat and brings me coffee and croissants. Soon after, he greets two older English women, clearly regulars, with a gallic twinkle. 'Hello you lovely ladies. Your usual table?' One takes her cardie off and he affects shock and delight. 'Oh my, she is taking her clothes off'. 'Yes, she normally does it to music' says her friend deadpan.

When I get to The Stump and enquire about climbing it, the nice blonde lady is very helpful but tells me I will have to leave my rucksack with her. 'People have been known to, you know,' – she mimes throwing – 'chuck things off.' To be let into the tower, I have to ask Mila in the gift shop to unlock it. She ushers me into the tiny cold stone space with its tight steep spiral of steps ascending into gloom. 'Good luck,' she whispers in an accent and tone that reminds me of Peter Lorre, and she locks the door behind me. Having no alternative, I start to climb. 'It was a very long and steep climb,' wrote Priestley 'up a staircase that got narrower and narrower and darker and darker until one was threatened with claustrophobia.' In truth it isn't that bad. Steep and cramped, yes, but there's a rope handrail. It's more the relentless mental spiral than the legwork that gets to you. Halfway up, amid the graffiti, is an old, faded message that says 'Fire Watch! This Leads to Roof!' and suddenly it's winter 1941, atop The Stump on a black night, watching bombs fall on the factories and RAF bases scattered across the flat Anglian plain, flames flickering in Grantham and Lincoln.

'At last, aching and exhausted, I tottered out to the tiny platform at the top,' said J B Priestley, being a bit of a wuss, I felt. The view is magnificent, though peering gingerly over the handrail brings that peculiar twinge in the most sensitive region. Looking inland, the Witham with its muddy brown banks goes die-straight past the Grand Sluice and off towards Grantham. In the other direction, it has the broad silvery back of a snake, sliding through and out of the town towards the lonely vastness of The Wash.

4

On the fine spring morning I make my way to Norwich, the talk is of nuclear war. Vladimir Putin, his addled mind boiling with Covid paranoia and rage at the loss of Russian might, is threatening 'consequences the like of which the world has never seen before.' A few years back I spent a week in Kyiv with a bunch of British writers. One of the many things we all loved about this wonderful old city was its grand and majestic Metro system, the deepest in the world. We timed the escalator ride down at six and a half minutes. My

Ukrainian friends told me that it was built so deep so that Kyiv's citizens could shelter down there from bombs. Last evening, this morning, that is what they are doing in Ukraine, huddled together as shells fall on their cities. On the Black Sea, fascists are hammering Mariupol into a new Guernica, and just as in the Spanish Civil War, an International Brigade of foreign volunteers is headed to fight alongside the brave Ukrainians. If I were a young single man with military experience and without little grandkids, I half think I might go. But this is vainglorious romantic valour. As it is, I am eastbound. But to Norfolk, by coach via Cambridge.

An M6 crash and the time restriction on the driver's hours mean we must wait for half an hour by a dull park in Cambridge. A loud young man takes part in a meeting at the top of his voice. 'What possibilities do you need me to factor into the proposal, Lindsay? Fridge capacity, yah?' Brilliant comic creation that Steve Coogan's Alan Partridge is, he has somewhat 'ironized' the reputation of two indisputably great things: Abba and Norwich. Like most of England's 'far east', you don't accidentally go to Norwich. No one is passing through here on the way elsewhere, except maybe a week's holiday in Great Yarmouth, a container run from Lowestoft or a bird hide near Caister. This would not always have been the case. Norwich was one of the great cities of Norman England and England's second city in medieval times. Protestants from the Spanish Netherlands, 'strangers' as they were known, came here escaping persecution and brought the weaving skills (and the yellow canaries that give the local football team its nickname and strip) that would mean, even as late as 1700, Norwich rivalled London as a trade and commercial hub. But the Industrial Revolution happened elsewhere, leaving modern Norwich with still a relatively small population and the unhurried, charmingly relaxed vibe of a city that's never been choked by heavy industry, apart from a bit of mustard-making at the local Colman's factory. I have to be here, since Priestley had been, but also because I have never set foot in what might be England's least-known city (alongside perhaps Carlisle) and I felt bad about that, or at least foolish.

I like Norwich straight away. A woolly-hatted man passing by indicated my shoes and, giving that chef's kiss gesture, says 'very nice'. Then a young woman sitting on some steps gives me the most winning smile and wishes me 'good afternoon' in an accent sweet and rich as cake. I realise she is homeless. She's sitting on the steps of the Norwich Union building, now disappointingly and meaninglessly renamed Aviva of course, but the giant clock still says Norwich Union. I thought about popping in and asking them how my pension is doing but figure they probably discourage that, preferring you to 'go through the channels'. It is balmy and with an hour or so before check-in I decide to take a little tour. Not a proper one with a guidebook or following a person with a little colourful umbrella. My favourite sort: a clueless wander.

St Stephens Street is big and broad with a crazily rich architectural mix. It's quirky, which I soon realise is an adjective applicable to Norwich as a whole. The Pure Electric Scooter shop – which should be destroyed of course along with all its hateful contents – is opposite Castle Meadow, a good name for what is a massive meadow with a gigantic castle on top. It's a castle that has loomed above the city for a thousand years of bloody history and now it has a mobile phone shop at its feet. When we have long outgrown or out evolved the need for electric scooters and mobile phones, when we finally get those hover jet packs and communicate by thought-transference data bursts, Norwich Castle will still be looking down on us and smiling impassively at our foibles and self-importance, an image that only really works if you can imagine a castle smiling, which I hope you can.

Just down the road is an impressive building with its own rich and storied past. I was lucky enough to grow up in 'Granadaland', the Manchester-based ITV regional franchise that made *Coronation Street*, *World In Action*, several brilliant sitcoms, and gave us Anthony

Wilson. Even as a kid, I would be scornful, pitying even, of the scattered and paltry televisual offerings of other regions. You knew when you saw their idents that there were only a few viewing possibilities ahead. Border TV's 'futuristic' graphic could mean only one thing: *Mr and Mrs* with Derek Batey (also station controller, fact fans). STV's logo meant rural Caledonian intrigue in *Take the High Road*. But the little revolving silver horseman that was Anglia's ident had two possibilities, either *Survival*, a wildlife show which pretty much every week would be a special on the wildebeest of Serengeti, or *Sale of the Century*, a campish game show introduced with the frankly inflated claim 'And now, from Norwich, it's the quiz of the week'. Nicholas Parsons was the host, compering it all with the gaiety of a man unsure whether to send all this up or not, wearing a candy stripe blazer and a tie that made the telly strobe.

My hotel is in Tombland. This sounds ominous but it is in fact the historic heart of the city. Its name is from the Norse 'Tomb' meaning open space and site of the Anglo-Scandinavian marketplace in the eleventh century. Now it is the quiet area around the cathedral, home to my hotel, The Maids Head. I had chosen this place deliberately as it's where Priestley stayed, finding it 'a fantastically rambling but comfortable old place … It would have served as an excellent background in an illustration for Barnaby Rudge.' It claims, with some justification, to be the oldest hotel in England, having sheltered travellers since at least 1287, when it was called the Myrtle Fish Tavern. The Black Prince and Catherine of Aragon both stayed here before Priestley. Fans of C J Sansom's detective novels will know that the seventh of the series is *Tombland* and it is set here. And so the plaque at the Maids Head hotel reads 'Matthew Shardlake stayed here in 1549, as featured in *Tombland* by C J Sansom.'

They've given this real guest the Wensum suite named after the river that flows nearby. I consult the menu in my room purely for research purposes. When Priestley stayed, he had the boiled beef and carrots, a real dish people ate then, and he loved it. Its 2022 equivalent is 'Marinated sirloin of braised beef brisket en crépinette, brown butter pomme purées, tenderstem broccoli, horseradish emulsion, pickled shallots, red wine jus.' It sounded mouth-watering but, as both Priestley and I arrived in a gathering dusk, I thought I should get in a spot of exploring while there was still a little misty East Anglian light about.

There were trams on Tombland's narrow side streets when Priestley stayed, which seems hard to believe. Best explored on foot. Magdalen Street is secretive and narrow, quirky junk and antique shops and delis jostle and it looked like a place to revisit in the morning. I pop into Ali's Tandoori, billed as 'nice and family run'. It seemed to be both. Clive, a well-dressed man with a copy of the *Financial Times* dining at the next table, orders a special dish. The waiter raises an eyebrow. 'You sure Clive? The super-hot one with the Scotch bonnets? The nuclear one?' 'Don't say nuclear tonight!' replies Clive in mock horror, indicating the doomy headlines in his paper. The FT seems to think economics might win this war. Let's hope so, Clive and I agree. We clink a glass and pass the rest of a pleasant hour here, getting yet more mango chutney on my battered Penguin edition of *English Journey*.

Priestley seemed to do most of his Norwich drinking in front of the roaring fire at the Maids Head. I feel I should cast my net a little further. Everyone has told me I simply must try The Fat Cat, whose bewildering array of ale would have bamboozled Priestley, used to a 1930s choice of bitter, mild or perhaps 'porter' for the maverick and the Irishman. The Fat Cat turns out to be a long schlep out to a gloomy part of town, but once through the door all is warmth and bustling activity. Many of the accents sound very familiar to me and I soon realised that the place is full of Mancunians connected with the Cloudwater brewery who are having a residency tonight. Fashionable breweries now tour to their devoted fans like rock groups, and many of the clientele look as if they might have been in Elbow or Everything Everything. Gentle hipsters with stylised beards scan the chalkboard beer menu as if flipping through the drum and bass 12-inches in a record shop. One of these turns out to be John from Cloudwater brewery itself; everything you'd imagine a modern microbrewer to be in his vintage American cattle feed cap and rolled jeans. One of the clientele, Robin, excitedly asks for a selfie. With John, obviously.

Next morning, I 'do' Magdalen Street properly. Norwich folk seem to have a great deal of affection for it, though not for the ghastly 1960s flyover which slices through it like the Berlin Wall. Magdalen Street is still, as it was when Priestley stopped by, a bewildering mix of antique shops. Priestley said that he 'bought a pretty set of syllabub glasses.' I hardly touch the old syllabub these days but there were many equally fascinating curios on offer. Surplus Trading Antiques Collectables and Militaria is a one-stop-shop for the man in need of a Toby Jug, an Everly Brothers album and a Gestapo dagger. Further down the road I come to something called a pledge store which seemed to mainly stock gas masks and orbs of mysterious function.

People are always telling me that their dad has a box with all the old Beatles Parlophone singles that 'must be worth a bob or two'. They aren't though, because The Beatles sold an awful lot of records and there are literally thousands of such boxes in lofts and lockups from Liverpool to Lahore. What you want is John and Yoko's *Wedding Album* which didn't get within a sniff of the British chart and peaked at 178 in the States. It isn't very good, but I reckon you'd get £200 for it here. In Looses Emporium, one of the biggest such places on this eccentric street, I see what seemed to be a Tudor halberd going for less than an Etch A Sketch. Go figure. In the visitor's book for Aladdin's Cave someone has written, 'I needed a cummerbund desperately and found one here. Great shop but wish you could pay with card.' At a little van outside on the street, I have a bacon roll and a cup of tea infused with CBD oil. Two crazy guys having an argument nearby scream at one other. 'You're a succubus!

You're a soul sucker!' one says, to which the other replies, 'Well, you're a dick!' Magdalen Street is that kind of place.

Turn up Waggon and Horses Lane and you're in a different Norwich. Elm Hill is as primly cute as Magdalen Street is roguishly down at heel. It's curvy and cobbled and painted in rust and turquoise and probably looks almost the same now as it did when most of the properties were rebuilt after the disastrous fire of 1507. It became home to Norwich's hoi polloi – wealthy wool merchants, skilled craftsmen, civic grandees – all living perfumed cheek by florid jowl in the fine houses with their pantile roofs. Amazingly, it was almost demolished during Norwich's swift, massive slum clearances of the 1920s and 30s but was spared to the eternal gratitude of scores of TV drama directors and location scouts.

The shops are very different from Magdalen Street's chaotic galli-maufry too. There's a Teddy Bear shop with a large Black Lives Matter poster in the window, a curious juxtaposition of cuddly toys and radi-cal activism. There's a classy bridal wear shop, a stamp collectors shop and Stoned and Hammered, makers of contemporary jewellery. Just to stop it becoming too rarefied there's also a Wetherspoon's and a café offering deals on toasties to celebrate what they are calling 'Cheesebruary', a shockingly ugly and upsetting non-pun.

Along the quiet River Wensum at the bottom of this sweet lane, marauding Vikings came in 869, slaughtering royal martyr King Edmund. Most of the city's river trade came this way too. Now there's just the phut phut of a little motorboat as a man in a hi vis jacket sails by. Along the riverbank are very desirable looking flats, the little balconies crammed with heaters, chimineas and barbecues and, in one case, a six-foot rabbit straight out of James Stewart's nightmares. Several of them have ladders leading down to moored rowboats. Nice commute into the city centre, I think. When Priestley came, the slum clearances were in full swing and the resi-dents of Fishergate and Thoroughfare Yard were dispersed to new estates on Norwich's outskirts. Thoroughfare Yard now boasts seven wheelie bins so they obviously decided they made a mistake and people have moved back. It's tiny, cramped and higgledy-piggledy, but at least people are living here again.

I have been told many times since arriving that Norwich Market is exceptional, and for once, public opinion is not wrong. But I do curse my luck that the mushy pea stall is closed. Overcome by thirst, I promise I did try to find a stall selling healthy fresh guava juice or a super vitamin enriched kale smoothie but I couldn't, not even here. Instead, I had to go to the craft beer stall and asked for a half of the coldest, tastiest, weakest thing they have. A couple of hearties are clearly here for the afternoon, and I recall a remark of Priestley's to the effect that 'The East Anglian is, of course, a solid man. Lots of beef and beer, tempered with east wind, have gone to the making of him.' The lads in Elements clothes shop are friendly and helpful. Great clobber, too, but nothing in my size, not after two years of lockdown snacks and takeaways. They pass on an old adage that Norwich has a pub for every day of the year and a church for every Sunday and they give me a few good recommendations for pubs to watch the Manchester City vs Peterborough FA Cup tie tonight. I had thought that there might be a rivalry between Norwich and Peterborough, one of the few nearby league teams, but eighty miles is clearly far enough to take the heat out of any ill feeling. Norwich's sworn footballing enemy is Ipswich with whom they contest the 'Pride of Anglia' match, the so-called 'Old Farm Derby'.

Norwich became famous for producing wool, then mustard and then writers. In 1970 Malcolm Bradbury, the son of a Sheffield railway worker, and Angus Wilson started Britain's first MA in Creative Writing at the University of East Anglia, UEA as all know it, in Norwich. In that first year there was one student, Ian McEwan who in that year wrote the twenty or so brilliant and disturbing short stories that initially made his name. The hundreds of writers who have emerged from the course since are some of the most respected names in modern letters, among them Kazuo Ishiguro, Anne Enright and Rose Tremain. They have won all the major prizes; Nobel, Booker, Whitbread, Betty Trask and the rest and have, as Bradbury said, 'changed the climate of writing in Britain … there were those who said writing couldn't be taught. There were those who said if it could, it shouldn't be anyway, because it wasn't an academic subject … and there were those who had been to Oxford and Cambridge and who couldn't understand why if this sort of thing was happening at all it was happening in a provincial university in the nation's flattest and probably most benighted county.'

It's a short bus ride out through Earlham to the city's rural fringe and the campus of UEA. This Brutalist classic is worth a visit in itself, its 'teaching wall', famous ziggurats and walkways in the sky designed by Denys Lasdun and now Grade II listed. In his brilliant blog Brutalist Constructions, Andrew Garford Moore sings UEA's and Lasdun's praises splendidly. 'The teaching block is a long, winding ribbon with a strong horizontal emphasis and appealing copper hued windows. The horizontal is broken up by Lasdun's characteristic roof furniture – concrete housed vents and lift shafts jutting dramatically above the roofline.'

My friend Charlie Higson, who met Paul Whitehouse when a student here, recalls how, staggering back from the Union to the modernist ziggurat bedrooms, freshers might bump into one of the many Antony Gormley humanoids lurking in darkened corners and jump out of their skinfuls. Brutalism can turn a little grim when it gets old, stained and dirty and, if they were in the inner city, some of the stone staircases and walkways here feel like ideal places to get stabbed rather than discuss Georgian poetry or mass spectroscopy. But on the outskirts of a ancient city, the combination of nature and uncompromising concrete makes it a unique and brilliant place. I know some people's student days were a horror but, for me, the laughing groups, books under arms, all football kits and hockey sticks, in an environment very much like the estate I grew up in brought a weirdly melancholic and satisfying ache. Priestley himself was a student in East Anglia, going 'up' to Trinity Hall, Cambridge in 1921. All universities were overwhelmingly middle class then, especially Oxbridge, and Priestley hated his time there. 'Cambridge regarded me as a North Country lout of no uncertain temper,' he wrote, and he was far happier out in the 'real' world of hack work.

Even though I was ravenous by now, and the café looked fantastic, I was put off by the excruciating thought of that *30 Rock* episode and 'undercover' detective Steve Buscemi with his reversed baseball cap and skateboard saying 'how do you do, fellow kids'. So, I walked to Earlham and the bus back to the city. I had a scribbled list of pubs, a recommended chip shop and one more night in Norwich, a place I was growing to like a lot. But before all that it was time for Evensong.

I'm not a churchgoer really. But, like Larkin in that poem of that name, I do like to soak up the atmosphere of such places, the 'serious house on serious earth' that leaves me in 'awkward reverence'. With Evensong, there's always the promise of a good tune too and Vaughan Williams, Byrd and Tallis draw me in this evening. It's full, and as the processional of choristers and priests enters with glittering gold and silver crosses and the incense billows, the sheer mystery and long ancient weight of ritual, combined with the heavenly music, is heady stuff. All this beneath a Ukrainian flag. The homily by the precentor Aiden Platten is quite brilliant, encompassing both T S Eliot's *Four Quartets* and *Strictly Come Dancing*. He concludes with a complex thought about Eliot's notion of time and the moment that is 'at the still point of the turning world,' and how for people of faith, like Aiden, the relationship with God is like that of a dancing teacher – of being held always close, sometimes uncomfortably so. And then the voices are raised again in stacked and radiant harmonies and the incense burns blue again and people go forward, heads bowed, to receive their cross of ashes.

Out into the misty East Anglian night, with that scribbled list of pub names. A pub called The Murderer's Arms feels like it should be landlord Alexei Sayle's local in a 'Young Ones' episode of the early 1980s. This pub on Timberhill (it's really the Gardeners Arms) got its grisly nickname from a horrible act of violence in 1895: the murder by a jealous ex-cavalryman of his young wife after seeing her with another man on the premises. These days it's popular with lads in caps and Superdry T-shirts and not really my vibe so I wander back to Tombland.

The Ribs of Beef is much more like it. The Cup match is on several big screens, but quietly so that those who aren't interested can go about the evening without the shrieking clichés and vapid chit-chat that come with every televised football match. Two Scousers burst in desperate for a drink after a seven-hour journey. 'Something went wrong at Ely,' they mutter darkly. The young barman is from Norwich but, for complicated family reasons, is a Wigan Athletic fan like me. He was there for the most glorious day in our history when we beat billionaire petro-dictatorship plaything Manchester City in the 2013 FA Cup Final ('I was only six. They passed me over their heads in the crowd when we won'). I buy him a drink and, not wishing to antagonise the local Canaries fans in the bar, we whisper that we will meet next year in the championship when Wigan go up from League One and Norwich are relegated from the Premier League.*

Next morning, I lie in bed in the Wensum suite of the Maids Head and check my messages. Here's one from Daniel Kitto suggesting a trip to Mousehole Common and Kett's Heights for some fine valedictory views of the city. I decide to head up there and then on to the station. The Pink Line No. 12 bus climbs steadily and windily and I get off at a weirdly-situated American diner on the hill before picking my way through muddy woodland tracks across the ridges that overlook the city. It's a delicious, misty Fenland morning. Winter's grip is loosening and spring is breaking out in green and gold everywhere. The Wensum is frosted silver below, and there are spires and towers,

---

* We did.

old and new, above the waking flowers and reviving trees and foliage. One of those towers belongs to Norwich Castle from whose walls Robert Kett was hanged in 1549. Kett lead a rebellion here against the cruel and unjust enclosures which took common land away from the people and gave it unlawfully to the rich and highborn. There it remains to this day, the basis of our class and economic system in what is still in many ways a backward and feudal nation. Kett and 10,000 followers took over Norwich and marched on London but were eventually defeated by the forces of the aristocracy, aided by thousands of German mercenaries with early handguns.

But Kett is not forgotten, this so-called traitor rightly turned folk hero. There is a pub named after him in the city, and also a junior and primary school nearby and a hall of residence at UEA. On the walls where they hanged him, there is now a plaque of commemoration. 'In 1549 AD Robert Kett, yeoman farmer of Wymondham was executed by hanging in this Castle after the defeat of the Norfolk Rebellion of which he was leader. In 1949 AD – four hundred years later – this Memorial was placed on the castle wall by the citizens of Norwich in reparation and honour to a notable and courageous leader in the long struggle of the common people of England to escape from a servile life into the freedom of just conditions.' Kett and Priestley would have got along famously, I think. Both good company over a pint at the Ribs of Beef or over a whisky by the fire in the Maids Head.

My English journey, like Priestley's, is almost at an end and I'm glad it's ending here in Norwich. It was a city I didn't know and has delighted me and raised my spirits; a city with an intoxicating, dark, rich tide of history flowing down nearly every street and lane. Yet, thanks to UEA and the nearby Silicon Fen, it is also a place where youth, progress and the future is being daily celebrated and embraced. A great city in a great country, one that would have been even greater perhaps if Robert Kett and his people had won the day.

12

TO THE END

By his own admission, Priestley does not so much conclude his English journey as ditch it, 'suddenly abandoning it, giving it up as a bad job.' He starts the day by breakfasting, as I did, in the cosy ambience of the Maids Head in Norwich, and ends it by his own fireside in foggy Highgate, having completely missed out a 'good fat slice of England' that he'd sketched into his itinerary: Newmarket, Cambridge, Bury St Edmunds, Ipswich, Colchester.

Had he gone there, then so would I. But he didn't, so I didn't and thus remain embarrassingly ignorant of them all. Newmarket is 'horsey', fantastically so I believe, and so probably not for me, having spent time at New Street Station on Cheltenham festival days.* Cambridge I know a little, mainly through attendance at the Folk Festival in the grounds of Cherry Hinton. My knowledge, therefore, is not of Silicon Fen innovation or punting on 'the backs' but of drinking mind-bogglingly strong ale made of goat's horns while

---

* Unworthy of me, I know, but if the Newmarket tourist board want me to 'check it out', perhaps at a luxury spa hotel with a couple of Michelin stars, well I'm sure I can swiftly become as equine as the next man, unless the next man is a member of the Royal family.

watching middle-aged men in brocade waistcoats singing about the arduous nature of the mid-nineteenth century whaling industry. Bury St Edmunds I regularly confuse with St Albans. Ipswich I have never been to and thus must remain silent upon. Colchester is hometown of Blur and my old *NME* and radio colleague Steve Lamacq and has a lot of squaddies knocking about. Err, that's it, as *Private Eye* used to say. I feel genuinely sheepish about this woeful lack of knowledge of Cambridgeshire and Suffolk. Then again, I've met many people almost proud never to have been north of Oxford and who cheerily confuse Manchester and Liverpool or Lancashire and Yorkshire, which for me beggars belief.

While Priestley apologises to Newmarket and the rest, some more glaring omissions go unmentioned. He didn't bother with Cornwall or Cumbria or Kent or Essex or the Sussex Coast and doesn't seem to care much. But the yawning gap at the heart of *English Journey* is London, glimpsed only from a motor coach window at the start and through a yellow murk at the end. The omission may be glaring, but it's also sensible. London is not England. It thinks that it is, just as New York, Chicago, Houston, Philadelphia and the other loud, confident, brash megalopolises do. But they're all wrong. London is London. A city state. A borderless interzone. Some 272 Tube stops clinging to an idea. This is part of its brilliance, and most of its lack of appeal for those of us who love to visit but could never live there.

Ensconced by his Highgate fireside, that damp, misty night at the window and, I like to think, a pipe and glass of something decent to hand, Priestley begins to marshal his thoughts. 'I had seen a lot of Englands. How many? At once, three disengaged themselves from the shifting mass. There was, first, Old England, the country of the cathedrals and minsters and manor houses and inns … guide-book and quaint highways and byways England.'

The guidebooks are online now and there's a QuaintByWays4UApp on the App Store (maybe). But that England is still there, and it is still, caught right, an amazing place. Again and again, travelling for this book, at dusk or in the dew fresh of the morning, I would find myself having to pause in pleasure and drink it all in. Not the biscuit tin loveliness of that over publicised honey stone, or the drooling estate agent pornography of thatched roofs and inglenooks. But the sheer, long, strange, sweet, bloody history that's steeped in the walls or stained in the cobbles or hangs like mist on ancient rivers like the Wensum, the Witham or the Soar. With a little imagination, and a couple of glasses of reasonable plonk inside me, I would take a moment in the twilight on old stone bridges and fancy I could see the paddles rising in the torchlight on a Saxon or Viking longship, berserkers coming slowly down the tide to wreak havoc. This was especially easy on the Saturday night I spent in Blackpool.

Standing on the castle walls in Lincoln one bright, gusty afternoon just before Queen Elizabeth II's Platinum Jubilee celebrations, I looked down on the ancient green to witness men in hi vis tabards putting up bunting and assorted ladies arranging feasts. It struck me like a battering ram that we may think we are astonishingly futuristic because our phones can take pictures, but England still has the same things on its mind as it had in 1933 and 1733 and 1533. Queens and feasts. Wars and jubilees.

Priestley's second England was the nineteenth-century one: an England of 'coal, iron, steel, cotton, wool, railways; of thousands of rows of little houses all alike, sham gothic churches, square-faced chapels, Town Halls, Mechanics' Institutes, mills, foundries, warehouses … It provided a good parade ground for tough, enterprising men who could build their factories in the knowledge that the world was waiting for their products … [but] the less fortunate classes were very unlucky indeed in that England. They had some sort of security, which is more than many of them have now, but it was a security of monstrously long hours of work, miserable wages and surroundings in which they lived like black-beetles at the back of a disused kitchen stove.'

He does not mourn its passing much. Anyone bored by those TV programmes in which Neil Oliver or similar extols the rugged individualism of some rich, cigar smoking, slave-driver in a frock coat will find Priestley's lack of admiration cheering. 'I felt like calling back a few of these sturdy individualists simply to rub their noses in the nasty mess they had made ... At one end of this commercial greatness were a lot of half-starved, bleary-eyed children crawling about among machinery.'

At least some of them salved their consciences through civic good works, like those town halls and such. But that too has gone. Public service. Self-improvement. Ethics. These notions seem as dreadfully quaint as sing-songs around the parlour piano and penny farthings. We probably must at some point get over the fact that we do not make things anymore. But that does not mean we have to become the spiv and horse trader to the world; a shady, money-laundering 'hand car wash' for oligarchs and sheikhs and tech billionaires. We may never get our hands dirty again, but we could keep our minds busy, as they are doing in Coventry designing driverless hydrogen cars, or in Stockton rethinking the way their town looks. Stockton, perhaps inspired by the pioneering work in Preston, which Priestley bypassed for the delights of Blackpool, has come to realise that our town and city centres will never be devoted to the making and selling of stuff again. The death of manufacturing and the rise of out-of-town and online shopping have seen to that. So, we need to embrace another future for our cities and towns, where all those deserted malls maybe become affordable social housing, work spaces, galleries (this has already happened in my home town, Wigan), parks, cafés, or drop-in centres. It may sound utopian; I think it's inevitable.

Then there was a New England, which appropriately enough Priestley saw as largely American. This was an England 'of arterial and by-pass roads, of filling stations ... of giant cinemas and dance-halls and cafés ... cocktail bars, Woolworths, motor-coaches, wireless ... factory girls looking like actresses ... swimming pools.' Priestley begins by seeming to welcome this, the democratising effect of popular culture, the 'Blackpooling' of England, where 'you are all as good as one another so long as you had the necessary sixpence.' Soon, though, a note of snobbish caution creeps in. 'Unfortunately, it is a bit too cheap,' says Priestley of this new demotic culture. Sadly, at this point, even a fan such as I regret Priestley's move into pop music journalism. He bemoans the new-fangled, mass produced, record company sponsored, wireless-promoted music taking hold in the 30s and pines for the days of his youth when music meant beery men singing lustily in the upstairs rooms of pubs. They 'were not falling in with any general movements or fashion; they were singing glees over their beer because they like to sing glees over their beer; it was their own idea of the way to spend an evening and they did not care tuppence whether it was anyone else's idea or not; they drank and yarned and roared away, happy in the spontaneous expression of themselves.'

This sounds bloody awful to me. Both personally and professionally, I have rubbed up against the 'real music' lobby a lot and they are as cloth-eared and wrong now as Priestley was then. I do not want to hang about in the upstairs rooms of pubs with roaring, beery men. None of the music I love has ever been made in this way and it never will. Authenticity in music is a specious notion beloved of bores and mansplainers. All music is 'manufactured'. None of it seeds in the ground like cow parsley or falls from the sky like rain.

As for the American influence Priestley detects, the decades of cross-pollination from Noel Coward to The Beatles to Adele coming from this side of the Atlantic alone (and that's just the pop music) mean that it's hard to say what qualifies as truly British and truly American now. I was once a huge Americophile. I loved its commitment to freedom and (small 'r') republicanism, its youthful vigour and boundless energy; its music, its comedy and its hot dogs. Naturally, the election of Donald Trump was a bracing cold shower upon this former ardour. What kind of country elects a man so shifty, craven, weak, entitled and self-regarding, so patently not up to the job? I ask you! (Pauses for ironic effect).

As for US pop culture, well I think any grown person who can use the phrase Marvel Comics Universe without blushing should have the vote taken away from them. But give me American mass-produced entertainment any day over drunken men upstairs in Bradford pubs. When the hard day's writing and travelling was done – it's been hell readers, honestly – and I looked for an evening's diversion I fired up Netflix and other choice streaming services and watched *Severance* and *Gaslit* or *The Bear* or any number of brilliantly daring TV shows that made our leaden parade of clichéd police procedurals look exactly that. Priestley liked a good yarn well told. I'm sure he'd have had a Netflix account. Or borrowed someone's log-in. He was from Yorkshire, after all.

2

Priestley's *English Journey* took him a single autumn. Mine occupied me for the best part of two years, for reasons that were macro and micro, societal and personal, of which more in a moment. Stories unfolded and seasons changed. England ebbed and flowed and sometimes seemed to be whirling down a plughole of mayhem. We appeared to be living through a state of constant churn and permanent crisis, so much so that that old Chinese curse about wishing your enemy to live in 'interesting times' felt written for us. Aside from a few wealthy (and therefore insulated and protected) 'disruptors' like Dominic Cummings and Jacob Rees-Mogg, most people pined for a safe, stable, healthy, competently run nation again. From Brexit to Covid to a dreadful European war to the Queen's death, I surely wasn't alone in wishing that things would just stop happening.

Like many people, I was a staunchly republican but quietly conflicted admirer of the Queen. She did an absurd job quite seriously and well without being massively racist, corrupt, sleazy or mad, and did it for a very, very long time. Only the Sun King, Louis XIV of France, has ever reigned for longer. But the sheer formulaic banality of her jubilee and its coverage was wearying, offering up a familiar, sappy version of Englishness for an ever-decreasing audience: Minis, Cliff Richard, a perfunctory nod to Bhangra, lots of campness and 'Pride', a comedy punk with a lime green Mohican and the cosier end of the Notting Hill Carnival. Very little about the various miners' strikes or the poll tax riots. Shame. I'd really like to have seen Lulu and Gloria Hunniford chatting about that. A popular TV gardener popped up to recount how the Queen had once commented on the size of his onions, referring to her unctuously as 'my sovereign'. The combination of vulgarity and a deeply conservative obsequiousness was very like the tenor of the 'Carry On' films we have to pretend to like; very English and mildly depressing.

It was also misleading. Every few minutes during this TV coverage, a tremulous-voiced flunkey told us that these 10,000 or so eccentrics waving flags along The Mall was proof of the tremendous esteem the Royal Family were held in, these relatively few folk in their weird Union Jack waistcoats and comedy headgear being, it was asserted, completely and definitively representative of Britain as a whole. Yet the 60,000 Scousers who'd lustily booed 'their' National Anthem at the League Cup Final at Wembley a couple of weeks before were aberrant, untypical sourpusses. The truth is that no one represents modern England, which is both a blessing and a curse. Yet we go on, aching to boss the world again like the lady in the Coventry car museum, fawning and flapping and waving our little flags. As Priestley wrote in his bitter late 30s tract, *Rain Upon Godshill* 'while everyone is gaping and cheering, no awkward questions will be asked.'

It didn't take long for the gaping and cheering to give way to the awkward questions, though, especially in the wake of Prince Harry's extraordinary memoir *Spare*. For some time the English had been nudged gently by the media to pick a side in this dysfunctional family spat; either the frosty, repressed Windsors or the unbuttoned, over-sharing, newly-Californian Sussexes. But *Spare*, with its filial fisticuffs, bawdy trysts with 'older women' in fields behind pubs, drugs, broken necklaces and offing the Taliban took things to a new level – high or low – depending on your taste. What would JB have made of it all, I found myself wondering again?

I wrote this book during wartime. Latterly, there was a real one in Ukraine, horrific and bloody. But there was also the Covid war footing. We were exhorted to a 'blitz spirit'; we carried masks and stayed at home and kept mum. We did as we were told, by and large. But we were not 'all in it together'. David Spiegelhalter and Anthony Masters point out in *Covid By Numbers* that three of the jobs with the highest levels of mortality in the UK were chefs, cab drivers and bus drivers. Workers in more poorly-paid, lower-status jobs were less likely to be able or allowed to work from home, and the jobs they did involved more sustained close contact with strangers. As Marxist art critic J J Charlesworth put it, 'There was never any lockdown. There was just middle-class people hiding while working-class people brought them things.'

Another war was also raging, so it was said, and the skirmishes and pitched battles were fought every day in the dying 'legacy' print press and the new, exciting, unpoliced frontier of social media. Just as in 1939, this war the commentariat talked up daily seemed entirely phoney. In 1991, the American Sociologist James Davison Hunter published a work entitled *Culture Wars: The Struggle To Define America*, describing the new fault lines and polarising disagreements running through US politics and culture, specifically between those on the traditionalist right and the progressive left. These new battlelines were no longer solely about political parties or class, ethnicity or religion but about worldview; about how one lined up on, for instance, abortion, gun control, drug use or gay rights. If you accept the terms of engagement, England's current culture wars are being fought on the pitted and scorched earth of a front that includes transgender rights, Brexit, vaccinations, slavery reparations and the like, between the 'woke' and the 'gammon'.

We're told this war is going on. But it is essentially a media creation and one that serves that media very well. What else would we fill 24-hour news channels and radio phone-ins with? Most ordinary English people, the inheritors and descendants of the people Priestley wrote for and about, the ones who don't tweet* or phone in to radio shows, seem reluctant to join up. As Adam Boulton pointed out in *Prospect*: 'Wokeism and anti-wokeism are not another Brexit, a great divider along party lines, because the great British public is stubbornly uninterested … Polls [have] recorded that 59 per cent don't know what "woke" means and that 67 per cent are "not following the gender identity debate closely" … In the UK, confusing fog is descending – but the culture wars never got properly started.'

If proof were needed of this, it has come in the (at least initially) dismal ratings for a couple of attempts to get Fox News-style right wing demagoguery off the ground in Britain, namely GB News and Talk TV. But make no mistake, with increasing desperation on both sides, it is in Piers Morgan and Owen Jones' and Nigel Farage's interest to keep this phoney war going, to stoke and reload the armoury of human unhappiness with insults and slanging, to keep the clicks and tweets coming. All have a vested interest in keeping a spurious culture war on a rolling boil because, put bluntly, it pays their wages. They are professional 'opinionators' of a kind that did not really exist when Priestley was writing. Perhaps because people had genuine problems and very real, not imagined, bogeymen on the rise.

Just after Russia invaded Ukraine and started on its campaign of murder, rape and torture, I took part in an event to mark the mass

---

* The total number of Twitter users in the UK as of October 2021 was 19.05 million out of a population of some 68 million. Most people who have a Twitter account never tweet.

trespass of Kinder Scout and, against my better judgement, bought a copy of the *Morning Star*. There was no mention of the invasion and war on the front page, nor on any of the next six pages. On page seven I found a few derisory paragraphs of shameful 'whataboutery', refusing to condemn Russia and heaping blame on Ukraine for daring to look to the west for its future. Opposite was a page of handwringing platitudes from Jeremy Corbyn. A paragraph from the concluding chapter of *English Journey* came immediately to mind, in which Priestley challenges the 'useful idiots', as Stalin called them, of the 1930s: 'Even Mr Bernard Shaw, who appears to favour iron autocracies, has continued his residency in a country where he can say what he likes to the next interviewer. A good many of my fellow authors who are for ever sneering at liberal democracy have still sense enough to keep within its tolerant boundaries, and do not venture into those admired territories where they would soon find themselves kicked about by uniformed hooligans or shoved into a gaol that knew nothing of *Habeas Corpus*.'

3

My mum and dad both passed away while I was writing and travelling for this book, within a year of each other. They both had that well-worn but precious consolation of those who pass and those who remain: the good innings. Though they were both in their late eighties when they grew ill, and both died in the national 'annus horribilis' of 2021, neither passed away from Covid, although it made their final days harder. My mum went into hospital after a fall and then, in the first nightmarish panic of the pandemic, was kicked out of her hospital bed to make room for other, I guess younger, more pressing Covid casualties, and sent to a care home. Given that British care homes were at the time Covid-infested death traps, it is extraordinary that she ever came out. But she did, after months of contact only though erratic, halting phone conversations with her that now feel heart-breaking. She wanted to be at home and could not understand why she was being kept here in this strange, sad, bare little room. My dad, who had probably never used the washing machine in his life, would wash and dry her nighties every few days and I would take them to the care home door to leave them with a masked nurse. The thought of him doing that makes my chest hurt. She did come home, yes, but she was never the same again. I imagine she was the same bewildered little girl she'd been in 1939, baffled by a world of masks and restrictions and gathering her small strength every day against fear.

They were married for sixty-two years. But the last couple were not easy, with mum ill and unhappy, alternating between hospitals and care homes. When she'd gone, dad seemed fine at first. I would visit every week, take him for a pint, get his favourite pies and we'd watch footie on TV. Liberated from mum's ultra-conservative taste in food, which regarded a tin of Heinz ravioli as being as outlandish as the rancid yak butter tea of the Mongolian high steppes, he began taking his first unsteady steps into the foothills of international cuisine; sweet and sour pork, lasagne, chicken tikka masala. I hoped for a few last good years with him like this – pubs, football, meals out – but it wasn't to be. Just after his ninetieth birthday he became very ill very quickly and again I had a parent who I couldn't visit – until it was the end.*

While I was taking trains and taxis to drop clean nighties washed by my dad to my lonely, sad, confused mum's care home; while I was burning CDs of my dad's favourite books (he never mastered his MP3 player) to leave with overworked nurses in the hope that he got them; while I was buying the protein drinks that were the only food or drink dad could manage; while I was not seeing them for the weeks and months that they grew sicker and lonelier; while I lay

---

* The wonderful Barry Cryer, raconteur, wit and British comedy legend also passed away while I was writing this book. He and Graeme Garden introduced me to JBP and this book is dedicated to them.

awake next to dad and held his hand all night before that winter Saturday afternoon he died, eventually having been allowed into the ward to say goodbye; while I did all this, and maybe you did too, Downing Street was having Wine Time Friday. It was holding ABBA parties. Braying staffers came back clanking from the off-licence with suitcases of booze and partied and fought and broke children's swings and drank themselves sick and left the minimum wage cleaners to mop up their mess in the morning. All these chummy little get-togethers were illegal as well as immoral when families could not hold their dying loved ones' hands. More breaches of the law happened at 10 Downing Street than any other address in the country. Some 126 fines were issued to eighty-three people. One of these was Alexander Boris de Pfeffel Johnson, member of Parliament for Uxbridge and South Ruislip, then leader of the Conservative Party and prime minister of the United Kingdom.

Naively, as we waited for the verdict of the Metropolitan Police, some of us thought, that if one of these fixed penalty notices or fines were issued to the Prime Minister, then he would have surely to resign. But then I remembered that I was still foolishly living in a different world, one where people in high public office were expected to have standards. We had somehow gone beyond all that and Boris Johnson knew it. The knowledge was written all over his face. He knew that he enjoys the security of that class who are beyond apology, beyond morality.

Except, apparently, we hadn't. No one was more surprised than me, other than possibly Alexander Boris de Pfeffel Johnson.

Johnson's short, queasily Trumpian, tenure was surely a low point in British history whatever your politics. It was a refutation of everything we teach our children, namely that fairness, hard work and decency are at the core of our country's soul and spirit. What I couldn't have known as I left Norwich for home, was that hot on its heels would come a different kind of nadir, the suicidal lunacy of Truss and Kwarteng and the descent of the Conservative Party into a kind of living death. Which would have been fine, except they took us down with them.

4

This final chapter of my English journey is shorter than Priestley's, and by design. When he was the brilliant TV reviewer for the *Observer*, Clive James' wife used to tell him that beyond a certain point it was counterproductive to go on being nasty about James Burke, the portentous, hyper-enthusiastic TV science presenter. In the same way, I realise that I want to stop before I wear your patience thin. But first, some notes on what I discovered.

Perhaps the one solid conclusion I have drawn from my journey is that the difference between England's towns and cities is pronounced. This has been the century of the city. Every one I visited felt resurgent and optimistic: Birmingham, Manchester, Coventry, Hull, Newcastle, Bradford, Norwich and so on. But not so England's towns (with a few notable exceptions like Ilkley). Under-resourced, vilified, sneered at, and, yes, left behind, they are viewed with suspicion by the big cities and their media. They are thought to be Brexity, insular, uncool, old, boring, and poor. Angry at being so labelled, those in our towns played up to this image, defining themselves against the 'wokery' and pretension of metropolises and so the self-defeating cycle goes on.

I saw some bleak and neglected places on this journey. I spent some grim days and forlorn nights in them. I won't name them here, but they were nearly all towns and the refrain in everyone was the same: 'this used to be a great place.' Some of the things I heard, the proffered reasons for this decline, were uncomfortable. I needed to hear them though, So do the people in the cities who make the decisions they have to live with in Boston, Longton and Shotton Colliery. There, I did name a few.

I also had some great times in some wonderful places. Time and time again. I stopped and looked around and thought 'I could live here', whether it was the lovely flats on New Walk in Leicester or the ones overlooking the sleepy Wensum in Norwich; whether it was the fine stone cottages in Ilkley or the grand houses overlooking the rugged coast in elegant Tynemouth. There were days and nights I will never forget: misty golden fenland mornings; a fabulous hot summer's night in Liverpool; walking snowy towpaths in deepest Lancashire; the view of 'blue remembered hills' from the Cotswolds escarpment; Spanish City and Whitley Bay in the gathering dusk; walking Southampton's ancient walls, looking out to the liners in the harbour; the Birmingham skyline, electric and radiant, from a roof-top bar in funky Digbeth; even the flicker of acetylene on the working boats in Seaham Harbour's chilly twilight hour. A mosaic of England in all its shifting, messy, variousness. 'World is crazier and more of it than we think/Incorrigibly plural,' as Louis MacNeice said. That goes for England too.

I was leafing through the pages of the *New Statesman* on the Newcastle Metro between Gateshead and Hebburn and came across a diary piece by Andrew Marr, the eminent political journalist and broadcaster. In it, he wrote 'Another conundrum I've been thinking about since rereading J. B. Priestley's *English Journey* of 1934, in which he tours what later became Brexit England, looking at how people made their living, where their sense of local and national pride came from, and much more … The conundrum is this: who do the English now want to be?' He concluded that the Labour movement and, by extension, the country: 'needs a political philosopher – a patriotic English thinker with a decent sense of history and a certain moral anger, a Priestley or Orwell for our times.' I suppose you could call this a very long letter of application.*

---

* That sounds terribly vain. I don't really mean it. But it was irresistible. This is the last footnote in the book by the way. Thanks for dropping by down here.

If Priestley could see England now (who knows, maybe he can?) I don't think he would have worried too much about the Americanisation of Britain. It happened JB. It was pretty painless and we got some great records and books and films and TV shows. I think he'd be more pained at the shrinking of the English mind and heart. He was a big man with big appetites. He loved food, booze, music, sport, the outdoors, cities, sex – pleasure in all its forms. He wrote a charming little book all about it called *Delight*, listing the things that made him happy, from waking to the smell of bacon to being silly with small children. What would not have delighted him, looking at the England of the last few years, was that a certain kind of England and Englishman still held sway. Five years after *English Journey*, which radicalized and angered him, he was sickened that so little had changed in this regard as he looked hard at England on the verge of war: 'This is a real country where men and women have to live out their lives and not a vast fancy dress ball. The tradition of feudal aristocracy and landed gentry hangs over our life like the pall of smoke over wintry London … We have amongst us thousands and thousands of Bertie Wooster's who do not know that Jeeves is dead.' He knew that a Nazi victory would bring from under stones a class of men who were 'rotten with unsatisfied vanity, gnawing envy, and haunted by dreams of cruel power … you will find that the laziest loudmouth in the workshop has been given power to kick you up and down the street.'

England is a country forever taking two steps forward and one step back. For every Battle of Britain, there's a Battle of Orgreave; for every NHS, a Brexit; for every Attlee, a Johnson. Seemingly astonished at the good it can do, how grown up it can be, England regularly retreats into stupidity and deference, still in thrall to the vain, the dim and the laziest loudmouth in the workshop. Jeeves is dead. But on shining Southampton Water and the misty Fens, in the busy streets of Birmingham, Bradford, Liverpool and Manchester, in ancient, secretive Lincoln and newborn, futuristic Coventry, we are still bowing and scraping to Bertie Wooster and his private club. The personnel may change. Some of them are asked to leave, having been particularly obnoxious or useless. But the club remains, and it remains members only. So, sorry, you're not coming in, England, dressed like that, looking like that, talking like that.

For a country that has been here for a thousand years, we are still taking our baby steps towards adulthood.

The journey is not over yet.

ACKNOWLEDGEMENTS

Thank you to the following who helped with my journey.

Dan Jackson, Steven Maddocks. Hollie Christian-Brookes, Jonathan Davidson, Chris Morris, Richard Howle, Steven at Notts County, Eleanor Rees and all at the Sweet Centre, Bradford.

Harper
North

BOOK CREDITS

HarperNorth would like to thank the following staff
and contributors for their involvement in making
this book a reality:

Laura Amos
Fionnuala Barrett
Claire Boal
Caroline Bovey
Charlotte Brown
Katie Buckley
Sarah Burke
Fiona Cooper
Alan Cracknell
Jonathan de Peyer
Anna Derkacz
Tom Dunstan
Kate Elton
Sarah Emsley
Simon Gerratt
Neil Gower
Lydia Grainge
Monica Green
Natassa Hadjinicolaou
Emma Hatlen

Graham Holmes
Ben Hurd
Patricia Hymans
Megan Jones
Jean-Marie Kelly
Taslima Khatun
Dan Mogford
Petra Moll
Alice Murphy-Pyle
Adam Murray
Genevieve Pegg
Natasha Photiou
Agnes Rigou
Florence Shepherd
Zoe Shine
Eleanor Slater
Hilary Stein
Emma Sullivan
Katrina Troy
Phillipa Walker

For more unmissable reads,
sign up to the HarperNorth newsletter at
www.harpernorth.co.uk

or find us on Twitter at
@HarperNorthUK

**Harper
North**